William Grigsby Bullitt

Review of the Constitution of the United States

Including Changes by Interpretation and Amendment

William Grigsby Bullitt

Review of the Constitution of the United States
Including Changes by Interpretation and Amendment

ISBN/EAN: 9783337112325

Printed in Europe, USA, Canada, Australia, Japan

Cover: Foto ©Suzi / pixelio.de

More available books at **www.hansebooks.com**

REVIEW

OF THE

Constitution of the United States

INCLUDING

CHANGES BY INTERPRETATION AND AMENDMENT

FOR

Lawyers and Those Not Learned in the Law

BY

W. G. BULLITT

Of the Frankfort, Ky., Bar

—()—

CINCINNATI
THE ROBERT CLARKE COMPANY
1899

PREFACE.

The tendency of the officials of every nation is to augment their own importance and powers by grasping additional powers for the government they represent.

The accomplishment of this augmentation of powers to the government must take place by periodic steps, each step appearing innocent at the time, or of too little importance to attract attention.

Every additional power seized for the government must be taken from the reserved powers, or from powers lodged elsewhere by the organization of the government.

In the United States, certain powers are retained in the states, and all powers not granted to the United States, nor prohibited to the states, are reserved to the states respectively or the people.

This division of powers between the United States and the several states, makes each, in guarding its own powers, necessarily guard the reserved powers of the people ; so that, whether the powers so seized for the United States be taken from the people, or the states, the people will be the sufferers ; hence, we must not only be watchful of the reserved powers of the people, but must be mindful of the powers of the states.

" It is very uncommon to see the laws and constitution of a state openly and boldly opposed ; it is against silent and gradual attacks that a nation ought to be particularly on its guard. Sudden revolutions strike the imaginations of men ; they are detailed in history ; their secret springs are developed. But we overlook the changes that insensibly happen by a long train of steps that are but slightly marked. It would be rendering nations an important service to show from history how many states have thus entirely changed their nature, and lost their original constitution.

" This would awaken the attention of mankind—impressed thenceforward with this excellent maxim (no less essential in politics than in morals) *principiis obsta*—they would no longer shut their eyes against innovations which, though inconsiderable in themselves, may serve as steps to mount to higher and more pernicious enterprises." *

Powers not granted by the letter of the constitution have been adjudged to the United States by the *supreme court* on the alleged theory that they were incidental to the sovereign government thereof.

Sovereignty, being *supreme, absolute, uncontrollable* authority, it can neither be divided nor put in the custody of two separate jurisdictions. Therefore, if it was reserved to the people (as is contended for by all) it must be wholly in the people ; and, if it is in the government, it must be wholly in the government.

---

* Vattel's Law of Nations, Chap. 3, p. 9.

Nor can it be divided between the United States and the respective states, as held by the supreme court in the McCulloch case; so that, unless that authority resides exclusively in the people, it must be exclusively in the the United States (as its authority must be paramount to that of the states), and the United States must be an *empire*, with the states as its provinces, instead of the federal republic the American people boast of.

The *executive* has also assumed powers not granted to it by the letter of the constitution, and in some instances has encroached on the powers expressly delegated to the legislative department by the constitution.

The *congress* has also assumed powers not granted to it by the letter of the constitution, or by the spirit of that instrument.

The assumptions of ungranted powers by each of said departments has been accomplished by the exercise of some apparently unimportant authority at periodic steps, or an authority claimed to be necessary for the time, and not to be repeated, though they have been invariably used as precedents to excuse the exercise, not only of the same powers, but to go further in their encroachments on the reserved powers of the people. Sometimes their assumptions of powers have been claimed as necessary to keep up with advancing civilization; but this plea is a mere apology to quiet the people while the construction of a new form of government, to be builded on interpretation alone, is being constructed step by step, to take the place of the republican form of government ordained by the constitution.

The constitution itself furnishes incontrovertible evidence of the bad faith of this plea. That instrument provides ample facilities for its own amendment whenever the advance in civilization shall require an amendment; and every substantial advance in civilization is encouraged by the constitution, by authorizing congress to protect inventions, writings, and developments in the fine arts, by patent rights and copyrights.

However, no amendment can be made to the constitution without the sanction of the people, and their sanction thereto can not be secured without informing them of the character of the desired change, and this information would likely divulge the secret object of the advisers of the change, and check their revolutionary schemes.

This Review is written in plain English, avoiding all unnecessary technicalities; and the provisions of the constitution are explained according to the general use and meaning of the words and phrases by which they are expressed, as used at the time the constitution was ordained. I have endeavored to give to each provision the meaning and functions it was intended to perform by the convention that made the constitution, and the construction given by the several departments of the United States, and the interpretation as advocated by each of the two great political parties, so that the reader may have the benefit of each interpretation.

Of course, I have used the strongest arguments in my

power to sustain my understanding of the provisions of that great instrument, and the office each is to perform, and wherever a different interpretation than the letter thereof is indicated, whether by the supreme court, the executive, or legislative departments, or by either of the two great political parties, I have argued in favor of the interpretation that sustains the letter thereof.

Instead of relying on the statements of any one as to what was meant by the several provisions thereof (except the letters of Messrs. Madison, Hamilton and Jay published while the constitution was before the people of the states for adoption, and compiled in a volume known as the Federalist), I have relied on the organization and lodgment of the powers and duties under the constitution; the manner they are required to be executed by the officials intrusted with them; the retention of the sovereign authority in the people as shown by the great Declaration of Independence, and the provision of the constitution authorizing the people of the states to amend or alter the constitution without the sanction of the United States, or any department thereof, by demanding a federal convention to propose amendments to be ratified by conventions of the states, as was done in making the constitution of 1787; the language used to express the several provisions, particularly that used in the preamble delaring the objects for ordaining the constitution: the language used in proposing the several provisions of the constitution by the delegates in the convention, and the action of the convention thereon, before adopting the

same as provisions of the constitution to ascertain the
intent and meaning the delegates in the convention
ascribed to each provision of the constitution ; and the
functions the convention intended each provision to perform in the government of the United States and in the
several states of the more perfect union.

While every provision of the constitution is to some
extent considered in this Review, that class of powers
relating to the civil rights and business interests of the
people more properly belong to a commentary on the
constitution, which is beyond the purpose of this work ;
they are therefore but briefly explained.

But that class of powers that relate to the form and
character of the government of the United States, and
its relations to the states and the people, are extensively
and minutely shown, together with the conflicting inter-
pretations by either of the three departments, and by the
two great political parties, with each of which the interpretation given by this Review is carefully compared.

The interpretation adhered to in this Review conforms
to the Declaration of Independence and the great American principles introduced into the science of government
by our colonial ancestors, which are shown to have been
incorporated into the constitution of 1787, and to form
the guiding principle of that great charter, so that by
those guides every power granted by the constitution
should be construed.

TABLE OF CONTENTS.

CHAPTER I.

CHAPTER II.

CHAPTER III.

CHAPTER IV.

CHAPTER V.

CHAPTER VI.

REVIEW

Constitution of the United States.

CHAPTER I.

ORGANIZATION OF THE STATES AND CONFEDERATION.

The first permanent settlement under English authority in this country, was made under a grant to two companies by the sovereign kingdom of Great Britain, in 1606, in the name of Sir Thomas Gates and others. The first company consisted of citizens of London and elsewhere, and the second company consisted of citizens of Bristol, Exeter, Plymouth and elsewhere.

The grant to both companies comprised all the territory between north latitude 34° and 45°, extending from the Atlantic ocean one hundred miles inland. The part thereof granted to the first company comprised all the territory between latitude 34° and 41°; and the part thereof granted to the second company comprised the territory between north latitude 38° and 45°. It will be observed that a conflict appears in the boundaries granted to these two companies, but an amendment of the charter of the first company, in 1609, changed the boundary of the territory granted to that company, so as to extend two hundred miles northwardly, and two hundred miles southwardly from Point Comfort, in Vir-

ginia, on the Atlantic coast, and to extend from sea to
sea.* The purpose of England in planting her colonies
in this country was to acquire vacant territory, and the
amendment of the charters of these two companies was
to extend the actual possession of that kingdom to the
Pacific ocean, with a view of appropriating the territory
between Canada and Florida from sea to sea.†

The first company sent over three ships laden with
emigrants to aid in settling the country (under said grant
to said first company), to be known as Virginia. But
the emigrants that came over in 1606 made no permanent
settlement, until another colony arrived in the spring of
1607, whose ships landed at James City (afterward called
Jamestown), on the James river. The charter of that
company was again amended in 1611–12, which amendment provided for a treasurer, and a London board or
committee, to manage the financial affairs, all of whom
were required to reside in England and hold their meetings in London, and a governor, to be appointed by the
king, to preside over the colony.

The London board of directors or committee was authorized to provide for and constitute such officers as that
committee and the governor should agree on, to manage
the affairs of the colony ; and at the instance of the board
of managers residing in England, a committee or board
of managers to reside in the colony was instituted to aid
the governor, which was authorized by the amendment
of 1611–12, and authority was also given to adopt rules
for the general welfare of the colony.

By selling the lands in small parcels to those who would
settle on them, this first colony prospered, and as it increased in wealth and population it grew in power, and

* Poore, " Fed. and State Const. and Col. Charters "—Virginia.
† Ibid.—Massachusetts.

with that increase in wealth and power came a desire for greater liberty and a more congenial government ; and the people began to show such a spirit of unrest as to cause Sir George Yeardly, the then governor, to call a general assembly, composed of representatives from the several boroughs and plantations, in 1619, to exercise the functions of legislation ; and this was the first legislature that ever assembled on this continent. This body of representatives of course acted in conjunction with the committee chosen by the English directors and the governor, which gave this first legislature some resemblance to the British parliament.

This example of a domestic parliament to regulate the internal affairs of the colony was found to be so indispensable to the welfare and quiet of the colony as to induce the English committee to issue a permanent ordinance in 1621, establishing a legislative representation of the colony fashioned after the British parliament. The English committee appointed the council, composed of citizens of the colony, which corresponded to the House of Lords ; and the citizens of the plantations and boroughs elected representatives to another house, which two houses acted separately. This lower house corresponded with the House of Commons in the British parliament, and the governor occupied the relation of chief executive. After 1627 the governors were elective by the two houses of the legislative department ; but if they failed to elect, then the king might appoint a governor, provided he appointed a citizen of the colony known to be favorable to the welfare of the colony.

The charter of the second company was renewed in 1620, and by that renewed charter the boundary was changed, so as to embrace the territory between north latitude 40° and 48°, which left a gap between the two

grants instead of a lap, as it was under the charter of
1606 ; and the second company was then named "*New
England,*" under the amendment of 1620.* Under
that amendment, or renewed charter, the Plymouth settlement first began by the emigration brought over on
the Mayflower.

As the colony of Virginia had demonstrated that a
liberal government would cause the colonies the more
readily to be settled up, and therefore greatly redound to
the interest of the stockholders, the Plymouth emigrants
were assured of the aid of their English committee in
giving them a liberal government for their colony. The
emigrants who came over on the Mayflower planned their
government while on board the ship, and proceeded to
organize under that government as soon as they were
landed.

The other colonies obtained their respective charters
many years after that of New England, and they were
generally granted with such form of government as those
who were deputed to apply for them would ask for, and
indeed they were often prepared and voted on by the
people before the charter would be applied for, and were
seldom, if ever, refused.

The colonies, settled by English people under authority
of the crown of England, brought with them the English
common law and constitution, as well as their British
charters ; and when the separation took place it left the
people clothed with English common law, and the entire
sovereign authority thereof ; although they may have
lost the provisions of their respective charters, as the
charters were entirely municipal, and were sustained
alone by the support they were getting from the sovereign kingdom of Great Britain ; and when the munici-

---

* Poore, "Charters," etc.—Massachusetts.

pal cord that bound the colonies to Great Britain was severed, they could no longer draw any municipal authority from that kingdom.

But as all sovereign authority originally comes from the people, and their rules and customs, or common law, antedate and constitute the basis of the government, it is never lost with the loss of the government, but survives the government, as a part of the civilization of the people of the country. Still, the colonies chose to retain the laws enacted by themselves under their British charters, and carried them into their respective state governments under constitutional sanction.

The colonies originating under British authority, and the people thereof, being clothed with the English common law and the British constitution, as far as applicable to the condition and needs of each colony, many valuable principles were drawn from the English constitution and common law, that enter into the American system, therefore a brief mention of the origin and growth of such of the principles of the English common law and constitution as enter into and become a part of the American system, may aid in reaching a clearer understanding of the American system.

Whatever may have been the laws or customs of the British, it is not necessary to inquire into, as they were supplanted by the Angles or English, a race of people who came in the fifth century from the heart of the peninsula that separates the Baltic from the North sea, who after many years of relentless struggle, with the aid of the Jutes and Saxons, succeeded in conquering the Britons. Therefore we must look to the customs and laws of the Angles, or English people, for the fundamental principles of the constitution of Great Britain.

The most important and guiding principle upon which

the English civilization and constitution was founded, consisted of the sacredness with which the family and family governments were regarded.*

Whether these conquerors drew their sacred regard for their home governments from biblical revelation, or from the natural inclination to sustain their domestic tranquillity and family governments, is not material to this inquiry.

However, Schlegel, in his great work on the philosophy of history, claims that the four great convulsions of the world became necessary to purge the world of the sins that grew out of a disregard of marital relationship.

It is true, the language used in pronouncing the curse, or judgment in each case, includes that sin; though other sins were also mentioned in the judgments, still it must be admitted that the sins named in each judgment were in some way connected with and arose out of disregard of monogamy in marital relationship.

However, wherever those unlettered invaders derived their sacred regard for their family government, and strict adherence to monogamy and loyalty in marriage, the moral life growing out of it constituted the foundation of their future greatness as a nation of people.

The recognition of marriage being instituted by God, as a sacred institution, necessarily carries with it the recognition of a government of divine authority; and as no government can subsist without a head, and rules to be obeyed, from the natural formation of man and woman, as well as the natural division of duties consigned to each, the man must necessarily constitute the head of the family government.

So that the husband and father, while acting as the head of his family, is authorized to bind them in compact

---

* Green's English People, ch. 1 (larger edition).

or covenant with other families, in order to secure the maintenance of the cherished religious and civil rights to be enjoyed by his family, together with the families of the other parties to the covenant or compact; this may be the foundation of representative government brought by that people with them to Great Britain, which is so thoroughly grounded in their system of government. We find in the earlier period of the history of that people, that their village assemblies or motes, consisted of males capable of bearing arms, or who had families; and those village motes selected representatives to a higher assembly known as the township or hundred mote. These motes not only made laws but decided controversies between adverse parties; the township mote having appellate or revisory jurisdiction over the decisions and acts of the village mote.*

There was still another assembly, variously styled Michel-gemote or great meeting, but better known by the name Wittena-gemote, or the meeting of the wise men. When this council first began is not known, though it was familiar to the different kingdoms of the Heptarchy, and after the union it was ordered by Alfred that this council should meet twice a year or oftener, perpetually.†

The Angles, or English invaders, brought with them another assembly known as the *war host*, or folk mote, which was supposed to be an assembly of the whole people, and all freemen and soldiers, as well as the leaders, were entitled to seats in this mote. The villagers generally selected the representatives to this assembly, which was not, however, a regular provision of the government, but was called into existence only in cases of

---

* Green, ch. I (larger ed.).
† Blackstone, vol. I, pp. 147–149.

emergency, to regulate wars, and was authorized to decide whether to engage in conquest of other countries; and it had jurisdiction to change the government so as to make it adequate to the exigencies of the wars, or movements in making new conquests. But as the management of armies in the contest with the Britons required a compact government and rulers, this assembly was permitted to fall into disuse, which brought about the establishment of kings to rule over that country.*

It is claimed that the sovereignty of that people resided in the village motes. But when we recall the fact that sovereignty is supreme, irresistible, absolute, uncontrolled authority, as said by Mr. Blackstone,† it must be above all law, and authorized to change the form of the government or its constitution at will; and that the actions of the village mote being subject to revision by the township mote, that arbitrary, uncontrolled authority could not reside in the village mote. The war host, or folk mote, alone was authorized to change the government, though this mote had no permanent existence, and whenever it should adjourn it ceased to exist; but another war host could be called into existence by the villagers at any time.

Exactly what steps were necessary to be taken to authorize calling into existence the war host, is not given with certainty. But when the villagers called into existence the war host, and selected the representatives to the same, there was no appeal from that action of the villagers to the hundred mote. It therefore follows that, whenever the village mote acted within its jurisdiction as a part of the organized government, an appeal would lie to the hundred mote; but as the folk mote, or war

* Green's English People, ch. 1 (larger edition).
† Blackstone, vol. 1, p. 49.

host, was outside of the government, the villages had no authority as a part of the government to institute it, or to select the representatives thereto. Therefore, whenever the folk mote, or war host, was instituted, it must have been by the action of the villagers individually, and not as representatives of the village mote. Consequently the sovereignty resided not in the village mote, but in the villagers, or the heads of the families residing within the boundary thereof. The only mode by which the villagers could give expression to their sovereign will was through the folk mote, or war host.

At that time it was thought that a government could not exist without possessing sovereignty within its organization; hence the authority of the villagers to change or modify the government through the folk mote must have been a reversionary right to regain the sovereign authority.

Mr. Blackstone says: "It must be owned that Mr. Locke and other theoretical writers have held that 'there remains still inherent in the people a supreme power to remove or alter the legislative, when they find the legislative act contrary to the trust reposed in them; for, when such trust is abused, it is thereby forfeited, and devolves to those who gave it.' But, however just this conclusion may be, in theory, we can not practically adopt it, nor take any legal steps for carrying it into execution, under any dispensation of government at present actually existing. For this devolution of power to the people at large, includes in it a dissolution of the whole form of government established by that people, reduces all the members to their original state of equality, and, by annihilating the sovereign power, repeals all positive laws whatsoever before enacted. No human laws will, therefore, suppose a case, which at once must destroy all law, and compel men to build afresh upon a new foundation; nor will they make provisions for so desperate an event, as must render all legal provisions ineffectual. So long, therefore, as the English constitution lasts, we may venture to affirm that the power of parliament is absolute and without control." *

The learned commentator might have gone further, and with great force have added, that as such forfeiture must depend on the conviction of a betrayal of the trust, and those to be so convicted being public officials, would necessarily have control of the forces of the government to enable them to execute the trust so betrayed, with those forces at their disposal they could prevent a trial of themselves; or they might permit a trial, and refuse to surrender the forces of the government.

Should the officials, in good faith, believe they were but discharging their duty, although, as matter of fact, they might be exercising doubtful powers, they ought not to surrender the forces of the government, but on the contrary they ought to hold on to them, and maintain the government and its general welfare, as they conscientiously believe to be their duty. Hence a mere reversionary right to reclaim the sovereign authority must forever remain a theory of no practical value to the people, particularly as the dissolution of a sovereign government would annihilate the laws enacted by that government, as Mr. Blackstone says.

When the great council or *Wittena-gemote* was divided into the two houses of parliament as they now exist, historians differ, but Mr. Blackstone says: "It is, however, sufficient to know that as early as the seventeenth year of King John, A. D. 1215, in the great charter granted by that prince, he promised to summon all archbishops, bishops, abbots, earls, and greater barons per-

* Blackstone, vol. 1, p. 162.

sonally, and all other tenants in chief under the crown by the sheriffs and bailiffs, to meet at a certain place, with forty days' notice, to assess aids and scutages when necessary. . . . Since the year 1266 (49 Henry III.) the parliament has continued to subsist.*

"The parliament has no fixed time of meeting, and can not assemble without being called by the king; it is, however, provided . . . upon the death of the king the parliament last summoned shall meet and may hold for six months.†

"The parliament consists of the king in his royal capacity and the three estates of the realm, the lords spiritual, the lords temporal (who sit together with the king in one house), and the commons, who sit by themselves in another house. The king and these three estates together form the great corporation, or body politic of the kingdom, of which the king is said to be *caput, principium et finis*. For upon their coming together the king meets them, either in person or by representation, without which there can be no beginning of a parliament, and he also alone has the right of dissolving them.‡

"The concurrence of all of the constituent parts of the parliament are necessary to enact any new law. . . . Whatever is enacted by one, or by two only of the three, is no statute, and to it no regard is due, unless in matters relating to their own privileges." ‖

The power and jurisdiction of the parliament, Mr. Blackstone, quoting from Sir Edward Coke, says: "It hath sovereign and uncontrollable authority in the making, confirming, restraining, abrogating, repealing, revising and expanding of laws, concerning matters of all

---

* Blackstone, vol. 1, p. 149.   † Id., p. 150.
‡ Id., p. 153.   ‖ Id., p. 160.

possible denominations. . . . All mischiefs and grievances, operations and remedies, that transcend the ordinary course of the laws, are within the reach of this
extraordinary tribunal. It can regulate or new model
the succession to the crown. . . . It can change and
create afresh even the constitution of the kingdom, and
of parliament themselves. . . . It can, in short, do
every thing that is not naturally impossible." *

It will be observed that the division of the legislative
department into two houses was fully established by
England before the separation of the colonies from that
kingdom.

The executive authority was originally lodged with the
king, and all executive powers were supposed to flow
from the king, including all judicial power. Under that
idea the king was regarded as the fountain of justice:
"not author, or original, but the distributor of justice."
And in earlier times the king often heard and determined
causes in person between party and party.

But by long usage the kings delegated their judicial
powers to the judges of the several courts, until the
courts attained a known and stated jurisdiction regulated
by certain and established rules, which the crown itself
could not alter except through an act of parliament.

Athough the judges had acquired a certain and known
jurisdiction, they were still but the agents of the king,
and derived their powers from the king as the chief
source of all executive authority, and their terms of
office expired with the death of the king who appointed
them.

But by statute of 1 George III., c. 23, it was enacted at
the request of the king that "the judges be continued in
their offices during their good behavior notwithstanding

---

* Blackstone, vol. 1, pp. 160–61.

any demise of the crown" (which was formerly held, immediately to vacate their seats), and their salaries are absolutely secured to them during the continuance of their commissions.*

This statute completed the liberation of the judiciary from the king, and the construction of it into a separate and independent department of the government of that kingdom.

As the commissions of the judges extended only through good behavior, they would necessarily be subject to removal whenever their behavior should cease to be good. But to impeach them they must be convicted of some willful misbehavior ; a mere mal-interpretation of the laws, or of the constitution, would be no cause of impeachment ; still a mal-interpretation of the constitution might have the effect of changing the character of the whole system of government.

To guard against such a calamity, it was provided in the constitution of that kingdom that the judges should be removable upon the address of two-thirds of each house of parliament. Hence, while the judiciary was removed from every influence of the king by said act of 1 George III., c. 23, they were still subject to the power of the people, who could elect a parliament to address an offending judge out of office, whenever he betrayed a disposition to so interpret the constitution, as to change the character of the government. The mere existence of this power in the people has caused the judiciary of that realm to guard with scrupulous care the reserved rights of the people.

The exact date the county courts were established in England is not known, but mention is made of them as

---

* Blackstone. vol. 1, pp. 266-67.

early as the reign of Ina, during the continuance of the Heptarchy. *

And the incorporated city is of ancient origin. So that, we drew from England—

First, the separation of the law making power from the executive power.

Second, the division of the legislative, or law making power, into two houses, requiring a concurrence of each house with the other to enact any law.

Third, the division of the executive into two departments; that is, carving the judiciary out of the executive, and constituting it into a separate department of government.

Fourth, the division of the nation into counties, as parts of the state, to aid in the enforcement of the laws.

Fifth, the subdivision of counties into villages, townships, shires, and incorporated cities and towns.

But as, up to the establishment of the American system, it was thought that every government however constituted, must be vested with sovereign authority (unless in cases of incorporated cities and colonies, for every charter presupposes a superior), and sovereignty being the supreme authority, that superior could not vest a city or colony chartered by it with sovereignty, without destroying its own sovereignty; so that the city or colony chartered by it always acts as the agent of the sovereign nation in exercising sovereign authority, and in doing sovereign acts, and must continually draw its life and existence from the sovereign authority that granted the charter; and whenever that sovereign nation ceases to exist, it will have no life left to continue to infuse into a city or colony it may have chartered.

In the event of the nation granting the charter ceasing

---

* Hallam's Middle Ages, p. 320.

to exist, the sovereignty of the colony would devolve on the people thereof, or on the family governments, which, if of divine origin, must always exist independently of any government established by man.

There was no danger of the sovereign nation of England ceasing to exist ; but that nation was threatening to revoke the charters of the colonies, and to put the colonies under special parliamentary laws, as provinces, which would have severed the connection between the colonies (as colonies) and that nation, and they would have a perfect right to resist any effort on England's part to reduce them to provinces.

By the terms of the respective colonial charters, they were vested with jurisdiction of the civil laws only, England retaining in itself exclusive jurisdiction of the political laws and sovereign authority.   To give a clearer conception of the respective jurisdictions of the colonies and of England, I will call attention to the fact that there are but two grand objects of government, to wit : The main object is to provide a government for the people, sufficient to protect them in the regulation of their property and religious rights, and a police management for their safety and pursuit of happiness, which is called civil laws.   The political laws include the organization of the government, its powers and the mode of exercising the same for the general welfare of the government itself ; and as the government, or the agent having jurisdiction of political laws, is the only organ through which the nation contracts and maintains treaties, or can carry on intercourse with foreign nations, it must have control of all of the forces of the nation.   And every complete government must have control, not only of the forces of the nation, but the people thereof, and the making of the civil laws for their welfare.

As before stated, the jurisdiction of the colonies was

limited to the civil laws only, though with that limited
jurisdiction their colonial governments were satisfactory
to the people, and they did not desire to change their
home or state government in their respective colonies.
But as their corporate colonial governments could not be
continued without a superior, and as their mother country (Great Britain) was threatening to desert them,
the colonists were not willing to entrust the sovereignty
and the political laws thereof to any other government,
so the people resolved to retain the sovereignty in
themselves. But history failed to point out to them
forms of government, or any system of governmental
agencies, by which they could retain the sovereignty in
themselves and at the same time continue the subjects
of themselves.

However, beyond the history of governments formed
by man, they found that the Divine Ruler of the
universe had shown the way by which the sovereign
could continue to be sovereign, and also constitute subjects of that sovereign authority, by placing the world
under a reign of laws by which He chose to abide as
long as He permitted those laws to stand, without surrendering His sovereign authority, or power, to change
those laws at will. And the folk mote or war host of
their English ancestors taught them how to provide a
separate assembly through which to express their will as
sovereigns, other than that provided for them to express
their will as subjects ; and they boldly resolved to introduce
this new principle of science in government in their system for the American states, and to retain the entire
sovereign authority in themselves, and make themselves
the subjects of whatever government they might establish for themselves.

The Colony of Virginia leading off by its bill of
rights on the 12th of June, 1776, and its constitution on

the 29th of June, 1776, declared that the officers of the government thereof were but agents, trustees, and public servants ; and also provided for calling conventions to alter, amend, or abolish the constitution, or plan of government, then being established.

That government, being but an inanimate entity, could do nothing except by and through its officers ; consequently the government itself must be but a trustee and agent. But as one may be vested with a naked trust, which is revocable at any time by the grantor, or he may be vested with a trust coupled with an interest, which interest may be sufficient to prevent a revocation thereof until the trustee be compensated for his interest, so a government may be simply an agent and trustee (as is the case with municipal corporations), or it may be an agent and trustee vested with an interest in the sovereign authority. However, as sovereignty is supreme it can neither be limited nor divided ; therefore, if the government be vested with any part of that authority by its organization, it must necessarily have the whole sovereign authority, and in that event the only way to get that authority out of the government would be by a forfeiture of it by the malconduct of the officials, or by forcible seizure of it by the people in a revolution.

But, as was thought at that time, every government must possess sovereignty within itself, to enable it to exercise that power, the language used in the Virginia constitution and bill of rights may have been thought insufficient to reserve that authority out of the government of that state. However, when the fact that the people reserved to themselves the power to call a convention to alter or amend their constitution is considered, in conjunction with the declaration in said bill of rights and constitution, it appears sufficient, to reserve the entire sovereign authority to the people of that state. The further fact that the government then ordained and established should forever remain, until altered or amended by the people, in sovereign convention assembled, thereby constituted the *sovereign convention*, as the only organ through which to express their sovereign will.

Therefore, whatever may be done in the way of making or changing laws, or of governing the people, through the government, or any of its departments, or officers, could not be regarded as *sovereign acts* or *of sovereign authority*. But should the constitution and bill of rights of Virginia be held insufficient to fully set forth the great American discovery in the science of government, the great Declaration of Independence proclaimed the Fourth of July, 1776, clearly sets forth that the right of life, liberty and the pursuit of happiness, are inalienable rights; and that whenever the government fails to protect these rights, the people have the right to alter or abolish the same, and to institute a new government, laying its foundation on such principles and organizing it in such form as to them shall seem most likely to effect their safety and happiness. But if the Virginia constitution and bill of rights fail to fully declare the American principles, this great declaration also falls short of doing so.

Most of the states failed to establish a constitution until after said declaration had been proclaimed, and many of them failed to construct a constitution and bill of rights until after the Articles of Confederation for the union had been agreed to by the congress, and ratified by all of the states. And nearly all of the states that adopted their respective constitutions, after the debates on the Articles of Confederation in the congress, and in the legislatures of the states, in ratifying the same, in some form of language, either in its constitution or bill of rights, declared that the sovereign authority, or all governmental powers, emanated from the people and were inalienable from them.

As long as this sovereign power is inalienable from the people, it can not vest in the government ; therefore, the declaration of Virginia, as well as other states, must be accepted as a positive reservation of this power, out of the government, and a retention of it, in the people.

Our colonial ancestors were aware of the difficulty of providing for the preservation of the principles upon which the government might be originally founded ; for they knew of the contention by philosophical writers on the subject, that governments had generally been founded in compact, whereby the reserved rights of the people had been apparently well guarded ; but, by gradual usurpation, arising out of interpreted powers, seemingly innocent at the time, which performed the function of precedent, to lead to other and more dangerous encroachments, until every reserved right of the people had been absorbed by the government. However, Mr. Blackstone denies that governments were formed in compact ; on the contrary, he claims that they were always the result of growth ; but it is not material how they were originally established, for in their earlier existence the officials would have less power to impose on the people than they have after the government itself grows richer and stronger than its inhabitants. But whatever may have been the origin of governments before the American system was established, our colonial ancestors were then engaged in establishing a system of government in compact, and to introduce new principles in the science of government, and were extremely anxious to guard the new system " of retaining the sovereignty in the people."

They were familiar with the advantages of dividing

the powers of government between three co-ordinate departments, and putting each under the management of a different set of officials. They were also familiar with the fact that the grand attributes or objects of government could be separated, and each of them committed to a separate government, as the colonists had seen and tried, in the cases of their colonial governments under their British charters, with jurisdiction of the civil laws only, in the colonies, while England retained exclusive jurisdiction of the political laws and the entire sovereign authority, though granting limited jurisdiction to the colonies to wield such sovereign forces as were necessary to enable them to carry into effect the trusts and duties imposed on them as municipal agents of England.

This new development in the science of government not only required the separation of jurisdiction of the civil laws from jurisdiction of the political laws, but also required a limitation on the exercise of jurisdiction of the political laws; for wherever jurisdiction of the political laws might be lodged, the whole forces of the country, needed for public defense, must also be lodged, and the danger of that jurisdiction absorbing the reserved powers of the people made it necessary to impose limits and enforcible checks. Consequently, it was necessary to construct two governmental corporations, the one to be vested with jurisdiction of the political laws, and the other to be vested with jurisdiction of the civil laws, the jurisdiction of each to be exclusive as to the objects and governmental functions committed to it; and as the jurisdiction of each necessarily had to extend over the same territory and the same people, who were to constitute the union, there was no way to define the boundary of each jurisdiction, except to divide the whole territory into fractional or component parts, and to give to each fraction jurisdiction of one of the great objects of government, to the extent of its boundary, which would necessarily subdivide the jurisdiction of that object between the different parts.

As the political laws relate to the government itself, and its maintenance against either foreign or domestic foes, and in its relations with foreign nations, it must have control of all the forces of the whole country. Jurisdiction of the political laws, therefore, must be given to the corporation of the Union, and jurisdiction of the civil laws to the states, or fractional parts of the country, or union.

The states had existed as colonies having jurisdiction of the civil laws only, under their British charters, which was satisfactory to the people; and they did not desire any greater jurisdiction for their states under the new system, nor did they desire any change in the boundaries of their respective colonies or states; they therefore retained their respective colonies to constitute the division of the country to mark the boundary of the jurisdiction of one of the objects of government. By dividing the jurisdiction of the objects of government was the only way the people could have secured the sovereign authority in themselves absolutely; for had the sovereignty been vested in the American people as one people, the people of the states could not have been vested with it, but it must abide in the people of the union, and there was great apprehension of the governmental agency of the union gradually absorbing the sovereign authority from the people, by usurping powers apparently innocent at the time, but to serve as precedents to enable them to revolutionize the entire system of government, as history showed had so often been done in former free governments, apparently well guarded against the ambition of their officials. There was no danger of that character of usurpation to come from the state officials as long as jurisdiction of the political laws continued to reside in the governmental agency of the union, and the main inducement for separating the two great objects of government, so as to put them under the control of two separate jurisdictions, was to guard against all danger of losing their sovereign control of either of said governments, as it required both to constitute a complete government.

As each state is vested with exclusive jurisdiction of the civil laws (with a few specified exceptions) and excluded from jurisdiction of the political laws, the governmental agency for the union must constitute a part of that of each state individually ; and as the agency of the federal union was vested with exclusive jurisdiction of the political laws, and (in the main) excluded from jurisdiction of the civil laws, each state individually must constitute a part of the governmental agency for the federal union, so that each must constitute a part of the other.

As neither the federal union nor the states have jurisdiction of both of the necessary objects of government, to constitute government, neither can be sovereign, and each must be a mere municipal or corporate agent of some higher authority. Consequently the United States, as well as the several states, must constitute a mere agent of that higher authority, and bear the same relation to that higher authority that municipal corporations bear to the state or nation that granted the charter.

As the people of the respective colonies granted the charters of their respective states, wherein they reserved to themselves the entire sovereign authority, the states constitute municipal corporations, deriving their respective existence and powers from the people.

And as the Articles of Confederation were constructed by the Colonial Congress, composed of representatives

from each colony, and had to be ratified by the legislatures of the several states to make it valid and binding
(the legislatures being mere agents of the people), the
ratification by the legislatures of the states was in law
the ratification of the people of the states. Hence the
confederation could not have been more than a municipal
corporation, deriving its existence and authority from
the concurrent act of the people of all of the states.

These three great principles, to wit: First, the discovery of a mode by which the people could retain the
entire sovereign authority in themselves, and at the same
time make themselves subjects of a government deriving
its entire authority from themselves; second, how a people may govern themselves through municipal corporations constituted by themselves, with power to revoke
the same at will; third, how to separate the powers that
belong respectively to each of the two grand divisions of
government, and to commit the execution of each to a
separate government, or municipal agent, are of American origin; and when coupled with the guards to absolute religious freedom, at least, excuses the idea of
the inspiration of our revolutionary fathers, so often
claimed in the pulpit and Fourth of July orations, as
a fulfillment of the Lord's promise to put the new laws
in the minds of the people and write them in their
hearts.*

These great American principles were not only put
into the minds of our colonial ancestors by existing circumstances, but they were written in their hearts in the
blood of a fierce war, cruelly and unjustly waged against
them by the most powerful nation of that age.

The events and circumstances connected with the or-

---

* St. Paul's Epistle to the Hebrews, vii, viii, ix.

ganization of the governments of the several states, and
the government of the confederacy under the articles of
confederation, will show that they were constructed
about the same time, as parts of each other, on the principles above stated.

The Colonial Congress, by resolution adopted, the 10th
of May, 1776, advised the colonies, "where no government sufficient to the exigencies of their affairs had been
established to adopt such a government as should, in the
opinion of the representatives of the people, best conduce
to the happiness and safety of their constituents in particular and of America in general." *

On the 10th of June a committee was appointed by that
congress to draft a Declaration of Independence. That
committee consisted of five members chosen in the following order, Mr. Jefferson, Mr. J. Adams, Mr. Franklin,
Mr. Sherman and Mr. R. R. Livingston. The committee
requested Mr. Jefferson to draft that instrument, and
after drafting it he submitted it to his said committee,
and they agreed to it ; it was then reported to the convention on the 28th of June ; but it was thought that the
states of New York, New Jersey, Pennsylvania, Delaware, Maryland and South Carolina were not ready to
take so serious and advanced a step, and by request it
was agreed to postpone its consideration until the 1st of
July. †

On the 1st of July, 1776, said report was taken up and
earnestly debated until late in the afternoon session of
the 4th of July, 1776. The Declaration of Independence
was considered in connection with the motion of the
members from Virginia to "declare the colonies free
states ;" the latter was agreed to first by a majority of

---

* Elliott's Debates, vol. 1, pp. 54-5.   † Id., p. 59.

the states, and the former was agreed to and passed late in the evening of that day, and signed by the delegates from each of the states, except the delegates from the state of New York who said that they were individually in favor of it, but thought that their instructions, which had been given more than a year before, did not authorize them to sign it. The great Declaration of Independence was, however, proclaimed on the evening of the 4th of July, 1776, without the signature of New York; however, that state at once authorized its delegates to ratify it, and they signed the great Declaration on the 9th of July, 1776.

On the 11th of June a resolution was passed to appoint a committee to prepare and digest the form of the confederation to be entered into between the colonies. * On the day following that committee was appointed consisting of the following persons, to-wit: Mr. Bartlett, Mr. S. Adams, Mr. Hopkins, Mr. Sherman, Mr. R. R. Livingston, Mr. Dickinson, Mr. McKeen, Mr. Stone, Mr. Nelson, Mr. Hewes, Mr. Rutledge and Mr. Guinnett. Upon the report of the committee the subject was from time to time debated until the 15th of November, 1777, when a copy of the Articles of Confederation being made out, and sundry amendments made in the diction without altering the sense, the same was agreed to and it was then sent to the legislatures of the states for ratification.

The Articles of Confederation were ratified by the states in the following order of time by their respective representatives in the congress, after being first authorized to do so by their respective state legislatures:

Connecticut, New York, Massachusetts, Pennsylvania,

---

* Elliott's Debates, vol. I, p. 55.

South Carolina and Virginia, ratified the same on the
9th of July, 1778 ; Delaware (in part) on same day, but
not fully until the 5th of May, 1779. North Carolina
(in part) ratified the same on said 9th of July, and completed its ratification on the 21st of July, 1778. Georgia
ratified the same the 24th of July, 1778 ; New Hampshire (in part), July 9, 1778, and completed its ratification in August, 1778. New Jersey (in part) ratified the
same July 9, 1778, and completed its ratification in November, 1778. And Maryland ratified the same on the
1st of March, 1781, which included all of the states except Rhode Island ; and on the next day (March 2, 1781)
the members of the Colonial Congress were sworn in as
members of the congress of the confederation.

New Jersey, Delaware and Maryland, being hemmed
in on their western boundaries, while other states had
large surplus territory on their western border (some of
them claimed to extend to the Pacific ocean), which excited the jealousy of these three states, and they each
declined to ratify the Articles of Confederation, in hopes
of inducing the other states to give up their surplus territory to be used for the common interest of all, in paying the war debt. New Jersey and Delaware, however,
fell in and ratified the confederation without any pledge
to so appropriate said surplus territory ; but Maryland
held back until Virginia agreed to surrender her territory
on the north-west of the Ohio, by resolution of her legislature in January, 1781.

While this activity in the construction of the confederation was going on, the colonies were equally as active
in forming their respective state governments. Several
of the colonies, however, had taken steps toward the
formation of governments for themselves before the
Declaration of Independence was proclaimed by the

Colonial Congress, and indeed before the resolution of the 10th of May, advising them to form separate governments for themselves, respectively, to-wit :

North Carolina, by its Mecklenburg convention, which met the 20th of May, 1775.

New Hampshire, by its congress, on the 5th of January, 1776.

South Carolina, by its legislature, constructed and declared for itself a free and independent government, the 26th of March, 1776.

Virginia, by a house of burgesses chosen for the purpose, met on the 6th of May, 1776.

New Jersey, by a convention that met the 26th of May, 1776.

Each of the other colonies met for the purpose of forming separate governments after the Declaration of Independence had been proclaimed, except Rhode Island, which did not form a new government until in 1842, and Connecticut, which adopted its British charter as its constitution.

North Carolina failed to carry out its Mecklenburg form of government, however, and by a congress elected for the purpose, which assembled in Halifax on the 12th of November, 1776, constructed a permanent form of government, and proclaimed the same on the 18th of December, 1776.

New Hampshire's first constitution was constructed by its congress on the 5th of January, 1776, but it was intended as a provisional government, and was to last only until matters could be adjusted with England, and on the 10th of June, 1776, a convention of delegates chosen by the people met at Concord, and constructed another constitution, which was submitted to the people and rejected by them; another set of delegates were then chosen, who met at Exeter the 12th of June, 1781, and they formed a constitution and submitted it to a vote of the people at their town meetings, with authority in said town meetings to propose amendments; this constitution was adopted by the people, but not in time to go into effect until the 2d of June, 1784.

The first constitution of South Carolina was constructed and adopted by its legislature on the 26th of March, 1776, which was amended by the legislature on the 19th of March, 1778; the supreme court of that state holding that both of said constitutions, being the work of the legislature, were but legislative acts, and that they could be changed by the legislature of that state; thereupon a convention was called, the delegates to which were chosen by the people, which met at Columbia and constructed another constitution, and proclaimed the same on the 3d of June, 1790, without submitting the same to the people for ratification.

New Jersey called its convention to construct its constitution, and the convention held its session with closed doors successively at Burlington, Trenton, and New Brunswick, from the 26th of May to the 3d of July, 1776, at which time it completed its labors and proclaimed the constitution for that state.

Virginia's house of burgesses, which constructed the bill of rights and constitution of that state, was elected for that purpose, and in order to hold the sessions thereof the members were compelled to drive back the British forces under Lord Dunmore (the then governor of that colony); only forty-five of the members took part in the labors. The house of burgesses being as much a part of the machinery of government of that colony under its British charter as the governor was, and the object of that house being to dissolve all connection between that colony and Great Britain (although the sovereign authority may have been in the people of that colony at that time), by the use of the house of burgesses to effect that dissolution was using a recognized agent of the sovereign nation of England ; so that, although it may have been treason on the part of each individual delegate who took part therein, yet the bill of rights and constitution being constructed and proclaimed by the principal arm of the corporate government, gave them the apparent sanction of law under English authority.

The bill of rights constructed by that body of free, thinking men will compare favorably with any state paper of that or any other age ; and the principles of free government declared therein so closely resemble those contained in the great Declaration of Independence as to cause some to suppose that Mr. Jefferson had a hand in preparing the same, or that he copied from it in drafting the Declaration. The bill of rights having been published the day after the committee was appointed to draft the Declaration of Independence, and it was some fifteen days before the committee reported, Mr. Jefferson, therefore, had the benefit of reading the bill of rights before drafting the great Declaration ; but that instrument is in language so strongly resembling the peculiar style of Mr. Jefferson, while the language of the bill of rights differs so widely from that peculiar style, makes it quite clear that the bill of rights was drafted by some other person or persons.

Delaware, by a convention chosen for that purpose, constructed and proclaimed a constitution for that state on the 21st of September, 1776.

Georgia, by a convention of delegates chosen for that purpose, which met on the 1st of October, 1776, constructed and proclaimed a constitution for that state on the 5th of February, 1777.

Maryland, by a convention of delegates chosen for that purpose, met on the 14th of August, 1776, constructed a constitution for that state and submitted the same to the people on the 11th of November, 1776, which was duly ratified.

Massachusetts, by its general court, constructed a constitution for that state ; but that constitution was rejected by the people. Then by a convention of delegates chosen by the people for that purpose, which met at Boston on the first day of September, 1779, another constitution for that state was constructed, and, on the second day of March, 1780, submitted to the people, who duly ratified the same.

New York, by a convention of delegates chosen by the people for that purpose, met at White Plains, July 4, 1776, but being molested by British forces adjourned, and after repeated adjournments and meetings in different places in that state, finally completed its labors at Kingston, April 20, 1777, and submitted the same to the people who duly ratified it.

Pennsylvania, by a convention of delegates chosen by the people for that purpose, who met in Philadelphia on the 15th of July, 1776, constructed a constitution for that state, and on the 28th of September, 1776, proclaimed the same without submitting it to the people for ratification.

Connecticut, during the early part of the summer of 1776, adopted its British charter as its form of government, and after dissolving its connection with England, declared that the people were the source of power in that colony and held the sole right to construct its government, adopted its British charter.

Each colony formed its charter, or corporate government, with the view of becoming a part of a corporate government to be constructed by the Colonial Congress, and ratified by the legislatures of the respective states for the union, as advised by the resolution of the 8th of May, 1776. Although Virginia and South Carolina each formed a government before said resolution was adopted, it is evident from their constitution and bill of rights that each of those states also formed its corporate government with the expectation of its constituting a part of a corporation for the government of the union.

The states respectively reserved the police powers and the management of its domestic affairs by express provision in the organization of the corporation, although authority to ratify a charter for the union was vested in the legislature, consequently the legislature being but agents for the sovereign people, they could not ratify a grant of the police powers, or the rights to manage the domestic affairs to the union. But the Colonial Congress was as careful in preserving these rights in the states as the states were, and provided in the Articles of Confederation that "each state retains its sovereignty, freedom and independence, and every power, jurisdiction and right which is not by this confederation expressly delegated to the United States in congress assembled." *

The people of the states having reserved to themselves the entire sovereign authority, this reservation of sovereignty to the respective states, was in effect a reservation of said authority to the people of the respective states.

But the compact was defective, principally because there was no direct connection between the people and their corporate agent to manage the affairs of the union, and the

---

* Article 2, Confederation.

union did not have sufficient powers to maintain its organization. Consequently it was necessary to amend its organization and perfect the union, and rearrange its powers. Not to do away with the old law, but to amend it so as to make it meet the needs and exigencies of the government. And the better to preserve the great American principles of government.

CHAPTER II.

CONSTITUTION OF 1787.

Although the Constitution of 1777 was not finally ratified until March, 1781, congress during the session of 1781-2, by resolution, appealed to the states for additional powers to enable it to provide adequate laws relating to duties and revenues.

In April, 1783, congress again appealed to the states to extend its powers, to enable it to levy certain duties on importations.

On the 30th of April, 1784, congress proposed to the states to extend its powers, so as to enable it to manage the commerce for fifteen years, which proposition was prepared and presented by a committee appointed for that purpose.

As appears by the report of that committee, most of the states responded favorably to that proposition, but placed such restrictions and limitations on the authority so granted, as to render it unavailing; and three of the states took no action on the proposition.

Various amendments to the Constitution of 1777 were proposed and discussed in congress, but none of them came to any final results.

On the 21st of January, 1786, the Virginia House of Delegates passed a resolution, requesting the appointment of a commission consisting of members from each of the states, hoping it would lead to an enlargement of the powers of congress. Messrs. Edmund Randolph, James Madison, Jr., Walter Jones, St. George Tucker, Meriwether Smith, David Ross, William Ronald and George

Mason, were appointed on that commission, who or any five of them, were authorized to meet such commissioners as may be appointed by the other states at a time and place to be agreed on, to take into consideration the trade of the United States ; to consider how far a uniform system in their commercial regulation may be necessary to their common interest, and their permanent harmony; and to report to the several states such an act relative to this great object, as, when unanimously ratified by them, will enable the United States in congress assembled, effectually to provide for the same ; that the said commissioners shall immediately transmit to the several states, copies of the preceding resolution, with a circular letter requesting their concurrence therein, and proposing a time and place for the meeting aforesaid.*

Pursuant to that resolution, the states of New York, New Jersey, Pennsylvania, Delaware and Virginia sent delegates to Annapolis, Maryland, the place previously agreed on for said commission to meet; there being but five states represented, the delegates concluded to prepare an address to congress, and report to the several states that had delegates at that meeting, to be called to meet at Philadelphia on the second Monday in May, 1787: they then adjourned.

On the 21st of February, 1787, a committee, theretofore appointed by congress, reported in favor of its calling a convention of the states, to meet on the second Monday in May, 1787, as recommended by the Annapolis convention; but there seemed some difficulty in passing an act to call the convention by congress. The delegates from New York proposed: "That it be recommended to the states, that a convention of the representatives of the

---

* Elliott's Debates, vol. 1, page 115.

states be held . . . for the purpose of revising
the Articles of Confederation," which motion was defeated.

The members from Massachusetts then moved the following: "*Whereas*, there is provision in the Articles of
Confederation and Perpetual Union, for making alterations
therein, by the assent of a congress of the United
States, and of the legislatures of the several states; and,
whereas, experience hath evinced that there are de-
fects in the present confederation; as a mean to remedy
which, several of the states, and particularly the state of
New York, by express instructions to their delegates in
congress, have suggested a convention for the purposes
expressed in the following resolution; and such convention appearing to be the most probable means of establishing in these states a firm national government—

"*Resolved*, That, in the opinion of congress, it is expedient that, on the second Monday in May next, a
convention of delegates, who shall have been appointed
by the several states, be held at Philadelphia, for the sole
and express purpose of revising the Articles of Confederation, and reporting to congress and the several legislatures, such alterations and provisions therein as shall,
when agreed to in congress, and confirmed by the
states, render the federal constitution adequate to the
exegencies of government and the preservation of the
union." Which was agreed to, and then passed by
congress.

To this resolution all the states responded, and appointed delegates, to meet on the second Monday in May,
1787, except Rhode Island.

Each state instructed its delegates to discuss and report how the Articles of Confederation could be amended
so as to meet the exigencies of the government and preserve the "*federal union*."

The time for the meeting was the second Monday in May, but it was the 25th of that month before enough of the delegates reported, to represent a majority of the states.

On Friday, the 25th of May, 1787, delegates from New York, New Jersey, Pennsylvania, Delaware, Virginia, North Carolina and South Carolina, seven states, being present by representation, on motion of R. Morris, General Washington was unanimously chosen to take the chair as president of the convention.

After the credentials of the delegates from seven states were read, door-keepers, messengers and committee on rules were severally appointed ; the convention adjourned over to Monday, the 28th of May, 1787.

On the 28th, the convention met, and the committee on rules reported. After several amendments thereto were proposed, the rules were referred back to the same committee. On that day delegates from Massachusetts and Connecticut reported, making nine states represented in the convention.

The convention, after receiving the delegates from said two additional states, adjourned to the next day, it being the 29th.

On the 29th met pursuant to adjournment, and Edmund Randolph, of Virginia, after an elaborate speech, offered a series of resolutions relating to a plan of government to be constructed, which were as follows :

"1. *Resolved*, That the Articles of the Confederation ought to be so corrected and enlarged as to accomplish the objects proposed by their institution ; namely, common defense, security of liberty, and general welfare.

"2. *Resolved*, Therefore, that the right of suffrage, in the national legislature, ought to be proportioned to the quotas of contribution, or to the number of free inhabitants, as the one or the other may seem best in different cases.

"3. *Resolved*, That the national legislature ought to consist of two branches.

"4. *Resolved*, that the members of the first branch of the national legislature ought to be elected by the people of the several states, every —— for the term of ——, to be the age of —— years, at least; to receive liberal stipends, by which they may be compensated for the devotion of their time to the public service; to be ineligible to any office established by a particular state or under the authority of the United States (except those peculiarly belonging to the functions of the first branch) during the term of service and for the space of —— after its expiration; to be incapable of re-election for the space of —— after the expiration of their term of service; and to be subject to recall.

"5. *Resolved*, That the members of the second branch of the national legislature ought to be elected by those of the first, out of a proper number of persons nominated by the individual legislatures, to be of the age of —— years, at least; to hold their offices for a term sufficient to insure their independency; to receive liberal stipends, by which they may be compensated for the devotion of their time to the public service; and to be ineligible to any office established by a particular state, or under the authority of the United States (except those particularly belonging to the functions of the second branch) during the term of service; and for the space of —— after the expiration thereof.

"6. *Resolved*, That each branch ought to possess the right of originating acts; that the national legislatures ought to be empowered to enjoy the legislative rights vested in congress by the confederation; and, moreover, to legislate in all cases to which the separate states are incompetent, or in which the harmony of the United States may be interrupted by the exercise of individual legislation ; to negative all laws passed by the several states, contravening, in the opinion of the national legislature, the articles of union, or any treaty subsisting under the authority of the union ; and to call forth the force of the union against any member of the union failing to fulfill its duty under the articles thereof.

"7. *Resolved*, That a national executive be instituted, to be chosen by the national legislature for the term of —— years, to receive punctually, at stated times, a fixed compensation for the services rendered, in which no increase or diminution shall be made, so as to affect the magistracy existing at the time of the increase or diminution ; to be ineligible a second time ; and that, besides a general authority to execute the national laws, it ought to enjoy the executive rights vested in congress by the confederation.

"8. *Resolved*, That the executive, and a convenient number of the national judiciary, ought to compose a council of revision, with authority to examine every act of the national legislature before it shall operate, and every act of a particular legislature before a negative thereon shall be final ; and that the dissent of the said council shall amount to a rejection, unless the act of the national legislature be again passed, or that of a particular legislature be again negatived by —— of the members of each branch.

"9. *Resolved*, That a national judiciary be established —to hold their offices during good behavior, and to receive punctually, at stated times, a fixed compensation for their services, in which no increase or diminution shall be made, so as to affect the persons actually in office at the time of such increase or diminution. That the jurisdiction of the inferior tribunals shall be to hear and determine in the first instance, and of the supreme tribunal to hear and determine in the *dernier ressort*, all piracies and felonies on the seas, captures from an enemy, cases in which foreigners, or citizens of other states applying to such jurisdictions, may be interested, or which respect the collection of the national revenue; impeachments of any national officer and questions which involve the national peace or harmony.

"10. *Resolved*, That provision ought to be made for the admission of states, lawfully arising within the limits of the United States, whether from a voluntary junction of government or territory, or otherwise, with the consent of a number of voices in the national legislature less than the whole.

"11. *Resolved*, That a republican government and the territory of each state (except in the instance of a voluntary junction of government and territory) ought to be guaranteed by the United States to each state.

"12. *Resolved*, That provision ought to be made for the continuance of congress, and their authorities and privileges until a given day, after the reform of the articles of union shall be adopted, and for the completion of all of their engagements.

"13. *Resolved*, That provision ought to be made for the amendments of the articles of union, whensoever it shall seem necessary, and that the assent of the national legislature ought not to be required thereto.

"14. *Resolved*, That the legislative, executive and judiciary powers within the several states ought to be bound by oath to support the articles of union.

"15. *Resolved*, That the amendments which shall be offered to the confederation by the convention ought, at a proper time or times, after the approbation of congress, to be submitted to an assembly or assemblies of representatives, recommended by the several legislatures, to be expressly chosen by the people to consider and decide thereon.

"16. *Resolved*, That the house will to-morrow resolve itself into a committee of the whole house to consider of the state of the American Union."

Mr. Randolph confessed that they were not intended to establish a federal government, but rather a strong, consolidated union, in which the states would be nearly annihilated. He then moved that they should be taken in committee of the whole.

Mr. C. Pinckney, a member from South Carolina, then stated that he had reduced his ideas of a new government to a system, in writing, which he then read, and stated that his plan was grounded on the same principles as the resolutions of Mr. Randolph.

The house then resolved to go into committee of the whole on the following day, for the consideration of the state of the union, and then adjourned to the next day.

On May the 30th the convention met pursuant to adjournment, and resolved itself into committee of the whole, and Mr. Gorham, of Massachusetts, was chosen as chairman.

Mr. Randolph then moved to adopt his first resolution. Mr. G. Morris observed that it was an unnecessary resolution, as the subsequent resolution would not agree with it. It was then withdrawn by Mr. Randolph and the following proposed in its stead:

"1. *Resolved*, That a union of the states, merely federal, will not accomplish the objects proposed by the Articles of Confederation, namely, 'common defense, security, liberty, and general welfare.'

"2. *Resolved*, That no treaty or treaties among the states, as sovereign, will accomplish or secure their common defense, liberty, or welfare.

" 3. *Resolved*, That a national government ought to be established, consisting of a supreme judicial, legislative, and executive."

Various modifications were proposed to the first resolution, and rejected ; at last Mr. Pinckney observed : " If the convention agrees to it, its business is at an end, as the convention met to alter or amend the Articles of Confederation *only*."

Thereupon the first and second resolutions were dropped and the third only agitated.

The third had difficulties also in the convention. The term *supreme* had to be explained ; it was asked whether it was intended to annihilate the state governments. The friends of the resolution assured the convention that the states would be interfered with *only* in so far as their powers would clash with those to be granted to the union. It was then supported by the votes of Massachusetts, Pennsylvania, Delaware, Virginia, North Carolina, and South Carolina, for ; Connecticut, New Jersey (and New York divided) against.

The next resolution taken up was as follows : " That the mode of the present representation is unjust ; that the suffrage ought to be in proportion to numbers or property."

To this Delaware objected and moved a postponement of its consideration, which was agreed to. The convention then adjourned to the next day.

From that time on the convention, in committee of the whole, was engaged in considering the Randolph resolutions, with the various amendments, changes, and substitutes offered thereto, until the 13th of June, on which day the committee of the whole reported said resolutions to the convention, after revising, amending, and correcting them.

The said resolutions, as reported to the convention by the committee of the whole, were as follows:

"1. That it is the opinion of this committee that a national government ought to be established, consisting of a supreme legislative, judiciary, and executive.

"2. That the national legislature ought to consist of two branches.

"3. That the members of the first branch of the national legislature ought to be elected by the people of the several states for the terms of three years, to receive fixed stipends, etc. (as in the original Randolph resolution).

"4. That the members of the second branch of the national legislature ought to be chosen by the individual legislatures; to be of the age of thirty years, at least; to hold their offices for a term sufficient to insure their independency, namely, seven years; to receive fixed stipend, etc. (as in the third resolution).

"5. That each branch ought to possess the right of originating acts.

"6. That the national legislature ought to be empowered to enjoy the legislative rights vested in congress by the confederation, and, moreover, to legislate in all cases to which the separate states are incompetent, or in which the harmony of the United States may be interrupted by the exercise of independent legislation; to negative all laws passed by the several states contravening, in the opinion of the national legislature, the articles of union.

"7. That the right of suffrage in the first branch of the national legislature ought not to be according to the rule established in the Articles of Confederation but according to the same equitable ratio of the representation; namely, in proportion to the whole number of white and other free citizens and inhabitants of every age, sex and condition, including those bound to servitude for a term of years, and three-fifth of all other persons not comprehended in the foregoing description, except Indians not paying taxes in each state.

" 8. That the right of suffrage in the second branch of the national legislature ought to be according to the rule established for the first.

" 9. That a national executive be instituted to consist of a single person, to be chosen by the national legislature for the term of seven years, with power to carry into execution the national laws, to appoint to office in cases not otherwise provided for, to be ineligible a second time, and to be removable on impeachment and conviction of malpractice or neglect of duty ; to receive a fixed stipend, by which he may be compensated for the devotion of his time to public service, to be paid out of the national treasury.

" 10. That the national executive shall have a right to negative any legislative act which shall not be afterwards passed by two-third parts of each branch of the national legislature.

" 11. That a national judiciary be established to consist of one supreme tribunal, the judges of which to be appointed by the second branch of the national legislature, to hold their offices during good behavior, to receive punctually at stated times a fixed compensation for their services, in which no increase or diminution shall be made so as to affect the persons actually in office at the time of such increase or diminution.

" 12. That the national legislature be empowered to appoint inferior tribunals.

" 13. That the jurisdiction of the national judiciary shall extend to cases which respect the collection of the national revenue, impeachment of any national officers, and questions which involve the national peace and harmony.

"14. That provision ought to be made for the admission of states lawfully arising within the limits of the United States, whether from a voluntary junction of government and territory, or otherwise, with the consent of a number of voices in the national legislature less than the whole.

"15. That provision ought to be made for the continuance of congress and their authorities, until a given day after the reform of the Articles of Union shall be adopted, and for the completion of all their engagements.

"16. That a republican constitution and its existing laws ought to be guaranteed to each state by the United States.

"17. That provision ought to be made for the amendment of the Articles of Union whensoever it shall seem necessary.

"18. That the legislative, executive and judiciary powers within the several states ought to be bound by oath to support the Articles of Union.

"19. That the amendments which shall be offered to the confederation by the convention ought at a proper time or times after the approbation of congress to be submitted to an assembly or assemblies of representatives, recommended by the several legislatures, to be expressly chosen by the people, to consider and decide thereon."

When this report came to the convention and was read it was agreed that consideration of it should be postponed until the next day, and the convention then adjourned.

On the 14th of June met in pursuance to adjournment. On motion of the Hon. Mr. Patterson, of New Jersey, the consideration of said report was again postponed and the convention adjourned to the next day.

On the 15th of June met pursuant to adjournment. Hon. Mr. Patterson offered eleven resolutions as a substitute for the report of the committee of the whole. As the first and second of said resolutions of Mr. Patterson will show the main difference between the Patterson or New Jersey plan (based entirely on federal principles) and the Randolph or Virginia plan (laid mainly on national principles), I will copy those two resolutions only.   They are as follows:

" 1. *Resolved*, " That the Articles of Confederation ought to be revised, corrected and enlarged so as to render the federal constitution adequate to the exigencies of government and the preservation of the union.

"2. *Resolved*, That, in addition to the powers vested in the United States in congress, by the present existing Articles of Confederation, they be authorized to pass acts for raising a revenue, by levying a duty or duties on all goods and merchandise of foreign growth or manufacture, imported into any part of the United States ; by stamps on paper, vellum, or parchment ; and by a postage on all letters and packages passing through the general post-office, to be applied to such federal purposes as they shall deem proper and expedient ; to make rules and regulations for the collecting thereof ; and the same from time to time to alter and amend, in such manner as they shall think proper.   To pass acts for the regulation of trade and commerce as well with foreign nations as with each other ; provided, that, all punishments, fines, forfeitures and penalties, to be incurred for contravening such rules and regulations, shall be adjudged by the common law judiciary of the states in which any offense contrary to the true intent and meaning of such rules and regulations shall be permitted or perpetrated ; with liberty of commencing, in the first instance, all suits or prosecutions for that purpose in the superior common-law judiciary of such state ; subject, nevertheless, to an appeal for the correction of all errors, both in law and fact, in rending judgment, to the judiciary of the United States."*

It will be remembered that under the Articles of Confederation there was but one branch of congress, and each state was entitled to but one vote, without regard to population ; the New Jersey or Patterson plan, proposed no change as to that provision. With that provision in the new form of government, it would have remained absolutely federal and have recognized the states as sovereign and have left their governments above that of the union, as was the case under the Articles of Confederation. And as the act of congress calling the convention advised that, "*the Articles of Confederation be so amended as to render them adequate to the exigencies of government, and the preservation of the union,*" and each of the states sending delegates to that convention made use of the same language, the New Jersey plan had the merit of being in conformity with the powers given to the delegates in the convention.

The Virginia, or Randolph, plan departing from instructions proposed to change the government of the Union, from a federal to a national form.

Upon the introduction of Mr. Patterson's resolution, it was moved by Mr. Madison and seconded by Mr. Sherman, to refer the Patterson resolutions to a committee of the whole, which carried.

Mr. Rutledge then moved to re-commit the Virginia resolutions as amended to the committee of the whole,

---

* Elliott's Debates, vol. 1, page 175.

which was seconded by Mr. Hamilton, and passed in the affirmative.

The convention then adjourned to the next day.

Those two plans for a government for the union were discussed by the committee of the whole, from day to day until the 19th of June, when on motion the committee agreed to rise and report that it did not agree to the Patterson resolutions, and that it adhered to its former report. Massachusetts, Connecticut, Pennsylvania, Virginia, North Carolina, South Carolina and Georgia, seven states for; and New York, New Jersey and Delaware against (and Maryland divided).

The committee of the whole then reported its action to the convention on the said 19th of June.

A motion to postpone the consideration of the first resolve until the next day carried, and the convention then adjourned to the next day.

On June the 20th met agreeably to adjournment. The convention then took up the report of the committee of the whole, and discussed it with great ability, earnestness and zeal, from day to day, until the 2d of July.

The zeal and earnestness with which the advocates of the two plans had been discussed, betrayed acrimony and bitterness, and it was seriously feared that the convention would have to adjourn without accomplishing any thing.

To show the want of confidence, as well as the state of feeling in the convention at that time, it may not be out of place to report a speech made by the Hon. Mr. Bedford on the 30th of June, which is as follows:

"That all of the states at present are equally sovereign and independent, has been asserted from every quarter of this house—our deliberations here are a confirmation of the position ; and I may add to it, that each of them acts from interested and many from ambitious motives.

Look at the votes which have been given on the floor of this house, and it will be found that their numbers, wealth and local views have actuated their determinations, and that the larger states proceed as if our eyes were already perfectly blinded.

"Impartiality, with them, is already out of the question ; the reported plan is their political creed, and they support it, right or wrong.

"Even the diminutive state of Georgia has an eye to her future wealth and greatness.

"South Carolina, puffed up with the possession of her wealth and negroes, and North Carolina, are all, from different views, united with the great states. And these latter, although it is said they can never, from interested views, form a coalition, we find closely united in one scheme of interest and ambition (notwithstanding they endeavor to amuse us with the purity of their principle and the rectitude of their intentions), in asserting that the general government must be drawn from an equal representation of the people. Pretenses to support ambition are never wanting.

"Their cry is, ' Where is the danger?' And they insist that although the powers of the general government will be increased, yet it will be for the good of the whole ; and although the three great states form nearly a majority of the people of America, they never will hurt or injure the lesser states. *I do not, gentlemen, trust you.* If you possess the power, the abuse of it could not be checked ; and what then would prevent you from exercising it to our destruction? You gravely allege that there is no danger of combination, and triumphantly ask, ' How could combinations be effected?' The large states, you say, ' all differ in productions and commerce, and experience shows that, instead of combinations, they would be rivals, and counteract the views of one another.'

"This, I repeat, is language calculated only to amuse us. Yes, sir; the larger states will be rivals, but not against each other—they will be rivals against the *rest of the states.* But it is urged that such a government would suit the people, and that its principles are equitable and just.

"How often has this argument been refuted, when applied to a *federal* government! The small states never can agree to the Virginia plan; and why, then, is it still urged? But it is said that it is not expected that the state governments will approve the proposed system, and that this house must directly carry it to THE PEOPLE for their approbation! Is it come to this, then, that the *sword* must decide this controversy, and that the horrors of war must be added to the rest of our misfortunes?

"But what have the people already said? 'We find the confederation defective. Go, and give additional powers to the confederation—give to it the imposts, regulation of trade, power to collect the taxes, and the means to discharge our foreign and domestic debts.'

"Can we not then, as their delegates, agree upon these points?

"As their ambassadors, can we not clearly grant those powers? Why, then, when we are met, must entire distinct and new grounds be taken, and a government of which the people had no idea be instituted? And are we to be told, if we won't agree to it, it is the last moment of our deliberations?

"I say, it is indeed the last moment, if we do not agree to this assumption of power.

"The states will never again be entrapped into a measure like this. The people will say, 'The *small* states would confederate, and grant further powers to

congress, but you, the *large* states, would not. Then
the fault would be yours, and all the nations of the earth
will justify us. But what is to become of our public
debts, if we dissolve the union?' Where is your
plighted faith? Will you crush the small states, or must
they be left unmolested? Sooner than be ruined, there
are *foreign powers who would take us by the hand.* I say
not this to threaten or intimidate, but that we should reflect seriously before we act. If we once leave this
floor, and solemnly renounce your new project, what will
be the consequence? You will annihilate your federal
government, and ruin must stare you in the face. Let
us, then, do what is in our power—*amend and enlarge
the confederation, but not alter the federal system.*

"The people expect this and no more. We all agree
in the necessity of a more efficient government—and can
not this be done? Although my state is small, I know
and respect its rights, as much, at least, as those who
have the honor to represent any of the larger states." *

This speech seemed to check the use of severe language, but the debate continued with earnestness until
the 2d of July, on which day it was agreed to form a
committee, to try to fall upon some plan, to bring the opposing delegates to an agreement that would avoid the
calamity of having to adjourn without accomplishing any
result by the convention. While but a few of the delegates who had been zealous in the debate, thought any
good could be accomplished by such a committee, an adjournment without an agreement to a plan of government of some sort, would have so disastrous an effect
that they agreed to the appointment of the committee to
consist of a member from each state, which was chosen
by ballot as follows: Hon. Mr. Gerry, of Massachusetts;

---

* Elliott's Debates (Yate's minutes), vol. 1, p. 471.

Hon. Mr. Ellisworth, of Connecticut; Hon. Mr. Yates, of New York; Hon. Mr. Patterson, of New Jersey; Hon. Mr. Franklin, of Pennsylvania; Hon. Mr. Bedford, of Delaware; Hon. Mr. Martin, of Maryland; Hon. Mr. Mason, of Virginia; Hon. Mr. Davie, of North Carolina; Hon. Mr. Rutledge, of South Carolina, and Hon. Mr. Baldwin, of Georgia. *

After the appointment of said committee (which was known as the grand committee, so-called because of its size), but which proved itself to be truly a grand committee by the result of its labors, the convention then adjourned to the 5th of July.

The grand committee met on the 3d of July and elected the Hon. Mr. Gerry, chairman; and soon agreed on the terms of a compromise and reported the same on the 5th of July as follows:

"The committee to whom was referred the eighth resolution reported from the committee of the whole house, and so much of the seventh as had not been decided on, submit the following report:

"That the subsequent proposition be recommended to the convention on condition that both shall be generally adopted.

"That, in the first branch of the legislature, each of the states now in the union be allowed one member for every 40,000 inhabitants of the description reported in the seventh resolution of the committee of the whole house. That each state not containing that number shall be allowed one member.

"That bills for raising or appropriating money, and for fixing salaries of the officers of the government of the United States, shall originate in the first branch of the legislature, and shall not be altered or amended by the

* Elliott's Debates, vol. 1, pp. 477-78.

second branch ; and that no money shall be drawn from
the public treasury but in pursuance of appropriations to
be originated in the first branch.

"That in the second branch of the legislature each
state *shall have an equal vote.*" *

Hon. Luther Martin, of Maryland, in a report to that
state, says, there were three parties in the convention ;
that one party favored the annihilation of the states and
the establishment of a strong monarchical government ;
however, those who openly expressed these views were
but few, though there were others who did not express
them openly, who were regarded as favoring them.

The second party neither favored the abolition of the
states nor establishment of a monarchy, but wanted a
government that would give their own states an advantage over others.

The third party favored amending the confederation
so as enable it to raise the necessary means to pay debts
and render it adequate to the exigencies of government.†

The compromise as reported by the grand committee,
was accepted by some of the delegates, as the best they
could secure from the convention, but others from
each side withdrew and went home. Those who approved it, and those who accepted it without approval,
proceeded to construct the constitution on the basis of
the compromise ; and but for the irrepressible conflict
between the delegates from the larger and smaller
states, they would have had but little difficulty. But
that unyielding conflict again tied the convention
up, on providing the mode in which the senators
should vote ; the smaller states, insisting that the
senators should vote their respective states as a unit ;
the larger states, however, insisted that the senators

* Elliott's Debates, vol. 1, p. 478.   † Id., pp. 344–45.

should vote individually; the mode contended for by the larger states was carried; and Mr. Madison, in a letter to Mr. Sparks, said the return of Mr. Morris to the convention was opportune to cut the Gordian knot which gave the larger states their plan.*

It is evident from the language of the compromise, and the character of the debates preceding the same, that the committee intended that the respective states should be voted as units in the senate, as the congress did by the Articles of Confederation; and when that provision of the compromise was set at naught by the larger states, it greatly irritated the delegates from the smaller states; and doubtless to appease them, it was provided that, in no event should the constitution be amended so as to deprive any state of equal suffrage in the senate, without its consent, which seems to have satisfied the delegates from the smaller states.

The convention was industriously engaged in reconstructing the constitution so as to conform to the principles of that compromise, from the 5th day of June (the day it was reported by the grand committee), to the 17th day of September, 1787—on which day the convention completed its labors.

On said 17th of September, 1787, the constitution having been completed, agreed to and signed by the delegates of the respective states present, the convention, on that day, prepared and adopted a resolution, to go with the constitution, in its report of that instrument, which is in words and figures as follows:

"IN CONVENTION,
"MONDAY, *September 17, 1787.*
"PRESENT—*The States of New Hampshire, Connecticut, Mr. Hamilton from New York, New Jersey, Pennsylvania,*

* Elliott's Debates, vol. I, page 507.

Delaware, Maryland, Virginia, North Carolina, South Carolina and Georgia.

"*Resolved*, That the preceding constitution be laid before the United States, in congress assembled, and that it is the opinion of this convention, that it should afterwards be submitted to a convention of delegates, chosen in each state by the people thereof, under the recommendation of its legislature, for their assent and ratification; and that each convention assenting to, and ratifying the same, should give notice thereof to the United States in congress assembled.

"*Resolved*, That it is the opinion of this convention, that, as soon as the conventions of nine states shall have ratified this constitution, the United States, in congress assembled, should fix a day on which electors should be appointed by the states which shall have ratified the same, and a day on which electors should assemble to vote for the president, and the time and place for commencing proceedings under this constitution. That after such publication, the electors should be appointed, and the senators and representatives elected. That the electors should meet on the day fixed for the election of the president, and should transmit their votes certified, signed, sealed and directed, as the constitution requires, to the secretary of the United States in congress assembled; that the senators and representatives should convene at the time and place assigned; that the senators should appoint a president of the senate for the sole purpose of receiving, opening and counting, the votes for president; and that, after he shall be chosen, the congress, together with the president, should, without delay, proceed to execute this constitution,. By the unanimous order of the convention.

"GEORGE WASHINGTON, *President.*
"WILLIAM JACKSON, *Secretary.*"*

* Elliott's Debates, vol. 1, page 16.

Although the delegates to that convention were appointed by the respective states represented in it, and derived their entire authority from the state appointing them, the only provision in the Articles of Confederation that authorized the same to be altered, required that all alterations should be approved by the congress of the United States and afterwards confirmed by the legislatures of all the states; therefore the constitution had to be reported to congress.

Congress approved the constitution and by the following resolution referred it to the legislatures of the states:

"*Resolved, unanimously*, That the said report, with the resolutions and letter accompanying the same, be transmitted to the several legislatures, in order to be submitted to a convention of delegates chosen in each state by the people thereof, in conformity to the resolves of the convention made and provided in that case." *

In conformity with said resolution the legislatures of the respective states passed acts calling conventions. The several state conventions ratified the constitution and reported its actions thereof to congress as follows:

Delaware ratified the same on the 7th of December, 1787.

Pennsylvania ratified same on the 12th of December, 1787.

New Jersey ratified same on the 18th of December, 1787, and proposed amendments thereto.

Connecticut ratified same on the 9th of January, 1788.

Massachusetts ratified same on the 7th of February, 1788, and proposed amendments thereto.

Georgia ratified same on the 2d of January, 1788.

Maryland ratified same November, 1788.

---

* Elliott's Debates, vol. 1, p. 319.

South Carolina ratified same on the 22d of May, 1788, and proposed amendments thereto.

New Hampshire ratified same on the 21st of June, 1788, but did not report its action to congress until the 2d of July, and proposed amendments thereto.

Virginia ratified the same on the 26th of June, 1788, and proposed amendments thereto.

New York ratified the same on the 26th of July, 1788, and proposed amendments thereto.

New Hampshire being the ninth state to ratify the constitution, when its report to congress came in on the 2d of July, 1788, on motion of Mr. Clark, seconded by Mr. Edwards, congress ordered that the ratification of the constitution be referred to a committee to examine the same, and report an act to congress for putting the constitution in operation.

On that motion New Hampshire, Massachusetts, Connecticut, New Jersey, Maryland, Pennsylvania, Virginia, South Carolina, and Georgia voted yea; Rhode Island was excused and New York was divided, Mr. Yates voting nay and Mr. Hamilton yea; and an act of congress was reported and adopted for putting the constitution in operation.

North Carolina ratified the constitution on the 29th of May, 1790, and proposed amendments thereto.

Vermont ratified the same on the 9th of February, 1791, on coming into the union after the amendments to the constitution had been proposed by congress.

The first congress at its first session held in New York on the 4th of March, 1789, proposed twelve articles of amendments to the constitution, and submitted same to the legislatures of the respective states for ratification; the respective legislatures took action thereon as follows:

New Hampshire agreed to all except the second.

New York agreed to all except the second.

Pennsylvania agreed to all except the first and second.

Delaware agreed to all except the first.

Maryland agreed to all of them.

South Carolina agreed to all of them.

North Carolina agreed to all of them.

Rhode Island agreed to all of them.

Virginia agreed to all of them.

New Jersey agreed to all except the second.

Massachusetts, Connecticut, Georgia and Kentucky took no action on said amendments, although Massachusetts had proposed substantially the same amendments by its convention at the time it adopted the constitution.

The first and second of said articles of amendment failing to receive the ratification of enough of the states to pass them into the constitution, were lost; but the remaining ten articles of amendment, receiving the ratification of ten out of fourteen states, were carried, and duly declared to be parts of the constitution.

As said ten articles were proposed by six of the states in convention, at the time each of these states ratified the constitution, and were proposed by the first congress during its first session, they may be considered as part of the constitution as originally adopted.

The changes made in the confederation by the Constitution of 1787 relate more to the mode of executing the government than to the fundamental principles thereof.

The following is a copy of the constitution with its fifteen amendments:

THE CONSTITUTION OF THE UNITED STATES.

WE, the People of the United States, in order to form a more perfect union, establish justice, insure domestic tranquillity, provide for the common defense, promote the general welfare, and secure the blessings of liberty to

ourselves and our posterity, do ordain and establish this
Constitution for the United States of America.

ARTICLE I.

SECTION I.

1. All legislative powers herein granted shall be vested
in a congress of the United States, which shall consist of
a senate and house of representatives.

SECTION II.

1. The house of representatives shall be composed of
members chosen every second year by the people of the
several states; and the electors in each state shall have
the qualifications requisite for electors of the most numerous branch of the state legislature.

2. No person shall be a representative who shall not
have attained to the age of twenty-five years, and been
seven years a citizen of the United States, and who shall
not, when elected, be an inhabitant of that state in which
he shall be chosen.

3. Representatives and direct taxes shall be apportioned among the several states which may be included
within this union, according to their respective numbers,
which shall be determined by adding to the whole number of free persons, including those bound to service for
a term of years and excluding Indians not taxed, three-
fifths of all other persons. The actual enumeration shall
be made within three years after the first meeting of the
congress of the United States, and within every subsequent term of ten years, in such manner as they shall by
law direct. The number of representatives shall not exceed one for every thirty thousand, but each state shall
have at least one representative; and until such enumeration shall be made the state of New Hampshire shall be entitled to choose three; Massachusetts, eight; Rhode Island

and Providence Plantations, one ; Connecticut, five ; New York, six ; New Jersey, four ; Pennsylvania, eight ; Delaware, one ; Maryland, six ; Virginia, ten ; North Carolina, five ; South Carolina, five ; and Georgia, three.

4. When vacancies happen in the representation from any state, the executive authority thereof shall issue writs of election to fill up such vacancies.

5. The house of representatives shall choose their speaker and other officers, and shall have the sole power of impeachment.

SECTION III.

1. The senate of the United States shall be composed of two senators from each state, chosen by the legislature thereof, for six years ; and each senator shall have one vote.

2. Immediately after they shall be assembled in consequence of the first election, they shall be divided as equally as may be into three classes. The seats of the senators of the first class shall be vacated at the expiration of the second year ; of the second class, at the expiration of the fourth year ; and of the third class, at the expiration of the sixth year ; so that one-third may be chosen every second year ; and if vacancies happen, by resignation or otherwise, during the recess of the legislature of any state, the executive thereof may make temporary appointments until the next meeting of the legislature, which shall then fill such vacancies.

3. No person shall be a senator who shall not have attained to the age of thirty years, and been nine years a citizen of the United States, and who shall not, when elected, be an inhabitant of that state for which he shall be chosen.

4. The vice-president of the United States shall be president of the senate, but shall have no vote unless they be equally divided.

5. The senate shall choose their other officers, and also a president *pro tempore*, in the absence of the vice-president, or when he shall exercise the office of president of the United States.

6. The senate shall have the sole power to try all impeachments. When sitting for that purpose, they shall be on oath or affirmation. When the president of the United States is tried, the chief justice shall preside; and no person shall be convicted without the concurrence of two-thirds of the members present.

7. Judgment, in case of impeachment, shall not extend further than to removal from office, and disqualification to hold and enjoy any office of honor, trust, or profit under the United States; but the party convicted shall nevertheless be liable and subject to indictment, trial, judgment, and punishment, according to law.

SECTION IV.

1. The times, places, and manner of holding elections for senators and representative, shall be prescribed in each state by the legislature thereof; but the congress may, at any time, by law, make or alter such regulations, except as to the places of choosing senators.

2. The congress shall assemble at least once in every year, and such meeting shall be on the first Monday in December, unless they shall by law appoint a different day.

SECTION V.

1. Each house shall be the judge of the elections, returns, and qualifications of its own members; and a majority of each shall constitute a quorum to do business; but a smaller number may adjourn from day to day, and may be authorized to compel the attendance of absent members, in such manner and under such penalties as each house may provide.

2. Each house may determine the rules of its proceedings, punish its members for disorderly behavior, and, with the concurrence of two-thirds, expel a member.

3. Each house shall keep a journal of its proceedings, and from time to time publish the same, excepting such parts as may in their judgment require secrecy ; and the yeas and nays of the members of either house, on any question, shall, at the desire of one-fifth of those present, be entered on the journal.

4. Neither house during the session of congress, shall, without the consent of the other, adjourn for more than three days, nor to any other place than that in which the two houses shall be sitting.

SECTION VI.

1. The senators and representatives shall receive a compensation for their services, to be ascertained by law, and paid out of the treasury of the United States. They shall, in all cases, except treason, felony, and breach of the peace, be privileged from arrest during their attendance at the session of their respective houses, and in going to or returning from the same ; and for any speech or debate in either house, they shall not be questioned in any other place.

2. No senator or representative shall, during the time for which he was elected, be appointed to any civil office under the authority of the United States which shall have been created, or the emoluments whereof shall have been increased, during such time ; and no person holding any office under the United States shall be a member of either house during his continuance in office.

SECTION VII.

1. All bills for raising revenue shall originate in the

house of representatives ; but the senate may propose or concur with amendments, as on other bills.

2. Every bill which shall have passed the house of representatives and the senate, shall, before it become a law, be presented to the president of the United States ; if he approve, he shall sign it ; but if not, he shall return it, with his objections, to that house in which it shall have originated, who shall enter the objection at large on their journal, and proceed to reconsider it.   If, after such reconsideration, two-thirds of that house shall agree to pass the bill, it shall be sent, together with the objections, to the other house, by which it shall likewise be reconsidered, and if approved by two-thirds of that house, it shall become a law.   But in all such cases, the votes of both houses shall be determined by yeas and nays, and the names of the persons voting for and against the bill shall be entered on the journal of each house respectively.   If any bill shall not be returned by the president within ten days (Sundays excepted) after it shall have been presented to him, the same shall be a law in like manner as if he had signed it, unless the congress by their adjournment prevent its return, in which case it shall not be a law.

3. Every order, resolution, or vote, to which the concurrence of the senate and house of representatives may be necessary, except on a question of adjournment, shall be presented to the president of the United States ; and before the same shall take effect, shall be approved by him, or being disapproved by him, shall be repassed by two-thirds of the senate and house of representatives, according to the rules and limitations prescribed in the case of a bill.

SECTION VIII.

The congress shall have power—

1. To lay and collect taxes, duties, imposts, and ex-

cises ; to pay the debts and provide for the common defense and general welfare of the United States ; but all duties, imposts, and excises, shall be uniform throughout the United States :

2. To borrow money on the credit of the United States :

3. To regulate commerce with foreign nations, and among the several states, and with the Indian tribes :

4. To establish a uniform rule of naturalization, and uniform laws on the subject of bankruptcies throughout the United States :

5. To coin money, regulate the value thereof, and of foreign coin, and fix the standard of weights and measures :

6. To provide for the punishment of counterfeiting the securities and current coin of the United States :

7. To establish post offices and post roads :

8. To promote the progress of science and useful arts, by securing for limited times to authors and inventors the exclusive right to their respective writings and discoveries :

9. To constitute tribunals inferior to the supreme court :

10. To define and punish piracies and felonies committed on the high seas, and offenses against the laws of nations :

11. To declare war, grant letters of marque and reprisal, and make rules concerning captures on land and water :

12. To raise and support armies, but no appropriation of money to that use shall be for a longer term than two years :

13. To provide and maintain a navy :

14. To make rules for the government and regulation of the land and naval forces :

15. To provide for calling forth the militia to execute the laws of the union, suppress insurrections, and repel invasions.

16. To provide for organizing, arming, and disciplining the militia, and for governing such part of them as may be employed in the service of the United States, reserving to the states, respectively, the appointment of the officers, and the authority of training the militia according to the discipline prescribed by congress.

17. To exercise exclusive legislation in all cases whatsoever, over such district, not exceeding ten miles square, as may, by cession of particular states, and the acceptance of congress, become the seat of government of the United States, and to exercise like authority over all places purchased by the consent of the legislature of the state in which the same shall be, for the erection of forts, magazines, arsenals, dock-yards, and other needful buildings; and,

18. To make all laws which shall be necessary and proper for carrying into execution the foregoing powers, and all other powers vested by this constitution in the government of the United States, or in any department or officer thereof.

SECTION IX.

1. The migration or importation of such persons as any of the states now existing shall think proper to admit, shall not be prohibited by the congress prior to the year one thousand eight hundred and eight, but a tax or duty may be imposed on such importation, not exceeding ten dollars for each person.

2. The privilege of the writ of *habeas corpus* shall not be suspended, unless when, in cases of rebellion or invasion, the public safety may require it.

3. No bill of attainder, or *ex post facto* law, shall be passed.

4. No capitation or other direct tax shall be laid, unless in proportion to the census or enumeration hereinbefore directed to be taken.

5. No tax or duty shall be laid on articles exported from any state. No preference shall be given by any regulation of commerce or revenue to the ports of one state over those of another ; nor shall vessels bound to or from one state, be obliged to enter, clear, or pay duties in another.

6. No money shall be drawn from the treasury, but in consequence of appropriations made by law ; and a regular statement and account of the receipts and expenditures of all public money shall be published from time to time.

7. No title of nobility shall be granted by the United States, and no person holding any office of profit or trust under them, shall, without the consent of the congress, accept of any present, emolument, office, or title of any kind whatever, from any king, prince or foreign state.

SECTION X.

1. No state shall enter into any treaty, alliance, or confederation ; grant letters of marque or reprisal ; coin money ; emit bills of credit ; make any thing but gold and silver coin a tender in payment of debts ; pass any bill of attainder, *ex post facto* law, or law impairing the obligation of contracts ; or grant any title of nobility.

2. No state shall, without the consent of the congress, lay any imposts or duties on imports or exports, except what may be absolutely necessary for executing its inspection laws ; and the net produce of all duties and imposts, laid by any state on imports or exports, shall be for the use of the treasury of the United States, and all such laws shall be subject to the revision and control of

the congress. No state shall, without the consent of congress, lay any duty of tunnage, keep troops or ships of war in time of peace, enter into any agreement or compact with another state, or with a foreign power, or engage in war, unless actually invaded, or in such imminent danger as will not admit of delay.

ARTICLE II.

SECTION I.

1. The executive power shall be vested in a president of the United States of America. He shall hold his office during the term of four years, and, together with the vice-president, chosen for the same term, be elected as follows :

2. Each state shall appoint, in such manner as the legislature thereof may direct, a number of electors, equal to the whole number of senators and representatives to which the state may be entitled in the congress ; but no senator or representatives, or person holding an office of trust or profit under the United States, shall be appointed an elector.

[3. The electors shall meet in their respective states, and vote by ballot for two persons, of whom one at least shall not be an inhabitant of the same state with themselves. And they shall make a list of all the persons voted for, and of the number of votes for each ; which list they shall sign and certify, and transmit sealed to the seat of the government of the United States, directed to the president of the senate. The president of the senate shall, in the presence of the senate and house of representatives, open all the certificates, and the votes shall then be counted. The person having the greatest number of votes shall be president, if such number be a majority of the whole number of electors appointed ; and if there be more than one who have such majority, and have an equal number of votes, then the house of representatives shall immediately choose, by ballot, one of them for president ; and if no person have a majority, then, from the five highest on the list, the said house shall, in like manner, choose the president. But, in choosing the president, the votes shall be taken by states, the representation from each state having one vote ; a quorum for this purpose shall consist of a member or members from two-thirds of the states, and a majority of all the states shall be necessary to a choice. In every case, after the choice of the president, the person having the greatest number of votes of the electors shall be the vice-president. But if there should remain two or more who have equal votes, the senate shall choose from them, by ballot, the vice-president.*]

4. The congress may determine the time of chosing the electors, and the day on which they shall give their votes ; which day shall be the same throughout the United States.

5. No person, except a natural born citizen, or a citizen of the United States at the time of the adoption of this constitution, shall be eligible to the office of president ; neither shall any person be eligible to that office who shall not have attained to the age of thirty-five years, and been fourteen years a resident within the United States.

6. In case of the removal of the president from office, or of his death, resignation, or inability to discharge the powers and duties of the said office, the same shall devolve on the vice-president, and the congress may, by law, provide for the case of removal, death, resignation,

----
* Altered. See Amend., art. 12.

or inability, both of the president and vice-president, declaring what officer shall then act as president, and such officer shall act accordingly, until the disability be removed or a president shall be elected.

7. The president shall, at stated times, receive for his services a compensation, which shall neither be increased nor diminished during the period for which he shall have been elected, and he shall not receive within that period any other emolument from the United States, or any of them.

8. Before he enter on the execution of his office, he shall take the following oath or affirmation :

9. "I do solemnly swear (or affirm) that I will faithfully execute the office of president of the United States, and will, to the best of my ability, preserve, protect, and defend the constitution of the United States."

SECTION II.

1. The president shall be commander-in-chief of the army and navy of the United States, and of the militia of the several states when called into the actual service of the United States ; he may require the opinion, in writing, of the principal officer in each of the executive departments, upon any subject relating to the duties of their respective offices ; and he shall have power to grant reprieves and pardons for all offenses against the United States, except in cases of impeachment.

2. He shall have power, by and with the advice and consent of the senate, to make treaties, provided two-thirds of the senators present concur ; and he shall nominate, and by and with the advice and consent of the senate, shall appoint ambassadors, other public ministers, and consuls, judges of the supreme court, and all other officers of the United States, whose appointments are not

herein otherwise provided for, and which shall be established by law. But the congress may, by law, vest the appointment of such inferior officers as they think proper, in the president alone, in the courts of law, or in the heads of departments.

3. The president shall have power to fill up all vacancies that may happen during the recess of the senate, by granting commissions which shall expire at the end of their next session.

<h3 style="text-align:center">SECTION III.</h3>

1. He shall, from time to time, give to the congress information of the state of the union, and recommend to their consideration such measures as he shall judge necessary and expedient ; he may, on extraordinary occasions, convene both houses, or either of them, and, in case of disagreement between them, with respect to the time of adjournment, he may adjourn them to such time as he shall think proper ; he shall receive ambassadors and other public ministers ; he shall take care that the laws be faithfully executed ; and shall commission all the officers of the United States.

<h3 style="text-align:center">SECTION IV.</h3>

1. The president, vice-president, and all civil officers of the United States, shall be removed from office on impeachment for, and conviction of, treason, bribery, or other high crimes and misdemeanors.

<h2 style="text-align:center">ARTICLE III.</h2>
<h3 style="text-align:center">SECTION I.</h3>

1. The judicial power of the United States shall be vested in one supreme court, and in such inferior courts as the congress may, from time to time, ordain and establish. The judges, both of the supreme and inferior courts, shall hold their offices during good behavior ; and

shall, at stated times, receive for their services a compensation which shall not be diminished during their continuance in office.

1. The judicial power shall extend to all cases in law and equity, arising under this constitution, the laws of the United States, and treaties made, or which shall be made, under their authority ; to all cases affecting ambassadors, other public ministers and consuls ; to all cases of admiralty and maritime jurisdiction ; to controversies to which the United States shall be a party ; to controversies between two or more states ; between a state and citizens of another state ; between citizens of different states ; between citizens of the same state claiming lands under grants of different states ; and between a state, or the citizens thereof, and foreign states, citizens or subjects.

2. In all cases affecting ambassadors, other public ministers and consuls, and those in which a state shall be a party, the supreme court shall have original jurisdiction. In all the other cases before mentioned, the supreme court shall have appellate jurisdiction, both as to law and fact, with such exceptions, and under such regulations, as the congress shall make.

3. The trial of all crimes, except in cases of impeachment, shall be by jury ; and such trial shall be held in the state where the said crimes shall have been committed ; but when not committed within any state, the trial shall be at such place or places as the congress may, by law, have directed.

1. Treason against the United States shall consist only in levying war against them, or in adhering to their enemies, giving them aid and comfort. No person shall be convicted of treason unless on the testimony of two wit-

nesses to the same overt act, or on confession in open
court.

2. The congress shall have power to declare the punishment of treason, but no attainder of treason shall
work corruption of blood or forfeiture, except during the
life of the person attainted.

ARTICLE IV.

SECTION I.

1. Full faith and credit shall be given in each state to
the public acts, records, and judicial proceedings of every
other state. And the congress may, by general laws,
prescribe the manner in which such acts, records, and
proceedings shall be proved, and the effect thereof.

SECTION II.

1. The citizens of each state shall be entitled to all
privileges and immunities of citizens in the several states.

2. A person charged in any state with treason, felony,
or other crime, who shall flee from justice, and be found
in another state, shall, on demand of the executive authority of the state from which he fled, be delivered up, to
be removed to the state having jurisdiction of the crime.

3. No person held to service or labor in one state under
the laws thereof, escaping into another, shall, in consequence of any law or regulation therein, be discharged
from such service or labor, but shall be delivered up on
claim of the party to whom such service or labor may be
due.

SECTION III.

1. New states may be admitted by the congress into
this union; but no new state shall be formed or erected
within the jurisdiction of any other state; nor any state
be formed by the junction of two or more states, or parts

of states, without the consent of the legislature of the states concerned, as well as of the congress.

2. The congress shall have power to dispose of, and make all needful rules and regulations respecting the territory or other property belonging to the United States ; and nothing in this constitution shall be so construed as to prejudice any claims of the United States, or any particular state.

SECTION IV.

1. The United States shall guarantee to every state in this union a republican form of government, and shall protect each of them against invasion, and on application of the legislature, or of the executive, when the legislature can not be convened, against domestic violence.

ARTICLE V.

1. The congress, whenever two-thirds of both houses shall deem it necessary, shall propose amendments to this constitution, or, on the application of the legislatures of two-thirds of the several states, shall call a convention for proposing amendments, which, in either case, shall be valid, to all intents and purposes, as part of this constitution, when ratified by the legislatures of three-fourths of the several states, or by conventions in three-fourths thereof, as the one or the other mode of ratification may be proposed by the congress ; provided, that no amendment which may be made prior to the year one thousand eight hundred and eight, shall in any manner affect the first and fourth clauses in the ninth section of the first article ; and that no state, without its consent, shall be deprived of its equal suffrage in the senate.

ARTICLE VI.

1. All debts contracted and engagements entered into, before the adoption of this constitution, shall be as valid

against the United States under this constitution as under the confederation.

2. This constitution, and the laws of the United States which shall be made in pursuance thereof, and all treaties made, or which shall be made, under the authority of the United States, shall be the supreme law of the land ; and the judges in every state shall be bound thereby, anything in the constitution or laws of any state to the contrary notwithstanding.

3. The senators and representatives before mentioned, and the members of the several state legislatures, and all executive and judicial officers, both of the United States and of the several states, shall be bound by oath or affirmation, to support this constitution ; but no religious test shall ever be required as a qualification to any office or public trust under the United States.

ARTICLE VII.

1. The ratification of the conventions of nine states, shall be sufficient for the establishment of this constitution between the states so ratifying the same.

Done in Convention, by the unanimous consent of the states present, the seventeenth day of September, in the year of our Lord one thousand seven hundred and eighty-seven, and of the Independence of the United States of America the twelfth. In witness whereof, we have hereunto subscribed our names.

GEORGE WASHINGTON, PRESIDENT, and deputy from Virginia.

New Hampshire.—John Langdon, Nicholas Gilman.
Massachusetts.—Nathaniel Gorham, Rufus King.
Connecticut.—William Samuel Johnson, Roger Sherman.
New York.—Alexander Hamilton.

New Jersey.—William Livingston, David Brearly, William Patterson, Jonathan Dayton.

Pennsylvania.—Benjamin Franklin, Thomas Mifflin, Robert Morris, George Clymer, Thomas Fitzsimons, Jared Ingersoll, James Wilson, Gouverneur Morris.

Delaware.—George Read, Gunning Bedford, Jr., John Dickinson, Richard Bassett, Jacob Broom.

Maryland.—James McHenry, Daniel of St. Thomas Jenifer, Daniel Carroll.

Virginia.—John Blair, James Madison, Jr.

North Carolina.—William Blount, Richard Dobbs Spaight, Hugh Williamson.

South Carolina.—John Rutledge, Charles Cotesworth Pinckney, Charles Pinckney, Pierce Butler.

Georgia.—William Few, Abraham Baldwin.

Attest :   WILLIAM JACKSON, *Secretary.*

AMENDMENTS TO THE CONSTITUTION.

ARTICLE I.

1. Congress shall make no law respecting an establishment of religion, or prohibiting the free exercise thereof ; or abridging the freedom of speech or of the press ; or the right of the people peaceably to assemble, and to petition the government for a redress of grievances.

ARTICLE II.

1. A well-regulated militia being necessary to the security of a free state, the right of the people to keep and bear arms shall not be infringed.

ARTICLE III.

1. No soldier shall, in time of peace, be quartered in

any house without the consent of the owner, nor in time of war but in a manner to be prescribed by law.

ARTICLE IV.

1. The right of the people to be secure in their persons, houses, papers, and effects, against unreasonable searches and seizures, shall not be violated, and no warrants shall issue but upon probable cause, supported by oath or affirmation, and particularly describing the place to be searched, and the persons or things to be seized.

ARTICLE V.

1. No person shall be held to answer for a capital or otherwise infamous crime, unless on a presentment or indictment of a grand jury, except in cases arising in the land or naval forces, or in the militia when in actual service, in time of war or public danger ; nor shall any person be subject, for the same offense, to be twice put in jeopardy of life or limb ; nor shall be compelled in any criminal case to be a witness against himself ; nor be deprived of life, liberty, or property, without due process of law ; nor shall private property be taken for public use without just compensation.

ARTICLE VI.

1. In all criminal prosecutions the accused shall enjoy the right to a speedy and public trial by an impartial jury of the state and district wherein the crime shall have been committed, which district shall have been previously ascertained by law, and to be informed of the nature and cause of the accusation ; to be confronted with the witnesses against him ; to have compulsory process for obtaining witnesses in his favor ; and to have the assistance of counsel for his defense.

ARTICLE VII.

1. In suits at common law, where the value in controversy shall exceed twenty dollars, the right of trial by jury shall be preserved ; and no fact tried by a jury shall be otherwise re-examined in any court of the United States than according to the rules at the common law.

ARTICLE VIII.

1. Excessive bail shall not be required, nor excessive fines imposed, nor cruel and unusual punishments inflicted.

ARTICLE IX.

1. The enumeration in the constitution of certain rights shall not be construed to deny or disparage others retained by the people.

ARTICLE X.

1. The powers not delegated to the United States by the constitution, nor prohibited by it to the states, are reserved to the states respectively, or to the people.

ARTICLE XI.

1. The judicial power of the United States shall not be construed to extend to any suit in law or equity, commenced or prosecuted against one of the United States by citizens of another state, or by citizens or subjects of any foreign state.

ARTICLE XII.

1. The electors shall meet in their respective states, and vote by ballot for president and vice-president, one of whom, at least, shall not be an inhabitant of the same state with themselves ; they shall name in their

ballots the person voted for as president, and in distinct
ballots the person voted for as vice-president ; and they
shall make distinct lists of all persons voted for as
president, and of all persons voted for as vice-president,
and of the number of votes for each, which lists they
shall sign and certify, and transmit sealed to the seat of
the government of the United States, directed to the
president of the senate ; the president of the senate shall,
in the presence of the senate and house of representatives, open all the certificates, and the votes shall then be
counted ; the person having the greatest number of votes
for president, shall be the president, if such number be a
majority of the whole number of electors appointed ; and
if no person have such majority, then from the persons
having the highest numbers, not exceeding three, on the
list of those voted for as president, the house of representatives shall choose immediately, by ballot, the president.   But in choosing the president, the votes shall be
taken by states, the representation from each state having one vote ; a quorum for this purpose shall consist of
a member or members from two-thirds of the states, and
a majority of all the states shall be necessary to a choice.
And if the house of representatives shall not choose a
president, whenever the right of choice shall devolve
upon them, before the fourth day of March next following, then the vice-president shall act as president, as in
the case of the death or other constitutional disability of
the president.

2. The person having the greatest number of
votes as vice-president, shall be the vice-president, if
such number be a majority of the whole number of
electors appointed ; and if no person have a majority,
then from the two highest numbers on the list, the senate shall choose the vice-president ; a quorum for the

purpose shall consist of two-thirds of the whole number of senators, and a majority of the whole number shall be necessary to a choice.

3. But no person constitutionally ineligible to the office of president, shall be eligible to that of vice-president of the United States.

ARTICLE XIII.

1. Neither slavery nor involuntary servitude, except as a punishment for crime, whereof the party shall have been duly convicted, shall exist within the United States, or any place subject to their jurisdiction.

2. Congress shall have power to enforce this article by appropriate legislation.

ARTICLE XIV.

1. All persons born or naturalized in the United States, and subject to the jurisdiction thereof, are citizens of the United States, and of the state wherein they reside. No state shall make or enforce any law which shall abridge the privileges or immunities of citizens of the United States; nor shall any state deprive any person of life, liberty, or property, without due process of law, nor deny to any person within its jurisdiction, the equal protection of the laws.

2. Representatives shall be apportioned among the several states according to their respective numbers, counting the whole number of persons in each state, excluding Indians not taxed. But when the right to vote at any election for choice of electors for president and vice-president of the United States, representatives in congrees, the executive and judicial officers of a state, or the members of the legislature thereof, is denied to any of the male inhabitants of such state being twenty-one years of age, and citizens of the United States, or in any

way abridged, except for participation in rebellion or other crime, the basis of representation therein shall be reduced in the proportion which the number of such male citizens shall bear to the whole number of male citizens twenty-one years of age in such state.

3. No person shall be a senator, or representative in congress, or elector of president and vice-president, or hold any office, civil or military, under the United States, or under any state, who, having previously taken an oath as a member of congress, or as an officer of the United States, or as a member of any state legislature, or as an executive or judicial officer of any state, to support the Constitution of the United States, shall have engaged in insurrection or rebellion against the same, or given aid and comfort to the enemies thereof ; but congress may, by a vote of two-thirds of each house, remove such disability.

4. The validity of the public debt of the United States authorized by law, including debts incurred for payment of pensions and bounties for services in suppressing insurrection or rebellion, shall not be questioned. But neither the United States nor any state shall assume or pay any debt or obligation incurred in aid of insurrection or rebellion against the United States, or any claim for the loss or emancipation of any slave ; but all such debts, obligations, and claims, shall be held illegal and void.

5. The congress shall have power to enforce, by appropriate legislation, the provisions of this article.

ARTICLE XV.

1. The right of citizens of the United States to vote shall not be denied or abridged by the United States or by any state on account of race, color, or previous condition of servitude.

2. The congress shall have power to enforce this article by appropriate legislation.*

———

It will be observed that, by the fifth article of the constitution, the legislatures may demand a convention similar to the one that made the Constitution of 1787, to propose amendments to the constitution whenever the legislatures of two-thirds of the states shall concur in its call, and the congress is obliged to call it,† and whatever amendment may be proposed by that convention, when ratified by conventions in three-fourths of the states, shall become parts of the constitution, notwithstanding such amendments may be opposed by every department and officer of the United States.

This provision, together with that of making the senate represent the municipal corporations of the several states in the congress of the United States, clearly retains the governmental authority of the several states, as members of the more perfect union of 1787 ; and the people of the several states, being represented by the members of the house of representatives in the congress, clearly shows that the more perfect union consists of a

———

* The first ten of the foregoing amendments were proposed at the first session of the first congress held under the constitution ; the eleventh amendment was proposed at the second session of the third congress ; the twelfth, at the first session of the eight congress ; the thirteenth, at the second session of the thirty-eighth congress ; the fourteenth, at the first session of the thirty ninth congress ; and the fifteenth, at the third session of the fortieth congress, and were all adopted by the number of states required by the fifth article of the original constitution. The thirteenth amendment was adopted December 18, A. D. 1865 ; the fourteenth, July 20, 1868, and the fifteenth, March 30, 1870.

† Letter 85, Federalist, Hamilton, Story's Com. Con. 1830.

union of the people of the respective states as separate
societies of people, and a union of the governmental authority of the respective states ; that, therefore, the confederation was not displaced by the new union of 1787,
but was retained and added to by the new union, so as to
make it adequate to the exigencies of government.

CHAPTER III.

CHARACTER OF THE GOVERNMENT.

The Preamble to the Constitution:

"We, the people of the United States, in order to form a more perfect union, establish justice, insure domestic tranquillity, provide for the common defense, promote the general welfare, and secure the blessings of liberty to ourselves and our posterity, do ordain and establish this Constitution for the United States of America."

This preamble has been made the basis for greater contrariety in the interpretation of the constitution than any other part of that instrument.

Able statesmen, and the Supreme Court of the United States, contend that the preamble should be taken literally, and that, when so taken, it shows that the people of the United States ordained and established the constitution, and also claim that the United States was changed from a confederation into a sovereign government.

There are others who claim that the states were never free and sovereign states; on the contrary, that, even while the states were but colonies, existing under their British charters, they derived their powers from the same common sovereign authority, and through that authority were connected as one people; therefore deny that the people of the several colonies were ever a separate people.

This class of statesmen and commentators also claim that it was the people in the aggregate of the United States who inaugurated the revolutionary war of 1776, and that they won their independence as one people.

It is also claimed by as able statesmen and commentators, that each colony had a separate existence under its British charter, and by its own act separated from England, and that, as each threw off its servitude to that kingdom, the sovereignty thereof devolved upon the people of that particular colony, who constructed a charter for the government thereof, to derive its powers from themselves as the sole sovereign authority ; that charter they called a constitution, and expressly reserved to themselves the sole authority to alter or abolish the same at will. And in the organization of the union under the Articles of Confederation, sovereignty was expressly reserved to the states.

They also claim that the people of the several states, acting as different societies of people, concurred in the constitution without changing the character of the government from a confederacy, and without the people of the respective states surrendering their authority to any extent, by adopting the Constitution of 1787 ; but, to the contrary, the Articles of Confederation were simply amended, so as to increase the powers of the confederacy, to make it equal to the exigencies of government, and to better preserve the union.

The strongest argument that may be conveniently found by general readers, in favor of the United States being a nation with sovereign governmental powers is contained in the decision of the Supreme Court of the United States.

That court, in the case of Chisholm *v.* The State of Georgia, decided, in 1792,* by a divided court, that the United States is a sovereign nation and government, to authorize it to take jurisdiction of the parties and the

---

* Reported in 2 Dall. 419.

subject of the action. That ruling of the court caused an amendment to the constitution, declaring that the constitution should not be so construed as to give jurisdiction to the federal courts, of actions against any of the states, by citizens of another state, or subjects of a foreign state.*

England under the heptarchy constituted a federal government, but the kingdoms were each recognized as containing sovereignty within itself.

Every confederacy must be composed of sovereign states or nations, and the confederacy must have control of that class of powers necessary to maintain the government itself, and its general welfare, so that it will be able to protect the component parts against each other and against the outside world; its forces, therefore, must be superior to those of the component parts; hence in any contest of authority between the central government and either of its constituent parts, the central government will always prevail; consequently, under the natural inclination of all governments to increase their powers, the sovereign authority of the petty kingdoms of the heptarchy were absorbed by the great kingdom.

The Irish republic was also federal in character, and in like manner the authority of the component parts were absorbed by the central authority.

And so it has been with all confederacies that have existed before the establishment of the United States, which all will admit still consists of a union of states having reserved powers; to which extent, at least, it is federal in character. Some who advocate the sovereignty of the states claim that that authority resides in the people of the states, and deny that any sovereignty exists

_____

* 11th Art. Amendment.

either in the United States government, or in the government of the states, though they concede that each is authorized to use such sovereign forces as may be necessary to enable it to discharge its corporate duties and trusts as agent of the sovereign people.

To hold, as the supreme court does, that the government of the United States, *itself*, is sovereign to the extent of the objects and powers committed to it, and that the state governments are sovereign to the extent of the objects and powers committed to them, practically revives the views of the English Heptarchy, and applies that system to this country, in total disregard of the great American principle of retaining the sovereignty in the people, as shown in the first chapter of this review.

In the case of Martin *v.* Hunter's Lessee,* which was taken from the court of appeals of Virginia (it being the court of last resort of that state), the Supreme Court of the United States again decided that the United States was a sovereign nation to authorize that court to take jurisdiction of the parties and subject of the action, and reversed the ruling of the Virginia court of appeals. But when the case was sent back to the Virginia court, with the mandate of the supreme court to render judgment in accordance with the supreme court's opinion, the judges of the Virginia court, in separate opinions, unanimously agreed that no federal question was involved in the case, and refused to obey the mandate of the supreme court. The case was again taken to the supreme court. On this second appeal, the supreme court adhered to its former opinion, and announced that, if the state court persisted in refusing to obey the supreme court's mandate, that it could send its marshals out to execute its writs, but, fortunately for the country, the parties set-

---

* Reported in 1 Wheaton, 304.

tled the case among themselves, without forcing the collision between the federal and state courts.

In the case of McCulloch v. State of Maryland.* the question was, whether that state could tax the United States bank, which brought into question the validity of the charter of the bank, the state of Maryland denying authority in the congress to grant the charter, there being no power within the letter of the constitution authorizing congress to charter banks. The supreme court held the United States to be a sovereign nation, and that the power to charter banks was incident to that sovereign authority. Having reached the conclusion that the charter was valid, that court went on, and held that the power of a state to tax a bank involved the power to destroy it; therefore refused the state of Maryland the right to tax the bank.†

When the charter of that bank was about to expire, the congress sought to renew it by re-enacting the charter; but President Jackson vetoed it.

The president was urged by the friends of the bank to approve it, claiming that the supreme court having decided that the congress had the constitutional authority to charter the bank, that his veto under the circumstances would be setting up his judgment against that of the congress on a question of policy. But the president denying the supreme court's authority to interpret the constitution for him, and claiming that each department must interpret that instrument for itself, and that his oath required him to execute the constitution as he understood it, and not as somebody else might tell him; he, therefore, vetoed the re-charter on the ground of its being unconstitutional.

It is, however, not the power of congress to charter

---

* Reported in 4 Wheaton, 316.   † 4 Wheaton, 316.

banks that I wish to consider in this connection, but to show that the judges of the Supreme Court of the United States are like the judges of the courts of every other country, inclined to augment the powers of the government of which they constitute a part.

As the sovereignty of the United States was more extensively discussed in the case of McCulloch *v.* Maryland, I deem it advisable to give some extracts from the reasoning of the supreme court on the question. That court said :

"The convention which framed the constitution was indeed elected by the state legislatures. But the instrument when it came from their hands was a mere proposal without obligation or pretension to it.

"It was reported to the then existing congress, . . . by the convention, by congress, and by the state legislatures, the instrument was submitted to the people. They acted upon it in the only manner in which they can act safely, effectively and wisely on such a subject, by assembling in convention. It is true they assembled in their several states, and where else should they have assembled ?

"No political dreamer was ever wild enough to think of breaking down the lines which separate the states and of compounding the American people into one common mass. Of consequence when they act, they act in their states. But the measures they adopt do not on that account cease to be the measures of the people themselves, or become the measures of the state governments.

"From these conventions the constitution derives its whole authority. The government proceeds directly from the people, 'ordained and established in the name of the people.' . .

"The assent of the states in their sovereign capacity is implied in calling the convention, and thus submitting that instrument to the people. It has been said that the people had already surrendered all their power to the state sovereignty and had nothing more to give.

" But, surely, the question whether they may resume and modify the powers granted to government does not remain to be settled in this country. Much more might the legitimacy of the general government be doubted had it been created by the states. . .

" The powers delegated to the state sovereignties were to be exercised by themselves, not by a distinct and independent sovereignty created by themselves.

" To the formation of a league such as was the confederation, the sovereignties were certainly competent. But when 'in order to form a more perfect union' was necessary to change this alliance into an effective government possessing great and sovereign powers, and acting directly on the people, the necessity of referring it to the people and of deriving its powers directly from them, was felt and acknowledged by all.

" The government of the union then (whatever may be the influence of this fact on the case) is emphatically and truly a government of the people. In form and substance it emanates from them. Its powers are granted by them, and for their benefit.

" This government is acknowledged to be one of enumerated powers. . .

" The government of the United States, then, though limited in its powers, is supreme ; and its laws, when made in pursuance of the constitution, form the supreme law of the land, any thing in the constitution or laws of any state to the contrary notwithstanding.

"Among the enumerated powers, we do not find that of establishing a bank or creating a corporation. But there is no phase in the instrument, which like the Articles of Confederation, excludes incidental or implied powers, and which requires that every thing granted shall be expressly and minutely described. . . .

"The creation of a corporation, it is said, appertains to sovereignty. This is admitted. But to what portion of sovereignty does it belong? Does it belong to one more than to another? In America the powers of sovereignty are divided between the government of the union and those of the states. They are each sovereign with respect to the objects committed to it, and neither is sovereign with respect to the objects committed to the other."

If the learned court in saying, "the government of the union is emphatically and truly a government of the people, in form and substance, it emanates from them, its powers are granted by them, and for their benefit;" means to say its powers emanate from, and were granted by, the people of the United States, then it is difficult to understand what that court means, in saying no political dreamer ever supposed the American people were compounded into one mass, for, if they acted in mass, or as one people in ordaining and establishing the constitution, they were compounded into one mass by that act *alone*.

Again, just what was meant by that court in saying, "but there is no phrase in the instrument, which, like the Articles of Confederation, excludes incidental or implied powers," etc. How this was made to harmonize with the tenth article of amendment to the constitution, was left to conjecture alone, for there is no comment by the court relating directly thereto.

It will be observed that the said tenth article of amendment provides that, the powers not granted *by the constitution* to the United States, nor by it, prohibited to the states, *are reserved to the states respectively, or to the people.*

Nothing can be granted by the constitution to the

United States, or prohibited to the state by it, unless it be expressed in that instrument; for it speaks only by the language and expressions made use of in it, and can speak in no other way; hence, unless a power be granted to the United States, or prohibited to the states, by express language of the constitution, it is expressly reserved to the respective states, or to the people.

Since all powers not expressly granted to the United States, or prohibited to the states by the language of the constitution, are reserved to the states respectively, or to the people, no incidental or implied powers can be accorded to the United States, without first taking them away from, either the states or the people. And as (the supreme court concedes) the United States was given jurisdiction over a different class of objects of government, than the class of objects over which the jurisdiction of the states were made to extend, the power of the judiciary, to take from either the United States, to give to the states, or to take from the states to give to the United States, any power not expressed, is in conflict with the letter of the constitution, and the exercise of such authority by the judiciary amounts to changing the powers of the government by the judiciary.

The court says in this Maryland case: " In America the powers of sovereignty are divided between the government of the union and those of the states. They are each sovereign with respect to the objects committed to it, and neither is sovereign with respect to the objects committed to the other."

Sovereignty is above the law, and whenever it acts, its actions are independent of legal restraint; it must, however, act in the manner provided for it to act, else whatever it may do would not be regarded as sovereign acts; and if, as Mr. Blackstone says, " it is supreme, irresistible, absolute, uncontrollable authority," it can neither be divided nor limited. It is, therefore, difficult to understand what that court means by the phrase just quoted, unless the court intended to say that each of the governments named was authorized to wield separate sovereign forces, merely as respective agents of the sovereign people. But as powers not delegated by the letter of the constitution were adjudged to the United States, on the sole ground that they were incident to sovereignty, and therefore within the scope of its powers, it is more than likely that the court was guided by the theory, antedating the American system, that every government, however constituted, or by whatever authority it may subsist, must possess sovereignty somewhere within itself, and wholly ignored the bold repudiation of that theory by our colonial ancestors, who, upon separating from England, received the sovereign authority as an inherent right in themselves, and in changing their colonies into state governments, based on constitutional limitations, reserved that authority to themselves.

That authority being in themselves, they could, by the concurrence of the people of the respective states, authorize the union to wield such sovereign forces as might be necessary or proper to enable it to execute its governmental duties and trusts as the agent of the people of the several states, and still retain the sovereignty absolutely in themselves, to the extent authority is given to the United States to wield sovereign forces, to that extent the authority of the United States would be paramount to any authority of any state; and on the other side, to the extent authority to wield sovereign forces are reserved to the states by the Constitution of the United States, to that extent the authority of the state would be paramount, and ought to prevail over the United States.

The supreme court again, in the case of Gibbon vs. Ogden, held the United States to be a sovereign nation, and in arguing the question uses strong expressions ; but the strongest argument produced by the court consists in the change from what the court calls a mere league, with a college of ambassadors, into a congress with authority to make laws, vests the government of the union with sovereign authority, and made it a sovereign nation.

It is well known that each colony existed under a British charter, and had power to enact laws within the scope of the authority contained in its charter, and no one will contend that the right to make laws in conformity with the limitations imposed by its charter had the effect of vesting the colony with sovereignty. The cities of the United States generally, if not universally, have a legislative board with authority to enact ordinances, yet no one will contend that the authority of any city to enact ordinances under the limitations of its charter has the effect to vest it with the sovereign authority of the state that granted the charter.

In this Gibbons case the court again says, there is no provision in the constitution requiring a strict construction of the grant of power to the United States as was the case in the Articles of Confederation.

If the ninth and tenth articles of amendment to the constitution, heretofore referred to, failed to perform that function, then the court is correct ; but how the court can so construe those provisions is not easy to understand.

But Mr. Pomeroy in his commentaries on the constitution, and Mr. John C. Hamilton, in his edition of the Federalist, contend that the American people were always a united people ; that while they were occupying separate colonies, each colony deriving its charter from the same sovereign authority, constituted an agent of the kingdom of Great Britain, so that by reason of being common agents of that kingdom they were united as one people, who inaugurated the revo-

lutionary war, and as one people they won the independence of the American states.   However this may have
been, the second article of the Articles of Confederation is
a sufficient answer.

But Mr. Pomeroy claims that the people ought to be
considered as constituting the nation or state, *not the government*, and that, under the American system, the people have the right to alter or abolish the government and
reconstruct it at will.   But he supposes the sovereignty
to be in the people of the United States in the aggregate
instead of being in the people of the respective states;
and, therefore, claims that the people of the United
States being sovereign may change the government at
will, even to the extent of annihilating the states.

If the sovereignty is, in fact, in the people of the
United States in the aggregate, they are certainly above
the constitution, and according to the provisions of the
Declaration of Independence they would have the right
to alter or abolish the whole constitution at will, and
construct a government on such principles as to them
may appear most conducive to their welfare and happiness, even to the abolishment of the states absolutely.

But I hope to show that the sovereign authority of
these United States is in the people of the respective
states, as separate people, under the Constitution of 1787.

On the side of those who advocate that the United
States constitutes a federal republic : some contend that
the sovereignty is in the political organization of the respective states ; this theory logically leads to the right of
the states individually to secede from the union at will.

There are others who accept the theory declared in
the bill of rights of several of the states, to-wit, that
the people retain all rights in themselves, and the officials
are but the agents, trustees and servants of the people,
without realizing the necessity of providing a distinct

organ through which to express their sovereign will, and another to express their will as subjects of the government. This theory must be based on a supposition that the people constitute the state, otherwise the officials could not be their direct agents, trustees and servants. Among those who advocate this theory Judge St. George Tucker is one of the clearest commentators that I have been able to find. In his edition of Blackstone's Commentaries, he gave copious notes of the Constitution of the United States, in the form of appendix to the first part of the first volume of said edition.

Judge Tucker, a learned jurist and great logician, ably presents his theory of the government of the union, showing it to have been formed by compact, and to be but a federal republic.

But in dealing with the *political authority*, commonly denominated the sovereign authority by writers on the subject, he fails to exhibit his usual clearness ; but, for fear I may be doing him injustice in saying this, and that the trouble arises out of my want of ability to understand him, rather than from his want of clearness, I give this extract :

"But, for reasons which will hereafter be explained, I prefer calling it the government, or administrative authority of the state, to which each citizen subjects himself, by the very act of association, for the purpose of establishing a civil society.   .   .   .

"The *government*, or administrative authority of the state, is that portion, only of the sovereignty, which is by the constitution intrusted to the public functionaries : these are the agents and servants of the people." *

The learned jurist accepts Mr. Blackstone's definition of sovereignty, and concedes it to be the supreme au-

* Tucker's Blackstone, Note B, pages 7-9 (Appendix).

thority and beyond control; therefore it is difficult to reconcile his theory of vesting the public officials with a part of that authority, even as agents only, for, if it is supreme and beyond control, it can not be either divided or limited, though agents may be authorized to exercise sovereign forces as officers of the sovereign authority.

And it is equally as difficult to understand how the public officials can be vested with any part or all of that authority, independently of the government, of which they are officers. Their title to the offices must flow from the corporate government, and can be maintained only by maintaining that entity, and they can be punished for malfeasance or misfeasance in office only through that government, and whatever powers they may have must flow to them through that entity or government.

For the present I will pretermit the discussion of theories, and draw attention to the organization of the United States under the Constitution of 1787; the lodgment of the powers; the mode of limiting the exercise of the granted powers; and the lodgment of the sovereign authority to ascertain the character of the government.

The preamble to the constitution declares that the constitution was ordained and established. No government was established, to be divided into departments, as was the case with the states. But each department was separately ordained and established by the constitution.

The legislative department was instituted by the first article thereof, and its powers and duties minutely defined; the first section of which reads as follows:

"All legislative powers herein granted shall be vested in a congress of the United States, which shall consist of a senate and house of representatives."

The second article institutes the executive department,

and vests it with specific and well-defined powers. The first section thereof is as follows:

"The executive power shall be vested in a President of the United States of America. He shall hold his office during the term of four years, and, together with the vice-president, chosen for the same term, be elected as follows."

As the executive has jurisdiction to enforce such laws only as may be authorized to be enacted, the meaning of this section limits the executive to such laws only as may be rightfully passed by the law-making department.

The third article institutes the judiciary department, and vests it with prescribed and well-defined jurisdiction. The first section of this article reads as follows:

"The judicial power of the United States shall be vested in one supreme court, and in such inferior courts as the congress may from time to time ordain and establish." . . .

No powers were granted to the United States as a whole. On the contrary, all powers granted by the constitution are vested by it, in one or the other of these three departments. This fact, coupled with the further fact, that, with but a very few exceptions, jurisdiction of the political laws only, is vested in either of these three departments, which leaves them and the United States, without jurisdiction of the civil laws, and without authority to make any laws for the government of any people, without which, neither the United States nor these three departments combined, can possibly constitute a complete government. The United States, failing to constitute a government, and having no powers, they can not even constitute an agent to conduct the affairs of the union. The three departments, therefore, must be separate agents, and the only agents of the people who ordained them to manage the affairs of the United States, therefore the United States is nothing more than a name to indicate the states united.

Since the jurisdiction of said departments is limited to the political laws, neither one of them, nor all of them combined, can constitute more than corporate agents of the people of the several states united ; and since neither one of them, nor all of them combined, can possibly constitute a complete government, with authority to make laws for the people, they must each be a separate agent of the sovereign people who ordained and established them, and each must perform the function and duties committed to it alone.

Though the duties and functions committed to each have relation to the duties and functions committed to the other departments, and the aid of each is necessary to enable them to perform their respective duties ; each, therefore, necessarily constitutes a part of the others, though separately ordained and vested with separate powers, and is prohibited from encroaching on the powers of the others, in executing its own duties. The powers and duties committed to these departments being necessary to the conducting of the affairs of the union, and each department being required to act in harmony and in aid of the others, they constitute parts of a whole ; and that whole constitutes a municipal agent or corporation, deriving its powers from the sovereign people who ordained them, and as such municipal corporation, they bear the same relation to the people that a city does to the state that incorporated it, or to that borne by the colonies to the sovereign kingdom of Great Britain, under their respective charters.

Furthermore, by article five of the constitution, the sovereignty of the United States is recognized to be in the people of the states exclusively and absolutely, by giving to the states authority to require a *federal convention* to be called to propose amendments to the constitution, whenever the legislatures of two-thirds of the states shall concur in demanding its call, the congress is obliged to provide for it, and call the convention so demanded, and has no option to refuse.*

The federal convention authorized by said article must have equal powers to that of 1787, and it may propose any amendments or changes in the constitution ; and when the changes or amendments proposed by that convention shall be ratified by conventions in three-fourths of the states, they will become parts of the constitution and the supreme law of the land ; but until ratified by conventions in three-fourths of the states such changes would have no force, but amount to mere proposals ; therefore, it is the ratification by conventions of the states alone that can give them any validity, particularly such amendments as will change the form of the government or enlarge its powers, or change the race or character of those who are to compose the society or family of sovereign people of the nation.

The supreme court said of the present constitution : " It was the ratification by conventions in the states that gave it validity, which might be doubted if it had been ratified by the state governments."†

Judge Story, however, in his Commentaries on the Constitution, treats the two modes of amending the constitution contained in article five of equal validity as to any and every amendment authorized by said article, whether by proposals made by the congress, to be rat-

* Letter 85, Federalist (Hamilton); Story's Com. on Con., Sec. 1830.

† 4 Wheaton, 316, supra.

ified by the legislatures of the states, or by proposals by the federal convention, to be ratified by conventions in the states; but as the act of congress would amount to proposals only, and be of no validity until ratified by the legislatures of the states, either mode of amending the constitution will answer my present purpose. I will, therefore, postpone further discussion of article five until it is reached in the course of this review.

Since the federal convention authorized by article five of the constitution will have the same powers and authority the Convention of 1787 had, it may propose any amendment or change in the constitution, which, when ratified by conventions in three-fourths of the states, or by the legislatures of three-fourths of the states, shall become parts of the constitution, and be regarded as part of the supreme law of the land. Hence, so far as it affects the power of the states to change the organic law, by amending the constitution, it is not material whether Judge Story's interpretation of article five be accepted or not. For if the legislatures of three-fourths of the states could compel the calling of the federal convention to propose amendments, and when whatever amendments or changes that convention may propose to the constitution shall be ratified by conventions in three-fourths of the states, the same shall be valid as part of the constitution.

Therefore, the states may change the constitution at will without the assent of the United States, or any department or officer thereof.

No government can possibly be sovereign as long as it is dependent on the will of any other nation or government for its existence.

The Articles of Confederation declared that the states retained their sovereignty and independence, but the assent of the congress was necessary to make any change in the Constitution of 1777 (better known as the Articles of Confederation), and the assent of every state was also required to any amendment thereof.

Therefore, under the Articles of Confederation, the sovereign authority to change the organic law was vested in the congress and the states together. But under the Constitution of 1787 (known as the more perfect union), the people of the respective states alone are vested with that sovereign authority. The time may come when one-fourth of the states may contain a majority of the popular vote; indeed, at this time, twelve of the larger states in the union choose a majority of the presidental electors, and there being forty-four states in the union, it would require eleven states to constitute one-fourth, but no eleven states contain a majority of the popular vote of the United States.

Furthermore, the United States never had any citizens except those of the several states; nor can the United States have citizens, independently of those of the states, without distroying its ability to protect all citizens of the United States alike. All who are citizens of any state constitute citizens of the United States, and the only citizens thereof, as will be shown a little further on in this chapter.

It is conceded by the supreme court, and nationalists generally, that the political organizations of the states (or, as the supreme court chooses to term them, *the state sovereignties*) are represented by the senate of the United States. But they claim that the American people are represented by the house of representatives in the United states congress; which, according to my understanding, is a mistake. On the contrary, the members in the house of representatives represent the people of their respective states only.

The Constitution of the United States provides that,

representation and direct taxes shall be apportioned among the several states, which may be included within this union, according to their respective numbers, which shall be determined by adding to the whole number of free persons, including those bound to service for a term of years, and excluding Indians not taxed, three-fifths of all other persons. *

This representation shall be apportioned among the states (*not* among the people), according to the number of persons of the class named, each state may have.

The number of representatives given to Connecticut, and each of the two Carolinas was five members to each state. Inasmuch as it was provided that the number of representatives should not exceed one for every thirty thousand (except in case any state should contain less than that number of inhabitants, in which latter event, the state below the requisite number should have one representative) it must have been thought that the Carolinas and Connecticut, each, contained one hundred and fifty thousand persons of the class named.

Now, suppose that each of these states contained one hundred and seventy thousand persons of the class named, they would each still have been entitled to but five representatives, making but fifteen representatives from these three states, whereas, the same population, in any one state, would entitle it to seventeen representatives. As it is more convenient to count by voters, than population, let us reduce the population to voters by dividing by five as a fair estimate ; the two Carolinas and Connecticut would each have five districts, containing six thousand and eight hundred voters. Let us suppose further that the political sentiment should be nearly equally

* Sec. 2, Art. 1, Con.

divided in each of the Carolinas, and in Connecticut it should be pretty much one way. In each of the Carolinas the district should give to one party an average of six hundred majority, which would give to one party three thousand and seven hundred votes, and to the other party three thousand and one hundred votes.

There being in the two Carolinas ten districts, those two states would give to the prevailing party thirty-seven thousand votes, and to the unsuccessful party thirty-one thousand votes. And in Connecticut the party that lost the two Carolinas, should get an average of five thousand votes, and the winning party in the Carolinas should get only eighteen hundred votes in each of the Connecticut districts, making twenty-five thousand to be added to the thirty-one thousand votes given in the ten districts in the two Carolinas, making fifty-six thousand votes in all, yet that party would get but five representatives in congress; while the other party, getting only thirty-seven thousand votes in the ten districts of the two Carolinas, and five thousand votes in the five Connecticut districts, making in all forty thousand votes, would elect ten out of fifteen representatives, while the fifty-six thousand votes would elect only five, out of fifteen representatives. This of itself ought to be sufficient to show that the provision was intended to secure representation for the people of the states.

But it is further provided, "that the house of representatives shall be composed of members chosen every second year by the people of the several states, and the electors in each state shall have the qualifications requisite for electors of the most numerous branches of the state legislatures."*

---

* Sec. 2, Art. 1, Con.

It will be observed that the representation in congress must be chosen by the people of the several states, and by no other people.

It is also provided that, "when vacancies happen in the representation from any state, the executive authority thereof shall issue writs of election to fill such vacancies."

If that branch of congress was intended to represent the people of the United States, why not have provided for the president to issue writs of election to fill such vacancies?

The president and vice-president of the United States are chosen by the states, that is, the electors are elected by the people of the several states; however, each state has as many electors as its quota of congressmen and senators together, and each elector votes individually, and is counted individually in the election, although the electors may be voted for by the state at large.

But should the election of president devolve on the house of representatives, the vote is to be taken by states, the smaller states amounting to as much as the larger states.

The judges of the supreme court, and of other courts, are named by the president and confirmed by the senate.

Therefore in no event can the people as a people of the United States have any thing to do with the filling of any office in the United States, and are in nowise recognized by the constitution as people of the United States.

It is true, the language of the constitution frequently refers to the people of the United States, but the people so referred to were evidently the people of the several states; for it is conceded by all that the United States, under the Articles of Confederation, was simply a league of states, and, as such, could have no citizens; yet, in fixing the qualifications of president, he is required to have been a native born citizen of the United States, or a citizen thereof at the time of the adoption of the constitution; and senators are required to have been nine years a citizen thereof; and members of the house of representatives are required to have been citizens thereof for seven years.

As a league of states, the United States could not be a government of a people, or a nation of people, for, its constituent parts being states only, they could have no people; therefore the United States was incapable of having citizens, or maintaining a people; and this inability to maintain a people must have continued until the new constitution could be ratified, even if that instrument had the effect of changing the relation of the United States to the states. The framers of the constitution, therefore, must have intended to indicate the citizens of the several states, who, it is true, were in a qualified sense citizens of the confederation, but the obligation of the confederation to them flowed through the state they inhabited, and their obligation to the United States flowed through their respective state, and depended on the compact of confederation.

As the United States was at that time incapable of having full citizens, the convention not only prescribed impossible qualifications for president, senators and representatives, but made it utterly impossible to ever put the constitution in operation, unless the citizenship indicated was intended to apply to the qualified citizenship, arising out of being full citizens of some one of the states within the confederation.

Since, no government was ordained for the United States as a whole; but, to the contrary, three separate and distinct departments (to wit), a legislative, executive, and judiciary, with exclusive jurisdiction of the

powers, respectively, granted to each of them, were ordained and established.   And as every power granted to
either of said departments, or all of them combined, related to authority to said departments to maintain themselves and the autonomy of the states in the union, as
established by the constitution.   And all police powers,
and authority to make laws for the regulation of society,
and the protection of the civil and religious rights of the
people, were reserved to the exclusive jurisdiction of the
states.

And, as the people of the states were authorized to elect
legislatures to demand the call of a convention to propose amendments or alterations in the constitution,
which when ratified by conventions in three-fourths of
the states shall become part of the organic law.

And, as the United States has no citizens except by
virtue of their being citizens of a state in the union
to make laws for, it is utterly impossible for the United
States to have a sovereign government ; or a complete
government of any sort.   As the United States has jurisdiction of the political division of the object of government only, and the states exclusive jurisdiction of the civil
division of the object of government, it requires both
to constitute one complete government ; they are each as
necessary to the other, to constitute a complete government, as the legislative, executive and judiciary departments of the governmental agency of the union ; or of
any of the states are, to constitute a whole.

But while no powers were granted to the United States,
in that name, and every power, authorized to be used in
behalf of the union, was granted to the exclusive jurisdiction of the legislative, executive, or judiciary departments, respectively, the powers granted to each, relate to
the powers granted to each of the other departments ;
for no law that might be enacted by the legislative could

possibly be of any force, unless it could be executed, hence these three departments were thus, in a measure, united, and as a whole may constitute a municipal corporation, or governmental agent of the several states united.

Therefore it may be safely claimed, that the great American discovery in the science of government, by which the people can retain, in themselves, the whole sovereign authority, and also be members of the corporation, or subjects of the municipal agent instituted by themselves, by ordaining a different organ to express their sovereign will through (as explained in the first chapter hereof), is retained as a principle of government under the Constitution of 1787. And that the American discovery, of dividing the two grand objects of government, and giving one of them to one jurisdiction, and the other to another and separate jurisdiction, was also retained in the more perfect union.

Hence, the governmental structure of the United States, constitutes a municipal agent or corporation—enacted by the people of the states united.

But although the structure for the management of the affairs of the union is merely a municipal corporation, or agent of the states united, as such it is a trustee of the powers and duties reposed in ordaining the constitution, and is in duty bound to execute the same. Among the duties and trusts reposed we find that of protecting the states in the equal enjoyment of their rights and privileges, as against each other and as against foreign interference, and to guarantee to each state a republican form of government.

These duties can not be properly performed without authority to maintain the union, and to compel each state to contribute to the public defense.

Hence, not only has the municipal corporation of the

union no authority to assent to the withdrawal of any state from the union, but is compelled by the character of the trust to prevent any one of the states from withdrawing from the union otherwise than by the conventions provided for by the constitution.

This does not, however, exclude every other mode of escaping from discriminations by a state, or tyranny by the public officials ; for, as clearly set forth in the Declaration of Independence, no people can bind themselves to a bondage of tyranny or slavery by *even* the most solemn compact, for their freedom is a gift of nature, and they have no right to part with it, and may forcibly recover it whenever lost from them.

However, there is no mode prescribed in the constitution for exercising this right ; hence, whenever it is attempted to be exercised by force, the attempt will amount to rebellion against the constitution, whether the attempt be made by authority of the state or otherwise, and it will therefore be the duty of the federal corporation or government to suppress it, and to use such force as may be necessary to put down the rebellion, and no more.

Although such attempts be rebellion, as long as any regard is entertained for the great Declaration of Independence, those who engage in rebellion against discriminations and tyranny imposed on themselves or their state will be respected for their manhood and love of freedom and devotion to the great principles of the Declaration of Independence and of the Constitution.

These views are not in harmony with the right of a state to secede, as contended for by so many able statesmen on the southern side of the late civil war. However, many who were with me in that war, neither claimed the right of the states, individually, to secede, nor denied the right of the United States to coerce the seceding states back into the union.

But while we laid no claim to the right of a state to secede, we claimed the right to forcibly resist the revolution gradually and silently going on, by repeated usurpations of ungranted powers, which we believed would sooner or later undermine the whole fabric of our American system of free governments, and reduce the people to a humiliating bondage to an arrogant national aristocracy. And as that resistance had to be maintained by force of arms, it was better to conduct it through state authority, as the states could suppress lawlessness and mobs, and conduct the war with order and on civilized principles, and to a great extent prevent the useless destruction of property, and avoid many of the hardships and ravages of an internecine war.

Still, holding the American system of government in high esteem, and entertaining a reverence for our revolutionary sires who gave us that system, and believing that under that system the people could maintain their freedom, and recognizing the duty of every generation to hand down to its succeeding generation a good and free government, bouyed many a soldier on the southern side of the late civil war to cheerfully submit to the hardships of camp life and the dangers of the battle field.

Technically speaking, the confederates were engaged in rebellion; but it was rebelling against the forms of the government, to save the great principles thereof, and the freedom and sovereign authority of the people, and the principles of liberty set forth in the Declaration of Independence and the bill of rights of the respective states, which are too deeply rooted in the hearts of the American people for them to permit the term rebellion to become odious.

CHAPTER IV.

ORGANIZATION OF THE LEGISLATIVE DEPARTMENT.

ARTICLE I.

Section 1.

"All legislative powers herein granted shall be vested in a congress of the United States, which shall consist of a senate and house of representatives."

"All legislative power herein granted," shows clearly that there are legislative powers that are not granted to the United States.

But whatever legislative powers were granted to the United States, were vested in the congress, consisting of a senate and house of representatives. This must, however, be taken with some qualification, for, by the seventh section of this article, all bills are required to be approved by the president before they can become laws; or, if the president disapproves any bill, he is required to so state in writing and return it to the house from which it originated. Though each house, by a two-thirds vote, can re-pass the bill over his veto—thereupon it will become a law, notwithstanding the president's veto.

The president may, therefore, check the congress in the exercise of its powers in making laws, and in his veto message he may suggest such changes in the bill as would make it acceptable to him, consequently, he is to some extent a factor in the making of laws in the United States.

In England, the chief executive constitutes a part of the parliament; indeed, the king (who is the chief executive of the realm) sits with the house of lords, either in person or by representation. But this has been more fully explained in the first chapter, and will be further treated of in considering the sessions of congress, to which a comparison more appropriately belongs.

Section 2.

Paragraph 1. "The house of representatives shall be composed of members chosen every second year by the people of the several states, and the electors in each state shall have the qualifications requisite for electors of the most numerous branch of the state legislature."

Par. 2. "No person shall be a representative who shall not have attained the age of twenty-five years, and been seven years a citizen of the United States, and who shall not, when elected, be an inhabitant of that state in which he shall be chosen."

Par. 3. "Representatives and direct taxes shall be apportioned among the several states, which may be included within this union, according to their respective numbers, which shall be determined by adding to the whole number of free persons, including those bound to service for a term of years, and excluding Indians not taxed, three-fifths of all other persons. The actual enumeration shall be made within three years after the first meeting of the congress of the United States, and within every subsequent term of ten years, in such manner as they shall by law direct. The number of representatives shall not exceed one for every thirty thousand, but each state shall have at least one representative; and, until such enumeration shall be made the state of New Hampshire shall be entitled to choose three; Massachusetts, eight; Rhode Island and Providence Plantations, one; Connecticut, five; New York, six; New Jersey, four; Pennsylvania, eight; Delaware, one;

Maryland, six; Virginia, ten; North Carolina, five; South Carolina, five, and Georgia, three."

Par. 4. "Where vacancies happen in the representation from any state, the executive authority thereof shall issue writs of election to fill such vacancies."

Par. 5. "The house of representatives shall choose their speaker and other officers; and shall have the sole power of impeachment."

The organization of the house of representatives was considered at length in the third chapter, to show that this house represents the people of the respective states, instead of a people of the United States in the aggregate; therefore, instead of repeating, reference is here made to the consideration of the house of representatives in that chapter.

By the fifth paragraph of this section, it is provided that the house of representatives shall have the sole power of impeachment.

This provision does not mean that the house of representatives shall be triers of impeachment, but that it shall determine whether impeachment proceedings shall be prosecuted in all cases, for it is provided that the senate shall try all cases of impeachment; but when the president is under trial, the chief-justice of the supreme court shall preside, as will be seen further along.

The house of representatives therefore acts as a barrier against all prosecutions by impeachment, and performs the functions of conservatism, in prosecutions for impeachment similar to those that grand juries do, in prosecutions for felonies or penal proceedings. But unlike grand juries, which take no part in a prosecution, the house of representatives, after finding the bill of indictment, choose a certain number of their members to conduct the prosecution in all impeachment cases before the senate, as a court.

The senate is required to be under oath or affirmation when sitting as a court to try an impeachment, and sits alone in all cases except where the president is under trial.

That the house of representatives should be vested with power to choose its speaker and other officers, is evidently necessary to enable this house to efficiently transact its business ; it therefore needs no other comment.

Section 3.

Par. 1. "The senate of the United States shall be composed of two senators from each state, chosen by the legislature thereof, for six years ; and each senator shall have one vote."

Par. 2. "Immediately after they shall be assembled in consequence of the first election, they shall be divided as equally as may be, into three classes. The seats of the senators of the first class shall be vacated at the expiration of the second year, of the second class at the expiration of the fourth year, and of the third class at the expiration of the sixth year, so that one third may be chosen every second year ; and if vacancies happen by resignation, or otherwise, during the recess of the legislature of any state, the executive thereof may make temporary appointments, until the next meeting of the legislature, which shall then fill such vacancies."

Par. 3. "No person shall be a senator who shall not have attained to the age of thirty years, and been nine years a citizen of the United States, and who shall not, when elected, be an inhabitant of that state for which he shall be chosen."

Par. 4. "The vice-president of the United States shall be president of the senate, but shall have no vote unless they be equally divided."

Par. 5. "The senate shall choose their other officers,

ORGANIZATION OF LEGISLATIVE DEPARTMENT. 113

and also a president *pro-tempore*, in the absence of the vice-president, or when he shall exercise the office of president of the United States."

Par. 6. "The senate shall have the sole power to try all impeachments; when sitting for that purpose, they shall be on oath or affirmation. When the president of the United States is tried, the chief-justice shall preside; and no person shall be convicted without the concurrence of two-thirds of the members present."

Par. 7. "Judgment in case of impeachment shall not extend further than removal from office, and disqualification to hold and enjoy any office of trust, honor or profit under the United States; but the party convicted shall nevertheless be liable and subject to indictment, trial, judgment and punishment, according to law."

It was shown in a former chapter that the members of the house of representatives represent the people of the states.

And it will be seen by the provisions of this section that the senators represent the political corporation of the state that elects them, therefore, as the members of the house of representatives represent the people of the states, and the senators represent the political corporations of the respective states, the United States is truly a union of the people of the respective states, and also a union of the political corporations of the several states. Since all agreed to retain the states, for the management of the home affairs thereof, it was necessary for the union to consist of a union of the political corporations of the states, as well as a union of the people of the several states, for the reason that the states could not be retained as states without the people thereof owing allegiance to their respective state corporations, which would clash with the allegiance due the governmental corporation of the union, hence there must also be a compact and

agreement between the corporations of the respective
states. Indeed, the only way to accomplish that harmony between the states and the union, and relieve the
people of the embarrassing attitude of owing allegiance
to two different corporations or municipalities was to retain the corporations of the states, as well as the people
thereof, in the compact of the union.

It is true, the people of the states entered into the
union as sovereigns, not as subjects of the political corporations of the states, and their action in that regard
was above the state corporation ; but it is a physical im-
possibility to make any one equally subject to two different governments at the same time and in the same way.

The confederation was a union of the political corporations of the states only. But the more perfect union
consists of a union of the sovereign people of the respective states, as well as the union that had been formed
under the Articles of Confederation. The sanction of
the political corporations of the states to the more perfect
union is shown by sending delegates to the convention
that framed the constitution, and by afterward calling
conventions of the people of the respective states to adopt
the constitution.

There are leading politicians who advocate the election of the senators by popular election, instead of by
the legislatures of the states ; therefore, I give this subject more attention than seems to be necessary.

The advocates of electing the senators by the people
admit that it will require an amendment to the constitution, but they say, "Amend the constitution so as to authorize it to be done."

There were delegates in the constitutional convention
that framed it who thought the people alone should be
represented in the congress. Among them were the
Hon. A. Hamilton, James Madison, and many others,

who favored a strong central government; but I name Messrs. Hamilton and Madison because they each wrote letters approving of the plan of choosing the senators, and had them published, while the constitution was before the states for ratification.

Mr. Hamilton said on the subject:

". . . So far as that mode of formation may expose the union to the possibility of injury from the state legislatures, it is an evil; but it is an evil which could not have been avoided without excluding the states, in their political capacity, wholly from a place in the organization of the national government. If this had been done, it would doubtless have been interpreted into an entire dereliction of the federal principles; and would certainly have deprived the state government of that absolute safeguard which they will enjoy under this provision. . . ." *

Mr. Madison said:

". . . It is equally unnecessary to dilate on the appointment of senators by the state legislatures. Among the various modes which might have been devised for constituting this branch of the government, that which has been proposed by the convention, is probably the most congenial with the public opinion. It is recommended by the double advantage of favoring a select appointment, and of giving to the state governments such an agency in the formation of the federal government as must secure the authority of the former, and may form a convenient link between the two systems. . . ." †

He further says in the same letter:

". . . In this spirit it may be remarked that the equal vote allowed to each state is at once a constitu-

* Letter 59, Federalist.   † Letter 62, Federalist.

tional recognition of the portion of sovereignty remaining in the individual states, and an instrument for preserving that residuary sovereignty. So far the equality ought to be no less acceptable to the large than to the small states, since they are not less solicitous to guard, by every possible expedient, against an improper consolidation of the states into one simple republic.''

Both of these gentlemen, while in the convention that framed the constitution, opposed any representation of the political organizations of the states in the federal, or, as they called it, the ''national government,'' and urged a representation of the people only, which would indeed have consolidated the United States into one single republic, and have left the states no more rights in the government than counties have in the government of their states; they had a strong following in the convention, and succeeded in getting enough support to carry this plan in the committee of the whole and to sustain it in the convention for quite a while; but it was developed in the debates that, if that plan was adhered to, many of the states would withdraw and the convention would be compelled to adjourn, or, rather, dissolve, without coming to an agreement. All of the delegates realized the disastrous effect an adjournment of the convention without agreeing to a plan would have on the union, which encouraged a spirit of compromise; and a committee was chosen consisting of a member from each state, who readily agreed to retain the political corporations of the states in the more perfect union, and provided that each state (in its political organization) should be entitled to equal representation in the senate, and that the house of representatives should be apportioned among the states according to the number of inhabitants thereof.

This compromise has been referred to before, and probably ought not to be repeated, but it serves the purpose of illustrating the importance attached to a representation of the political corporation of the respective states. It serves to show that, without a representation of the corporation of the respective states in the legislative department of the union, the more perfect union itself would not have been agreed to, and could not have been formed. In addition to the great importance attached to a representation of the corporations of the states, in the federal congress, by the makers of the constitution, a critical examination of the great American principles will show that it is necessary for the states, as corporate organizations, to have a representation in the congress of the union, of sufficient strength to prevent improper legislation against the states, and to enable them to maintain jurisdiction of the civil laws and domestic affairs, as provided by the American system of government.

But the advocates, of electing the senators by the people, instead of by the legislatures, claim that the election by the people would not prevent the senators from still representing the states as political corporations.

But unless the states, in their organized characters, can elect their own representatives in the federal congress, how can they be represented therein?

It is true the people of the states elect the legislature thereof, and those legislatures are the only organs of the states to elect their respective senators, but, when so elected, they are commissioned as representatives of the corporations of the states, and pledged to maintain the states in controlling the civil laws and domestic affairs thereof, according to the American system, and to elect them by the people would annihilate the states, and simply amount to adding two more representatives of the people from each state to the congress of the United States.

The senators being elected by the political organiza-

tions of the states, they would naturally be more likely
to feel their obligations were due to the political organizations thereof, and more closely guard the rights of their
state governments than they would be if elected by the
people of the states.

By the charters or constitutions of the several states,
and by the charter or Constitution of the United States,
the legislatures of the respective states are made the
organs to elect the senators to represent the states in the
congress of the United States; and the distinction
between representation of the people of the states, and
the organization of the states, was closely drawn by the
framers of the constitution, when they provided that the
constitution should not be amended so as to deprive any
state of equal suffrage in the senate. They clearly
meant to provide perpetually for the equal representation
of the political organizations of the several states; therefore, the constitution can not be amended so as to authorize
the senators in the United States congress to be elected by
the people, without ignoring the compromise agreed to by
the grand committee, and accepted by the whole convention, and afterward ratified by the state, which was,
probably, the only plane upon which those favoring a
union of many republics, consisting of the several states,
and those who favored a consolidation of the states into
a "simple republic" (as Mr. Madison expressed it),
could have been brought together on, and should be sa-
credly kept and closely adhered to.

It was contended ·in the convention that there was
danger in permitting the president to appoint senators to
offices of trust, etc., during the continuance of their respective terms in office; but they were overruled, on the
theory that the president ought to have the right to select the best qualified persons for the various offices he

was authorized to fill, although they might be then holding office of honor, trust and profit.

Recent events show the wisdom not only of prohibiting the president from appointing senators to offices of honor, etc., but that it would have been wise to have prohibited him from appointing any one to a position on the recommendation of any senator, so as to cut him off from exerting any influence over the senators through his appointing power. The authority of the senate to choose its own officers is so manifestly necessary that it requires no comment.

The vice-president is required by the constitution to preside over the senate, but the senate may elect one of its members to preside in the absence of the vice-president, or when he may be performing the duties of president.

When the original draft of the constitution was completed by the committee on detail, the senate was not vested with jurisdiction to try impeachments ; that jurisdiction was at first reposed in the judiciary.

But, while the constitution was in the hands of the committee on style, it was changed, and jurisdiction of impeachments was vested exclusively in the senate. As the senators represent the political organizations of the states, they constitute the proper tribunal to try all impeachments, and experience shows this to have been a wise provision. Though it may be unwise theoretically to allow so small a proportion as two-thirds of one-half to convict, which is only possible, however, for, while one-half of the members thereof constitute a quorum, and two-thirds of those present may convict, which is equal to one-third of the whole, it is not probable that only one-half of the members of the senate will ever be present on any impeachment trial.

Section 4.

This brings us to the consideration of the powers and duties of the two houses of congress when acting together.

Par. 1. "The times, places and manner of holding elections for senators and representatives shall be prescribed in each state by the legislature thereof ; but the congress may at any time by law make or alter such regulations, except as to the places of choosing senators."

Par. 2. "The congress shall assemble at least once in every year, and such meeting shall be on the first Monday in December, unless they shall by law appoint a different day."

The congress has prescribed the times, places and manner of electing senators and representatives, except as to the place of choosing senators.

The act of congress being a statute, and liable to be altered at any time, is out of place in a treatise on the constitution. Though it is of such importance to have the election for congress and presidential electors held on the same day throughout the United States, it may not be out of place to insert it here, particularly, as the several states have changed their constitutions, fixing their respective state elections on the same day, to avoid the holding of more than one election in any one year ; it is not likely that the congress will change that day.

The congress, in the exercise of its authority under the latter part of section 4 of article 1, just quoted, provided for the election of senators and representatives, as follows : *

Sec. 14. "The legislature of each state, which is

---

* Title 2—Revised Statutes of the Congress. Chapter 1—Election of Senators.

chosen next preceding the expiration of the time for which any senator was elected to represent such state in congress, shall, on the second Tuesday after the meeting and organization thereof, proceed to elect a senator in congress."

Sec. 15. "Such election shall be conducted in the following manner : Each house shall openly, by a *viva voce* vote of each member present, name one person for senator in congress from each state, and the name of the person so voted for who receives a majority of the whole number of votes cast in each house, shall be entered on the journal of that house by the clerk or secretary thereof ; or if either house fails to give such majority to any person on that day, the fact shall be entered on the journal. At twelve o'clock meridian of the day following that on which proceedings are required to take place as aforesaid, the members of the two houses shall convene in joint assembly, and the journal of each house shall then be read, and if the same person has received a majority of all the votes in each house, he shall be declared duly elected senator. But if the same person has not received a majority of the votes in each house, or if either house has failed to take proceedings as required by this section, the joint assembly shall then proceed to choose, by a *viva voce* vote of each member present, a person for senator, and the person who receives a majority of all the votes of the joint assembly, a majority of all the members elected to both houses being present and voting, shall be declared duly elected. If no person receives such a majority on the first day, the joint assembly shall meet at twelve o'clock meridian of each succeeding day during the session of the legislature, and shall take at least one vote until a senator is elected."

Sec. 16. " Whenever on the meeting of the legislature

of any state, a vacancy exists in the representation of such state in the senate, the legislature shall proceed, on the second Tuesday after meeting and organization, to elect a person to fill such vacancy, in the manner prescribed in the preceding section for the election of a senator for a full term."

Sec. 17. "Whenever, during the session of the legislatures of any state, a vacancy occurs in the representation of such state in the senate, similar proceedings to fill such vacancy shall be had on the second Tuesday after the legislature has organized and has notice of such vacancy."

Sec. 18. "It shall be the duty of the executive of the state from which any senator has been chosen, to certify his election, under the seal of the state, to the president of the senate of the United States."

Sec. 19. "The certificate mentioned in the preceding section shall be countersigned by the secretary of state, of the state."

This provision has gone before the senate of the United States several times for interpretation, and it seems finally settled that it requires a majority of the members elected to the senate and house of representatives of the state, when in joint assembly for that purpose to elect a senator to the congress of the United States, and they must be *present* and *voting* to constitute a quorum for that purpose ; that is, a majority of the two houses added together, must not only be present, but must vote, to constitute the quorum for that purpose.*

By this act of congress, each state that is entitled to more than one member in the house of representatives, is required to elect its members by districts composed of contiguous territory, but the state or territory is au-

---

* McCrery on Elections, etc.

thorized to lay off the congressional districts within its borders. And representatives to congress are required to be elected on "the Tuesday after the first Monday in November."*

"All votes for representatives in congress must be by printed or written ballots."†

"The time for holding an election to fill a vacancy of a member to congress in a state or territory may be prescribed by the laws of such state or territory."‡

Section 22 of said chapter and title, providing that, if a state prescribes any disqualification to the male inhabitants thereof, who are citizens of the United States, other than for participation in the rebellion or other crime; shall be curtailed in its representation in congress, was intended to force the state to allow colored persons residing therein to vote. But if literally interpreted, must include all lunatics, idiots, and illiterates, not only of that state, but those of any other state who may be temporarily residing therein, consequently it can not be enforced; and, therefore, must be treated as void.

By the second paragraph of section 4, the congress is required to assemble once every year, and is required to meet on the first Monday in December in each year, unless a different day be fixed by act of congress.

As the congress must meet in every year, no session can be longer than a year, for every session must adjourn in time to give place for the incoming session, as no two sessions can exist at one and the same time.

By the second section of article one it is provided that, the members to the house of representatives shall be elected every second year; hence, not only is the congress compelled to meet every year, but the members of

---

* **Sec. 25, Chap. 2, Title 2, Rev. Stats.**　　　† 27 id.　　　‡ 26 id.

the house of representatives must go out of office every two years.

The senators are elected for six years, but they are divided into three classes, of one-third each, and the terms of the classes were made to begin at different times, and so arranged as that one-third thereof go out of office every two years, at the same time the members of the house of representatives go out.

Hence, the term of each congress is two years, with a session thereof every year, making two sessions, usually spoken of as the first, and second session, of a particular congress.

So, that, the congress of the United States has a time provided by law to convene and a time that it must adjourn, though it may adjourn on its own motion at an earlier date, and generally does adjourn before the sessions expire by limitation.

As shown in the first chapter, the British parliament has no time fixed by law to meet, and must be called by proclamation or royal letter of the king, to be elected before it can meet, and its sessions may be prorogued by the king, or the king may dissolve the parliament at pleasure.

Hence, the American congress has vastly more power, as a department of the government of the United States, than the parliament possesses in the government of England.

The congress can enact no law without the approval of the president, unless the congress can pass it over his veto. Still the president constitutes no part of the congress, either in theory or in fact, and it is no part of his duty to suggest any particular legislation, except through proclamations, or messages addressed to the congress, giving information on subjects that need legislation ; and it would be grossly improper for him to interfere with the congress in matters of policy, for if he can interfere with the congress as to its legislation, the congress to that extent would be reduced below a co-equal department of the government.

The appointing power of the president is immense, and by giving to one member of congress authority to put his friends in office under his appointing power, and refusing that advantage to others, he may secure the re-election of a favored member, so that by the exercise of that power, he may exert quite a pernicious influence over the members of congress, and induce them to support legislation they are actually opposed to. The exercise of that power in that way, is as criminal, as any other bribery, and ought to be equally a cause of impeachment.

This comparison between the American Congress and the British parliament is drawn because the former was evolved out of the latter, and shows the advance in the direction of representative government, and the corresponding curtailment of the one-man power, and the determination of the American people to so guard the representative system as to maintain it against the natural inclination of the government to extend the power of the chief executive.

Section 5.

Par. 1. "Each house shall be the judge of the election returns and qualifications of its own members, and a majority of each shall constitute a quorum to do business; but a smaller number may adjourn from day to day, and may be authorized to compel the attendance of absent members, in such manner and under such penalties as each house may provide."

Par. 2. "Each house may determine the rules of its proceedings, punish its members for disorderly behavior, and, with the concurrence of two-thirds, expel a member."

Par. 3. "Each house shall keep a journal of its proceedings, and from time to time publish the same, excepting such parts as may in their judgment require secresy ; and the yeas and nays of the members of either house on any question shall, at the desire of one-fifth of those present, be entered on the journal."

Par. 4. "Neither house, during the session of congress, shall, without the consent of the other, adjourn for more than three days, nor to any other place than that in which the two houses shall be sitting."

The first paragraph of this section is so definite that it needs no comment to explain its meaning, and it is necessary that they should be authorized to determine the election returns and qualifications of its members, to be able to know who is entitled to take part in the proceedings in their respective houses.

The provision that a bare majority shall constitute a quorum, while arbitrary, is perhaps as reasonable and just a rule as could have been agreed to. And all will concede that each house should have power to prescribe its own rules of proceedings, compel the attendance of its members, punish them for disorderly behavior and expel them when necessary ; and the concurrence of two-thirds of the members is a reasonable limitation on the exercise of this latter power.

It is necessary in a free republic to publish the proceedings of the legislative department, in order to let the people know how their business is being conducted, which can not be done without keeping a journal of the proceedings thereof. It is, however, claimed by some that one-fifth of the members is too small a number to be intrusted with authority to demand a yea and nay vote in each house, for the reason, as claimed, it weakens the powers of the legislature of the United States.

It may cause delay in conducting the business ; but if calling for the yea and nay vote would have the effect of changing the vote of any one member of either house, that effect will always be worth the delay caused by it, and doubtless many a member would look more carefully into the subject under legislative consideration if he knew that his constituents would know how he voted, than if that fact was to be concealed from them.

As no law can be enacted without the concurrence of each house, prohibiting either house from adjourning longer than three days at a time without the consent of the other, is not only necessary to secure economy and dispatch in conducting the business of the congress, but without that provision either house might adjourn to prevent action on some bill that had been voted for by the other house ; as it might be that the vote to adjourn could be carried without a yea and nay vote, although whenever a vote could be reached on the bill it would pass in the house voting to adjourn.

Sometimes any tactics will be resorted to by either party when hard pressed by the other, to defeat the enactment of laws relating to the political policy of the respective parties, and prohibiting either house from adjourning without the consent of the other cuts off resorting to that scheme to defeat legislation.

Section 6.

Par. 1. " The senators and representatives shall receive a compensation for their services, to be ascertained by law, and paid out of the treasury of the United States. They shall in all cases, except treason, felony and breach of the peace, be privileged from arrest during their attendance at the session of their respective houses, and in going to and returning from the same ; and for any speech or debate in either house, they shall not be questioned in any other place.''

Par. 2. '' No senator or representative shall during the time for which he was elected, be appointed to any civil office under the authority of the United States, which shall have been created, or the emoluments whereof shall have been increased, during such time : and no person holding any office under the United States shall be a member of either house during his continuance in office.''

That the members of each house should be paid for their services, was thought to be necessary, for the reason that many of those who would make the best representatives of the interests of the people, were too poor to devote their time to the service of their constituents without pay ; and to adopt the English rule of not paying the members of parliament, would tend to build up an aristocracy in the congress, and bring about a system of legislating to enable the members of both houses of congress to get rich out of legislative speculations.

That the members of each house should be privileged from arrest while attending the session of congress, and in going to and from the same, was probably prompted by the fact that imprisonment for debt prevailed in some of the states at the time the constitution was framed ; however that may be, the members of each house while attending the sessions, and in going to and from the same, would be engaged in serving the public, therefore they ought not to be interfered with by arrests, except in cases of treason, felony or breach of the peace.

The second paragraph, prohibiting the appointment of members of either house to offices created while they were in congress, or to offices the emoluments of which shall have been increased while they were in congress, is of but little practical value.

Section 7.

Par. 1. "All bills for raising revenue shall originate in the house of representatives ; but the senate may propose or concur with amendments, as in other bills."

Par. 2. "Every bill which shall have passed the house of representatives, and the senate, shall, before it becomes a law, be presented to the president of the United States ; if he approve he shall sign it, but if not he shall return it, with his objections, to that house in which it shall have originated, who shall enter the objections at large on their journal, and proceed to reconsider it. If after such reconsideration two-thirds of that house shall agree to pass the bill, it shall be sent, together with the objections, to the other house, by which it shall likewise be reconsidered, and if approved by two-thirds of that house, it shall become a law. But in all such cases the votes of both houses shall be determined by yeas and nays, and the names of the persons voting for and against the bill shall be entered in the journal of each house respectively. If any bill shall not be returned by the president within ten days (Sundays excepted) after it shall have been presented to him, the same shall be a law, in like manner as if he had signed it, unless the congress, by their adjournment, prevent its return, in which case it shall not be a law."

Par. 3. "Every order, resolution or vote to which the concurrence of the senate and house of representatives may be necessary (except on a question of adjournment), shall be presented to the president of the United States, and before the same shall take effect, shall be approved by him, or, being disapproved by him, shall be repassed by two-thirds of the senate and house of representatives, according to the rules and limitations prescribed in the case of a bill.''

This section defines the process of making laws by the congress, and it seems so explicit that it can not be made any plainer.

However, it will be seen that it requires every order, resolution or vote that requires the concurrence of the senate and house of representatives, except that of adjournment, to be laid before the president and approved by him or passed over his veto before it can take effect.

Therefore, while the president constitutes no part of the law-making authority of the United States, he is a potent agent in preventing the enactment of laws, and in that way may dictate what laws may be passed by the congress.

This brings us to the general powers vested in the congress.

It should be borne in mind that every power the congress is vested with must have been delegated by the letter of the constitution, hence, unless it can be found in the letter of that instrument, or is a necessary part of a power granted by the letter thereof, or is necessary to the execution of a power plainly granted by that instrument, it must be construed to have been reserved to the states respectively, or to the people.

CHAPTER V.

TO LAY AND COLLECT TAXES—TO COIN MONEY—TO REG-
ULATE COMMERCE.

ARTICLE I.

Section 8.

Par. 1. "The congress shall have power—

"To lay and collect taxes, duties, imposts and excises,
to pay the debts and provide for the common defense
and general welfare of the United States; but all duties,
imposts and excises shall be uniform throughout the
United States."

This provision taken by itself appears to vest the congress with unlimited taxing powers, provided the tax be
laid, for the purposes of paying the debts, or providing
for the common defense or general welfare of the United
States, and also provided all duties, imposts and excise
taxes be uniform throughout the United States.

As to the purpose of such taxes, there is no other department or officer of the government that has authority
to inquire into it, except the president, who may veto
any taxing bill, but, after the president approves the taxing bill, the only relief against it is by the action of the
people themselves, who can elect members to a succeeding congress who will pledge themselves to repeal it.

Uniformity throughout the United States applies to
the whole people and country, without regard to state
boundaries, with a hope of reaching equality through
that means.

But neither exact uniformity nor exact equality can
be expected in a country so large, extending over so

many degrees of latitude, and embracing such a diversity of climate and soil, as to cause the cultivation of different productions; for even the respective states, being so much smaller, and confined to a more homogeneous climate and soil, fail to reach exact equality; however, the United States, as well as the states, may closely approximate equality in all taxation.

While the term impost includes various exactions that may be imposed on a people, it includes an import or tariff tax, and was doubtless intended to vest the congress with the power of laying an import tax, and as the congress is authorized to designate what articles shall be taxed, it may, by selecting the articles to be put under an import tax, cause that tax to fall more heavily on one class of the people than other classes; or it may be made to fall heavier on the people of some of the states than those of other states; and if the congress is authorized to lay a particular and separate rate of tax on each article designated to be taxed, instead of an *ad valorem* tax, as contended for by one of the political parties. By the designation of the article to be taxed, and the rate of tax to be imposed on it, great injustice may, through party zeal, be imposed on one class of the people, or on the people living in different degrees of latitude. But, as the limitation of uniformity in the paragraph under consideration relates to the effect of the tax rather than the power to impose it, the judiciary may relieve those imposed on from the unequal burden, without inquiring into the validity of the act of congress imposing the tax. No case involving this question has ever been passed on by the supreme court, that I know of.

This is, however, the correct interpretation of said paragraph. Said paragraph proceeds to vest the congress with power to lay and collect taxes, duties, imposts and excises, and then proceeds to say, "but all duties, imposts and excises shall be uniform throughout the United States;" this provision, therefore, applies to the operation of the taxing law, *not to its passage;* indeed, a taxing law might be uniform when enacted, and subsequent circumstances might arise that would destroy that uniformity; it is true, the congress could repeal it as soon as it lost that uniformity.

But, suppose a personal interest of a majority of the people should be so strongly in favor of retaining the unequal law as to prevent its repeal. Or suppose a majority of the congressional districts should send representatives to congress pledged to enact a taxing law that would bear unequally on different classes or localities; in neither case could the law be uniform, and must impose unequal burdens on certain classes or sections of the United States, whenever it should be put into operation.

If this language had been put in form of a proviso, it would have applied to the enactment of the law, *not to its operation;* the meaning of the language, therefore, is that the effect of every law imposing duties, imposts and excises shall operate uniformly throughout the United States. So that whenever the want of uniformity may appear in any of said modes of taxation, it will be the duty of the courts to enjoin its enforcement. The congress is not likely to intentionally impose excise taxes unequally without a motive.

But there are some sections of the United States in which the agriculture or planting industries prevail, and in other sections manufacturing and mercantile enterprises prevail. The more dense the population may be, the better roads and other conveniences for carrying manufactured articles and raw material to and from the factory, and the greater facility merchants will have for selling and shipping. Therefore, if the tariff tax be high enough for the manufacturers to divide the profits with the merchants, they will want a tariff tax to protect them in their business, and to enable them to control the trade of the agricultural or planting section of the United States. While those who may be engaged in agriculture or planting, having no competition from abroad in the sale of their production at home, would not desire any protective tariff to aid them, particularly as a large part of their productions must go to a foreign market for sale, and as they sell to a foreign market, they would wish to buy their supplies from that foreign market, and to get them as cheap as possible. This conflict in interest necessarily leads to a conflict in political policy, and has built up two great political parties in the United States, one in favor of arranging the tariff taxation so as to protect home industries without regard to revenue for the United States. The other party denying the right of the congress to tax one part of the country for the benefit of another, or to tax the people engaged in one occupation for the benefit of those engaged in other occupations. And while they admit the authority of the congress to designate the imported articles to be taxed, they deny the authority of congress to impose higher rates of duty on some articles than on others, and insist that the congress must tax all imported articles at the same rates according to the value thereof—this is known as the *ad valorem* system, and the former is known as the specific tariff system.

If the powers of the congress is limited to the *ad valorem* system, it will greatly weaken its ability to impose unequal burdens upon some sections of the country, for the benefit of other sections, or from imposing unequal taxation on one or more classes of occupations for the benefit of other occupations.

For the character of clothing, and other merchandise, used in the agricultural parts of the union are of a much cheaper grade than those used in the mercantile cities and manufacturing districts.

So that to provide the protection demanded by the merchants and manufacturers, the articles taxed by the tariff must be limited to the articles used mostly in planting states, or sections, of the union ; and those cheap goods must be taxed at a higher rate than the better grade of goods used in the manufacturing districts and mercantile cities. As the tariff on home goods is high enough to prevent importation, the manufacturer with the aid of the merchant is enabled to force all laborers within any part of the United States to use goods of that grade, manufactured under that tariff protection; and there being more laboring people to be clothed in the United States than idle, fine dressing people, such a tariff tax would reach the whole laboring class of citizens, for the benefit of the manufacturers and merchants.

The other political party insists that it is the duty of the United States to protect the manufacturing enterprises, in the discharge of the duty imposed on the congress, to provide for the general welfare of the United States, and that the congress has the right to tax the people in any authorized way, to build up manufactures in the interest of the general welfare of the United States. It is, however, beyond my purpose in giving this review to discuss the political features of any question any further than they may be necessary to elucidate some provisions of the constitution. I will leave this branch of the question, and take up the constitutional authority of the congress to discriminate in the matter of taxation, or any other imposition on the citizens, in the nature of governmental duties.

The congress, undoubtedly, is authorized to "lay and collect taxes, duties, imposts and excises, to pay the debts and provide for the common defense and the general welfare of the United States," and may select the objects of such taxation.

"But all duties, imposts and excises shall be uniform throughout the United States," and "no capitation or other direct tax shall be laid, unless in proportion to the census or enumeration hereinbefore directed to be taken."*

"No tax or duty shall be laid on articles exported from any state."†

"No preference shall be given by any regulation of commerce or revenue to the ports of one state over those of another; nor shall vessels bound to, or from one state, be obliged to enter, clear or pay duties in another."‡

While the word equality is not used in either of these provisions, they show that equality in the burdens of the government was the design of each one of them. But for the purpose of inquiring into the power of the congress to lay and collect taxes, etc., suppose we admit that equality is not required by said provision of the constitution, and if uniformity throughout the United States be followed by the congress, in taxation and laying burdens on the people, nothing else can be required; still it will be difficult to see how the congress can lay and collect a tariff tax for the purpose of protecting manufacturing enterprises, although they may redound to the general welfare of the United States, for the simple reason that any tariff tax that will afford protection to any particular character of industry, can not be made uniform throughout the United States.

For, to protect an industry by means of a tariff tax,

---

* Art. 1, Sec. 9, Par. 4, Con.   † Id. Par. 5,   ‡ Id. Par. 6.

that tax must fall exclusively on other industries in
order to protect the favored industry, every tariff tax
must therefore bear unequally, to favor any one industry
over others.

However, a tariff tax intended to be both equal and
uniform may operate more beneficially to one character of
industry than to another; in all such cases the object of
the taxing law is equality, therefore, its unequal bearing
must be so slight as not to impose heavy burdens on any
class or classes.   But whether the inequality of the tariff
tax proceeds from design or accident, the United States
includes such a variety of climate, and the productions
and industries are of such a heterogeneous character,
as to make it impossible for the congress to enact a
tariff law that discriminates between classes of occupations, that will not also discriminate between localities,
and, therefore, lack the uniformity required by the constitution.

Such discriminations are further guarded against by
the following provisions:

"No tax or duty shall be laid on articles exported
from any state."

"No preference shall be given by any regulation of
commerce or revenue to the ports of one state over those
of another; nor shall vessels bound to, or from, one
state be obliged to enter, clear or pay duties in another."

These two paragraphs clearly show the right of the
states to require uniformity of tariff or import taxation, but they appear to be limitations on the power
of the congress to enact a law taxing articles exported from any state, or showing a preference to the
ports of one or more states over those of other states,
and when such discrimination is shown the law itself is
void, because the congress had no authority to pass it :

on the contrary was expressly prohibited from passing it.

It is not clear what steps the states can take to enforce their rights to uniformity in that character of burdens. However, the importer of the articles so taxed may raise the question by refusing to pay the duty, and let the custom officer seize them to be sold for the duty on them; then the importer can sue for the articles, and use the name of his state, if it had been discriminated against, in conjunction with his own name; and should the court find that a preference had been shown to the ports of one state over those of another, the court would be compelled to hold the law void; or if it should be found that the tax was not uniform throughout the United States, the court being required to look to the effect of the act of congress relating thereto, *not* to the validity thereof, would be compelled to grant the relief, and have the articles delivered without payment of the duty on them.

There is still a further limitation on the power of the congress to lay and collect taxes, as follows:

"No capitation, or other direct tax, shall be laid, unless in proportion to the census or enumeration hereinbefore directed to be taken."

Every direct tax is not necessarily a capitation or personal tax, as in the case of taxing lands, which are always taxed specifically, without regard to the ownership of them, or liens upon them, though every capitation or personal tax must be direct.

The language "no capitation or other direct tax" was evidently intended to include every character of personal tax, and probably the tax on land was not on the minds of the framers of the constitution, as either a capitation

or direct tax ; for no people can constitute a nation, or
state, without a territorial boundary to own and possess
to the exclusion of all other people.   Hence, to constitute a state or nation, there must be a people separate
from and distinguishable from every other people,
who must have possession and control of a territorial boundary, separated and distinguishable from the
balance of the territory of the world, with power to
exclude it from the use or occupation of all other
people, except by sufferance of themselves ; therefore, no
state treats the lands within its borders as personal
property in its taxing laws, but lays taxes on the lands
specifically.   It is true the owner of the land is named in
the tax levy or assessment as the one who is to pay the
tax, though not as following his person as owner thereof,
but rather as the occupant paying a rent charge to the
state as lord of the fee than as a tax due from the occupant
as owner thereof.

The facts are, the final and absolute title to the lands
in the several states of this union belongs to the state in
which they are situated, and the citizen to whom it appears to belong owns simply an estate therein, which
must always be subject to the support of the state, as the
only safe reliance from which to obtain the necessary
means to defray the expenses of the state government ;
and in order to retain absolute control of the lands
therein, the state retains the absolute title and eminent
domain of all the lands within its borders as a necessary
attribute of its sovereignty.

Furthermore, at the time the constitution was
adopted, many of the states had more vacant land
within their respective borders than had been appropriated or settled, and as the apportionment of direct
taxes was required to be made according to the enumera-

tion of the population, without regard to the property, or the value of the taxable property within each state, the small states with but little vacant and unappropriated lands would have been imposed on by an unequal taxation by the terms of a provision intended to give them equal protection under the constitution.

If the absolute title and eminent domain to the lands within the states be recognized to be in the state, or the great body of the people thereof, as sovereign owners of it, and that nothing passes by the patent for the land except an estate less than the absolute fee, the state retaining the absolute title in itself, as lord of the fee, and therefore not subject to be taxed by the United States, it will greatly simplify the method of laying and collecting direct taxes by the congress. As all valuable stocks in corporations, and all mortgage bonds, are secured by liens on whatever estate in land that passes under the patent to the grantee, hence if the patentee gets less than the absolute title by the grant, nothing more than that which passes to the patentee can be pledged to secure such stocks or bonds; therefore, neither can be treated as part of the land. The absolute title in the lands themselves being retained in the state, they could not be mortgaged or pledged. Though whatever estate may have passed by the patent would be subject to be pledged to secure the stocks or bonds aforesaid, and such stocks and bonds would depend on an estate carved out of land, and not on land itself, therefore, while such stocks and bonds may be said to constitute a part of the estate in the lands pledged to secure them, they could not be held to be any part of the lands so pledged, any more than a lease for a term of years of the land, and the profits arising out of such a lease, and such estates in lands being equitable charges, carved out of the estate granted by the state in the patent to the land ; the right thereof attaches to the person, and follows the stocks and bonds into the hands of whomsoever they may pass, and the courts of any state having jurisdiction of the person of the holder thereof may adjudicate as to the right, though by special laws of the respective states, statutes to foreclose mortgages therein have been made local.   But this provision of the legislatures of the states can not be strictly adhered to, for in case of a mortgage on a railroad extending through two or more states, the courts of either state have jurisdiction to foreclose the mortgage and order a sale.

Stocks and bonds constitute the great bulk of the money capital of this country, and if they are to be treated as a part of the lands in regard to taxation, it will so limit the powers of congress in laying and collecting taxes to pay the public debt and provide for the public defense as to cause great embarrassment and delay in providing for the general welfare of the United States, while if such stocks and bonds be treated as part of an estate carved out of the land, they may be taxed on excise principles in form of an income tax, and thereby do away with the necessity of apportioning that tax among the states as a direct tax.

The difficulty in laying and collecting taxes on land by the congress is sufficient to prevent them from being taxed at all for purposes of the United States, and if the stocks and bonds of railroads, telegraph lines, street railroads, ice factories, and the like, are to be regarded as a part of the land included in the mortgage to secure them, they will also escape federal taxation ; and as that character of property has grown to such a large volume of the taxable property, if the congress is to be deprived of the use of that source of raising revenue to provide for the payment of the debts and the common defense and general welfare of the United States, it will amount to a serious obstacle in the exercise of the taxing power of congress, and may interfere with providing for the public defense.

Power to Borrow Money and to Coin Money—State Prohibited from Coining Money.

Article I, Sec. 8. " Congress shall have power—"

Par. 2. " To borrow money on the credit of the United States."

Par. 5. " To coin money, regulate the value thereof, and of foreign coin, and fix the standard of weights and measures."

Sec. 10, Par. 1. " No state shall . . . coin money; emit bills of credit; make any thing but gold and silver coin a tender in payment of debts; pass any bill of attainder, *ex post facto* law, or law impairing the obligation of contracts; or grant any title of nobility."

These three provisions relate to each other, and constitute part of the same objects provided for by the constitution, and should be considered together as one subject. The money authorized to be borrowed by the congress, was intended to be current and final redemption money, without a guarantee from the United States, or any other government, or any bank or company to redeem it.

For should the United States obligate themselves to guarantee the redemption of the money so borrowed, every borrowing might include an obligation to pay twice for the same loan, in the event the maker of the money so borrowed should fail to redeem the same.

Money had a known meaning at the time, and long before the constitution was made, it was used long before the birth of Christ, and in all nations, it was understood to indicate that which had been agreed on to express values, a medium of exchange to pay debts on final settlement, or as expressed by Abraham in the purchase of Machpelah, "current money with the merchant," as the only indorsement of it.

The business world had agreed that gold and silver were the best metals of which to make money; indeed, as far back as history reaches, gold and silver coin were both used as redemption money; the coins, however, were not always stamped by government authority, nor by individual guarantee.

Mr. Hallam, in his Middle Ages, gives an account of tampering with the coins, by the Jewish and Lombard usurers; he says the coins, in some instances, were reduced by them, to one-half weight, which caused great distress in France; but as prices went up on the clipped coin, in England, that nation was benefited by it for a short while;* but they soon grew into disfavor, and a company of German traders, who used the coins of a higher grade, both of gold and silver, the stamp value of which, both as to the fineness and weight, were entirely satisfactory to the English people. As those traders came from the east of England, they were called Easterlings, and their coins were also called easterlings, and then abbreviated into sterlings; those coins were esteemed so highly by the English people that the parliament by act of Edward III, ch. 13, adopted that system of coinage for that kingdom, both as to the gold and silver coins; however, the English shilling was retained as a unit of values.†

Without a legislative act fixing the weight and fineness of coins, and making them a tender in payment of debts, by force of law, their value will be regulated by common consent, and that consent is not likely to be

---

* Hallam's Middle Ages, pp. 483-486, 497-500.
† Blackstone's Com., vol. 1, p. 278.

given unless the coins contain sufficient precious metals to make them approximate their coin or stamp value. And, as the coins of all redemption money must be taken together, to arrive at their relative value as money, to the commodities they represent, and also the commercial ratio between the metals of which they are made must be considered, in ascertaining the quantity of metal to be put into the coins of each; it must remain difficult to determine what shall constitute the sign by which to express values, particularly as the precious metals themselves fluctuate in value.

Mr. Blackstone says: "As the quantity of precious metals increases, that is, the more of them there is extracted from the mines, this universal medium or common sign will sink in value and grow less precious. Above a thousand millions of bullion are calculated to have been imported into Europe from America within less than three centuries; and the quantity is daily increasing. The consequence is that more money must be given now for the same commodity than was given an hundred years ago. And, if any accident were to diminish the quantity of gold and silver, their value would proportionately rise. A horse that was formerly worth ten pounds is now perhaps worth twenty, and, by any failure of current specie, the price may be reduced to what it was." *

This fluctuation in the value of the precious metals must be estimated by combining the value of both, to get at their true value or relation to the commodities they are to be used to give expression to the value of. For, if the coins of both gold and silver be recognized as final redemption money, and the coins of only one of these metals be estimated in ascertaining the relation of the

* Blackstone. vol. 1, p. 276.

final redemption money to the commodities to be represented by both, the value of the sign, or coins, would be
too high, and the commodities measured by one only
would be correspondingly too low, and the trading public
would not agree to such expression of the value of their
commodities.

Consequently, the coin of both metals must be counted
together, to indicate their relation to the commodities
they are to express the value of.

Coins, or specie, used as final redemption money, being
estimated partly by the commercial value of the precious
metal in them, and partly by the uses they may be put
to, as a measure of values, and exchange for all articles
of trade, the precious metal put in them need not have
a commercial value equal to the coin or stamp value to
make them pass at their stamp value ; indeed, the value
of the convenience of their use to express the price of
all articles of commerce, and of being used in exchange
of all articles of trade, constitute the principal value of
the coins ; neither gold nor silver, as metals, deprived of
being used as money, would sell for half as much as the
bullion thereof will bring, as long as it may be converted into money of final redemption, for, whenever
the use of either of them as materials of which to
make money ceases, more than half of the demand for
them will also cease, and the metal of each will necessarily sink to less than half of its present value, if not
more.

Whenever the coins become more or less numerous,
the value of them will change in obedience to the laws of
supply and demand ; however, as they have a fixed sign or
index by which to express values stamped on them when
coined, which can not be changed, the price of the articles of commerce they are used to express the value of
must change to comport with the changed value of the

coin to be used as a sign or index thereof, so that whenever the signs are scarce, commodities must go down, and whenever they are abundant, the prices of commerce must go up.

And, if the specie of the country shall consist of two or more metals, the coins will be estimated by the ratio of the supply and demand of each metal of which they are made, unless the government making the coins shall coerce the people to take them, by making them a legal tender, in which event it will become a matter of but little concern to the trading public what the value of the metal in them may be ; but, unless the coins be made a legal tender, they will not take them, unless the metal in them has a commercial value, approximately, equal to their coin value.

However, as the law, making the coins a legal tender can not be made to operate any where except in the nation making them a legal-tender, it will be better for the people of the nation making its coins a legal-tender, that the value of the metal of which they are made should have a commercial value approximately equal to the stamp value. The precious metal in the coins of the United States has always had a commercial value equal to the coin value, except in the case of the silver coins under what is known as the Bland-Allison Act of 1878, and what is known as the Sherman Act of 1891. Under each of said acts, the silver coins, as well as the silver metal in them, was so hostilely decried against by the government of the United States, as to cause the price of the metal in the coins to sink below the coin value. And the mints, by those acts, being closed against the coinage of silver on individual account, and open *only* on account of the government of the United States, and, the coins being made legal tender in the payment of *only* such debts as should not otherwise be provided for by contract; the silver coins therefore fell in value.

The prohibition against the coinage of silver on individual account, and the government being limited in the quantity of silver it could coin, at once destroyed the market for a large part of the silver bullion, which necessarily reduced its commercial value. Moreover, the authority to destroy the legal tender feature of the silver coins by contract, while the gold coin was to remain a legal tender, so decries the silver coins themselves, as to make them form a lower grade of money than that which is represented by the gold coins; and, therefore, establishes two grades of money, the one based on gold coins, and the other on the decried silver coins; to the great injury of the producing classes, and to the advantage of brokers and persons who deal in exchange and investments in bonds.

As silver coins are used in the small transactions, and in purchasing the daily subsistence of life, the people become more familiar with them than with gold coins; and as nations usually begin their existence with a people of moderate means whose trade is small in amount, the first coins are usually made of silver, and then, as the people grow in wealth, they need gold.

It is claimed that England in adopting the pound sterling, as its criterion of coinage both as to silver and gold in the same act of its parliament, constituted its unit of gold, but that is a mistake, for England had coined her shilling of silver long before tha act of its parliament, though the quantity of pure metal in the shilling and probably the weight of it had been changed; however, every

coin authorized by that act (adopting the pound sterling), indirectly related to the English shilling, and its
value measured by that shilling; so that really no part
of the easterling system of coinage was adopted by said
act of parliament, except the quality thereof.

By the act of congress of 1873 an attempt was made to
establish a gold unit as follows: " The gold coins of the
United States shall be a one dollar piece, which, at the
standard weight of twenty-five and eight-tenth grains
shall be the unit of value; a quarter eagle, or two and a
half dollar piece; a three dollar piece; a half eagle, or
five dollar piece; an eagle, or ten dollar piece; and a
double eagle, or twenty dollar piece.   .   .   ."*

Although the congress declares that the gold dollar
shall be the unit of value, unless we accept the dollar
as established by the second congress of the United
States, the term dollar, as used in that act of congress,
must be entirely without meaning, and the mention of
the one dollar piece; the three dollar piece; the five
dollar piece; the ten dollar piece, and the twenty dollar
piece, would all be so much jargon and entirely without
meaning.

But if the silver dollar, as established by the second
congress, be recognized as the unit of value of the United
States, the act of congress quoted from becomes perfectly
plain and comprehensible.

I do not question the authority of the congress to
change the unit of value, and to establish such unit
as may please the congress; but, inasmuch as that
unit is a sign by which to express value, it must be
understood and agreed on by the trading people of
the United States, and should bear such relation to
the unit of values agreed on by the commercial na-

---

* Revised Statutes U. S. 3511.

tions with which the American people carry on trade, as
to make it useful to the people ; it should also bear relation to the value of the commerce it is to be used to
express the value of, otherwise it would not express the
true value thereof, and would prove a serious obstacle in
the way of carrying on commerce with foreign nations.
Consequently, unless the congress shall take its new
unit from some foreign nation, or from the existing
unit of the United States, it will be compelled to
look to the commerce of the world and the nations
with which the people of the United States trade, and
compare it with the money of those nations, or rather
the facilities of those nations to acquire bullion, of which
to make final redemption money, to ascertain a correct
unit by which to express values.   The congress without
entering into this investigation attempted to make the
unit of value of gold, as aforesaid, but, in fact, retained
the unit as established by the second congress.

The second congress declared that the money of account shall be expressed in dollars as units; dimes,
or tenths ; cents, or hundredths ; mills, or thousandths,
in decimal proportion each to the other.   That all gold
coins should be eleven parts pure gold and one part of
alloy, consisting of copper and silver, the proportion of
silver not to exceed one-half of said alloy.   And the
proportion between pure gold and pure silver should be
fifteen to one in value.   And the dollar of the United
States should be the same as the Spanish milled dollar,
containing 371¼ grains of pure silver, making the standard silver in it 416 grains.*

It will be observed that the second congress borrowed
from Spain and adopted the unit of that nation, viz., the
dollar.

* 30 L. U. S. Second Congress, CC. 15-46.

The power of congress to coin money does not necessarily include authority to make the coins thereof a
tender in payment of debts, as is manifested from the
custom in Europe, at the time the constitution was made,
of granting that authority to bishops and others, which
was never held to include authority to make the coins
a legal tender; and the coining of the precious metals
had frequently been done by individuals without any
grant of authority to do so by any government. However, authority to regulate the value thereof, and of
foreign coin, may with some plausibility be claimed to
include authority to make the coins a legal tender; but
a careful examination of all of the provisions of the constitution relating to the subject will show that the
authority to regulate the value thereof was not intended
to grant power to make the coins a legal tender, and can
not be so construed, unless we concede that the convention desired to vest the congress with authority to
give to the coin a fiat value, as the power to make them
legal tender can in nowise aid in regulating their value
except by enabling the congress to force the people to
take spurious coin in payment of debts; therefore I assume for the present, but will present the proof later,
that the states alone are vested with authority to make
the coins of gold and silver tenders in payment of debts,
and the only power the congress has is to coin and
regulate the ratio between gold and silver and the size of
the coins. Though congress may coin any metal to be
used as currency, the coins thereof can not be made legal
tender without the sanction of the legislatures of the
several states; and the states are prohibited from making
any thing a tender in payment of debts except gold and
silver coin.

The whole country was disgusted with the paper
money, whether it was continental money or that which

was issued by the respective states, and the delegates in the convention were impressed with the importance of establishing a stable and sound monetary system for the United States. But how to vest congress with power to make money and limit the exercise of that power so as to prevent it from following the example set by the continental and confederate congresses, was a matter of serious concern among the delegates.

Therefore, why not divide the power to make money between the congress and the states? The objects of government were divided between the states, and the United States, by giving the union exclusive jurisdiction of that class of powers necessary to enable it to conduct the affairs thereof with foreign nations; and to the several states exclusive jurisdiction of the domestic affairs and police powers thereof, and no amendment to the federal constitution could be made without the concurrence of two-thirds of each house of congress, and although concurred in by so large a vote of each house, such amendments could not become parts of the constitution until ratified by the legislatures of three-fourths of the states, or by conventions in three-fourths of the states; or be proposed by a federal convention and ratified by three-fourths of the states.

A stable and high grade of money being so earnestly desired by the convention, why should the monetary system not be guarded by dividing the power to make money between the states and congress?

The power to declare what shall be a tender in payment of debts can not be practically exercised by both the congress and the states. For, suppose the great state of New York should declare the gold and silver coin of the United States to be equally legal tender, without regard to any contract against the silver coin, (which that state clearly has a right to do, by the plain letter of

the constitution), any judgment in the courts of that
state could be satisfied by the payment of either gold or
or silver coin.   But either party would have a right to
appeal the case to the supreme court of the United
States, to test the validity of the act of congress, in attempting to delegate its authority of deciding when, and
in what character of cases, silver coin should be legal
tender.   If discretionary authority to declare gold and
silver coin a tender in payment of debts is vested in congress, the congress alone must exercise that power, for
congress can not delegate it to any other jurisdiction, not
even to the people themselves.*

Should the supreme court hold the act of congress
valid, in all judgments in the courts of that state, the
New York law would be sustained, and any judgment for
money could be satisfied by a payment in either gold or
silver coin.

But in actions in the United States courts, held in that
state, the New York law would be ignored and the debt
would be required to be paid in gold.

The authority to make gold and silver coin tenders in
payment of debts, is expressly reserved to the states by
the plain letter of the constitution.

"No state shall .   .   .   coin money, emit bills of
credit, make any thing but gold and silver coin a tender
in payment of debts."

But the congress is authorized, not only to coin money,
but to regulate the value thereof, and of foreign coin.
Though as has been shown, authority to coin money does
not include authority to make the coins a legal tender.
Neither does authority to regulate the value thereof include authority to make the coins a legal tender.

The value of the coins of every nation must be regu-

---

* Cooley's Con. Lim., Sixth Edition, p. 137.

lated by law ; but as the coins of every nation constitute
the money with which the national debts are to be paid,
they ought to be good enough to pass current without the
fiat of being made a legal tender by the nation.   Still, a
unit of value by which all values may be expressed is
essentially necessary to enable the people to sell or exchange their commodities, and every coin, whether fractional parts of that unit or multiples thereof, should refer
to that unit, as is the case in the United States.   The
dollar being the unit, the fractions thereof do refer to it,
as half dollars, quarter dollars, etc.   So do the multiples
refer to that unit, as the five-dollar gold coin, the ten-
dollar gold coin, etc.   Again, in fixing the size of the
fractional parts of the unit and multiples thereof and the
size of said unit, is but exercising authority "to regulate
the value thereof ;" and by declaring the relation of
foreign coins to that unit, is a regulation of the value of
foreign coins.

As authority to the manufacturer of coins to make
them a legal tender includes authority to give them a fiat
value, if the use of the words, "and to regulate the
value thereof and of foreign coins" means to vest the
congress with authority to make them a legal tender, the
convention must have intended to give the congress unlimited control of making money, and authority to nullify
that provision of the constitution reserving to the states
authority to make gold and silver coins a tender in payment of debts ; for, as has been shown, that authority
can not be exercised by the congress and the states both
at the same time.

The congress having exclusive authority to manufacture the coins of the United States without limitation,
and no limitation or restriction on the congress relating
to making legal-tender money appearing any-where in
the constitution, what will prevent the congress from

splitting the coins half in two and making them legal
tenders, and thereby reducing the public debt one-half
and relieving the debtor class of one-half the difficulties
of paying their obligations? For there is no prohibition
against the congress passing laws that will impair the obligation of contracts. Or what is there to prevent the
congress from increasing the amount of metal in the
coins, and thereby doubling the obligations of the debtor
class? Or what will prevent the congress from declining
to manufacture either or both of said metals into money,
and making the promises to pay of the United States a
legal tender, as was done with the treasury notes, commonly known as greenbacks, during the civil war, which
were paid out at par for army supplies, while they were
not worth more than from thirty to fifty cents to the dollar, which amounted to taking private property without
just compensation?

Some of the ablest statesmen that ever lived in the
United States were in the convention that made the constitution, and they certainly foresaw all of these dangers,
and knowing that the continental congress and the congress of the confederation had each shown themselves incapable of managing so delicate a trust, they, therefore,
could not have meant to vest the congress with such plenary
powers by the use of the language "to regulate the
value" of the coins.

As the states and the congress can not both exercise the
power to declare the coins of gold and silver tenders in payment of debts, the express reservation of that authority to
the states was intended, in part, as a limitation on the powers of the congress; but mainly for the purpose of guaranteeing to the people of the United States a specie, to consist of gold and silver coins alone, of full weight of pure
metal, and the coins of each metal to be of equal value,
and to constitute but one grade of money. The congress

having exclusive authority to coin money, and the states exclusive authority to determine whether they shall constitute tenders in payment of debts, and the states being prohibited from making any law that will impair the obligation of contracts, no changes that will impair the obligation of contracts could be made in the coins of the United States.   Under this view, the congress would not be likely to attempt to make any such changes in the coins, particularly as they would become a dead expense on the United States; unless the states could accept them and make them tenders in payment of debts, which the states could not do, if they were changed sufficiently to impair the obligation of contracts.

As the states would not be likely to agree on coins, unless they were of full weight of pure metal (and no one state could afford to accept coins as tenders in payment of debts that were refused by the other states), and the states being prohibited from passing laws that will impair the obligation of contracts. not only a high grade, but the most stable monetary system of any nation, was secured by the constitution.

The specie *must* consist of both gold and silver coins, the silver for small and gold for large transactions; the gold can not be used for subsidiary coin, for but few persons could see or feel a five cent gold piece, particularly those who labor. The gold dollar can not be easily handled by but few persons; and coins smaller than a dollar are absolutely needed to get the daily necessities of living; therefore, the silver is absolutely necessary for one class of business, and the gold is necessary for another and different class of business.

The value of the coins of each metal ought to be equal, and to pass current at their stamp value in the payment of

debts, and in exchange for all commodities on exact
equality.

There is, however, a strong party in the United
States that advocates what they call "the single gold
standard." A single gold standard is an utter im-
possibility; no nation ever had, and no nation can,
confine itself to a single gold standard of values, because
gold can not be used for making subsidiary coins of;
therefore some other metal must be used for that purpose. As the subsidiary coins are used to provide
the daily necessities of life, the people are made more
familiar with them, and their value; they will, therefore, measure the values of all things by the unit of
that coin, and every wise government will give to its
subsidiary coin a fixed value, by prescribing its unit of
values in the metal of which its small coins are made,
for all values are relative and fluctuate; even the
precious metals fluctuate in value, and, as before shown,
the coin, or specie, fluctuates in value, in obedience to
the supply and demand. Whenever a nation uses the
more precious metal to prescribe its unit of values in,
that act of itself decries the value of the less precious
money metal; for no nation can get its citizens to
consider what is called a gold standard of values unless
it decries the *coins* made of its less precious metal;
and as the people can not surrender the subsidiary
coin, to express the value of the things they are bound
to buy for their daily living, the gold standard necessarily results in another standard, without destroying
the unit recognized in the subsidiary coin, consequently
that attempt must result in establishing two standards,
which two standards will fluctuate in value according to
the supply and demand of the coins of each metal.

A discussion of the evils of two grades, or standards,

of money, more properly belongs to economics than
to the powers granted by the constitution.   However, it
may not be out of place, to call attention to the fact
that just at this time bonds made payable in gold sell
more readily than bonds made payable in American
coin; it should be borne in mind that, if the congress is authorized to declare what shall be a tender in
payment of debts, there is no limit on that power, and
the congress may make a bond contracted to be paid in
gold payable in paper alone, but if authority to declare
what shall be a tender in payment of debts is vested
exclusively in the states, they can never make any
thing a tender in payment of such bonds except gold
and silver coins; but the states must make the gold
and silver coins equally tenders in payment of debts.
Attention should be directed to the further fact, that,
as long as this country attempts to maintain two or
more grades of legal-tender money, American exchange
will necessarily take rank with the lowest grade of legal-
tender money, because of the natural inclination of man-
kind to pay debts in the cheapest money authorized by
law.   It should also be mentioned that, as long as this
country attempts to maintain two or more grades of
legal-tender money, it will be impossible to maintain a
merchant marine, because there will be no money with
which to pay the sailors, to make their wages, on American ships, equal to the wages they get on ships conducted
under foreign flags.   It is against human nature to pay
a debt in the highest grade of money that the law authorizes to be paid in the lowest grade; but if ship owners
could be found who would pay their sailors in the highest grade of money, the smallest piece of gold money
men accustomed to climb ropes can conveniently han-
dle is the two and a half dollar gold piece, American

ship owners are obliged to follow the custom of letting a
part of the crew off of duty in each port they may enter, and whenever sailors go ashore they want to spend
money, so that, unless they buy two and a half dollars'
worth, they will be compelled to take the subsidiary coin
of the port in change, which is not likely to be worth its
coin, or stamp, value in any other port; therefore the
sailors will be losers whether they are paid in gold or
silver coin of the United States. Hence, although the
merchant ships may offer and agree to pay their sailors
as much as they are to get on ships of other countries,
the character of the money they are to be paid in reduces
their wages below the wages paid on foreign ships.

In support of this theory, at the beginning of the late
civil war the merchant marine of the United States was
second only to that of England, and now it is inferior to
that of five or six nations, although it is claimed that the
United States furnishes about one-fourth of the commerce
of the world.

It is also claimed that the United States is more richly
endowed with silver deposits than any other nation in
the world.

The demonetization of silver and destroying its equal
legal-tender value with gold not only destroys the immense
wealth this country ought to derive from carrying the
commerce of the United States, but destroys one-half of
the value of the silver ores so bountifully deposited in
the mountains of this country.

The destruction of these two valuable sources of wealth
without cause, or at least without a reasonable cause, conclusively shows the inability of the congress to manage so
delicate and important an interest as that of regulating the
money of the United States, and the wisdom of the constitution makers in dividing the authority to make final

redemption money between the congress and the state legislatures.

The claim that the United States can not maintain its silver coins on a par with its gold coins is without foundation or common reason ; for that which gives specie its money value is the uses it may be put to, and if it is true that the United States furnishes one-fourth of the commerce of the world, by giving her coins of each metal equal sanction under the law, all coins so sanctioned could be maintained at par, and be gladly received in every country using articles exported from the United States.

ARTICLE I.

Sec. 8, Par. 3. " To regulate commerce with foreign nations, and among the several states, and with the Indian tribes."

Sec. 9, Par. 6. " No preference shall be given by any regulation of commerce or revenue to the ports of one state over those of another ;   . . ."

ARTICLE IV.

Sec. 2, Par. 1. " The citizens of each state shall be entitled to all the privileges and immunities of citizens in the several states."

Par. 2. "A person charged in any state with treason, felony or other crime, who shall flee from justice and be found in another state, shall on demand of the executive authority of the state from which he fled, be delivered up, to be removed to the state having jurisdiction of the crime."

These four provisions relate to the subject of commerce among the states and should be considered together, to reach a clear understanding of the extent of the power of congress on the subject.

"Among the states" was held by the supreme court of the United States, in the Gibbon-Ogden case,* to mean, "within the states;" indeed it is difficult to see how it can be construed otherwise. That was a case involving the validity of an act of the legislature of the state of New York, granting to two persons exclusive authority to navigate all the waters in that state, that were navigable by steam, for the period of ten years. This act of the New York legislature was clearly against the act of congress regulating domestic navigation, and therefore unconstitutional, and the decision was right, but it was not based on that ground.

While some of the navigable waters, by steam, of that state may have extended into other states, that feature was not discussed by the court in its opinion in the case, but the court held that the navigable waters by steam of that state, constituted channels of commerce, and notwithstanding the fact that some of the waters included in the grant were navigable by steam only within the state of New York, and the commerce to be carried on them must be taken on, and discharged, within the state; still the court construing the phraseology "among the states," to mean "within the state," held that as the navigable waters by steam, although entirely within the state of New York, constituted channels of commerce over which congress had control, and that the act of the New York legislature could not defeat the congress in its authority to regulate commerce, therefore the act of

---

* Reported in 9th Wheaton, p. 1.

the state legislature was void. This is held to be a leading case on the subject, and it has been uniformly adhered to, to the extent that congress has jurisdiction of commerce between the states, and over the means of carrying commerce. So that a discussion of these questions will cover all that has been decided on the subject by the supreme court.

While I concur with that part of the decision that interprets the phrase "among the states" to mean "within the states," I can not understand how the court could construe "among the states" also, to mean, "between the states;" nor can I concur with the court in holding that authority to regulate commerce includes authority to regulate the means of carrying commerce.

I will discuss these questions in the order they are here named.

In arguing the case, the court refers to no authorities (probably because the counsel cited none), but among other things, that court said : "The subject to be regulated is commerce, and our constitution being, as was aptly said at the bar, one of enumeration, and not of definition, to ascertain the extent of the power, it becomes necessary to settle the meaning of the word.

"The counsel for appellee would limit it to traffic, to buying and selling, of the interchange of commodities, and do not admit that it comprehends navigation.

"This would restrict a general term applicable to many objects, to one of its significations.

"Commerce undoubtedly is traffic, but it is something more ; it is intercourse. It describes the commercial intercourse between nations, and ports of nations in all of its branches, and is regulated by prescribing rules for carrying on that intercourse.

"The mind can scarcely conceive a system for regulating

commerce between nations, which shall exclude all laws
concerning navigation, which shall be silent on the admission of the vessels of the one nation into the ports of
the others, and be confined to prescribing rules for the
conduct of individuals in the actual employment of buying and selling, or of barter.

"All America understood the word commerce to com-
prehend navigation. It was so understood, and must
have been so understood when the constitution was
framed."

It is not the word commerce that is to be interpreted,
to fully understand the extent of the powers of congress
over commerce in the states ; what the phrase "*among the
states*" means is of the highest importance, for it is upon
that phrase that the whole question turns. If that shall
be interpreted as the makers of the constitution evidently
intended it to be understood and interpreted, the congress has no power over commerce between the states.
Commerce and intercourse between the states is unaltera-
bly provided for by the constitution itself as the very es-
sence of the compact of the union. It is provided that
" the citizens of each state shall be entitled to all of the
privileges and immunities of citizens in the several states."
Privileges and immunities, as has been said, include the
right of going into any state in the union and buying, owning, selling and conveying any thing therein that is recognized as property in the state ; to transmit the same by will,
deed, or descent and distribution, according to the laws
of the state ; to attend all lawful meetings and to freely
enter into any discussion on any lawful subject, whether
it relates to religion, politics or science, or any law of
physics or morals; to import, export, raise or manufacture any article of trade, and to use every railroad, canal,
river, turnpike, plank-road, dirt-road, or bridle-path over
the mountains, on the same terms and conditions the

citizens thereof are subjected to, no more and no less. It is impossible to prescribe any rules for the regulation of commerce between the states, without in some way interfering with these provisions of the constitution.

Congress never passed any act to regulate commerce between the states, except between rebelling states or parts thereof, and states adhering to the union during the late civil war, and to regulate steamboats navigating rivers that pass along or through several states; indeed, it is utterly impossible to pass an act to regulate trade between the citizens of the several states, without its restraining the states from extending equal privileges and immunities to the citizens of all the states; or to pass an act regulating the carrying of commerce on railroads, canals, turnpikes, plank-roads, dirt-roads or mountain paths, without interfering with the ability of the states to extend to the citizens of all of the states equal privileges and immunities. The extending equal privileges and immunities to the citizens of all the states by every state; the giving full faith and credit to the public acts, records, and judicial proceedings of each state in every other state; the capturing of one guilty of crime committed in a state, who flees to another state, by the authorities of the state where he may be found, to be taken to the state having jurisdiction of the act to be tried; and the feeling of security established by uniting the forces of all of the states to make common defense, constitutes the cohesive principles of the union, and without any one of these provisions the cohesion of the union would be greatly weakened, and without any of them the states, having no common interest, would likely drift apart and let the union go to pieces.

As these provisions are necessary to hold the union together, any interference that tends to destroy or weaken them, or either of them, must constitute acts hostile to the union, let it come from whatever source it may.

The authority to regulate steamboats on navigable waters arises out of an entirely different class of powers; navigable rivers are public highways, and it is the duty of the congress to keep them open for the use of all of the states, and by the terms of the cession of the surplus territory by the several states it was made the duty of congress to keep the Ohio and St. Lawrence rivers and their tributaries open for the use of all of the states. In addition to this source of authority, the congress is authorized to regulate domestic navigation among and between the states.

The federal judiciary has assumed jurisdiction of not only commerce between the states, but to regulate the means constructed by the several states for carrying commerce out of their borders to a seaboard town situate in another state, for exportation; but the courts have not as yet succeeded in arriving at an exact and uniform rule for regulating the same, and it is doubtful whether an exact and uniform rule can be discovered to regulate the means of carrying commerce between states without coming in collision with the fourth article of the constitution, and the right of the states to manage their police affairs.

At the time the constitution was being made the institution of slavery was a question of serious concern with the delegates in the convention; and to interpret the language "among the several states" to mean "between the several states," would have necessarily authorized congress to regulate commerce in slave property between the states, and carrying slaves from one state to another, and have destroyed the right of any state to regulate that institution within its borders.

The regulation of the liquor trade between states, and the carrying of the same from one state to another, must also be within the jurisdiction of congress, if the term "among the several states" be construed to mean "between the states."

If the reader will call to mind the facts that the United States had no citizens except the citizens of the several states, and, unless congress could bind the citizens of the several states to its commercial treaties with foreign nations, no foreign nation would make such a treaty with the congress of the United States. That there is no authority given to congress to bind the people of the respective states to commercial treaties by the letter of the constitution, unless this paragraph authorizing congress to regulate commerce with foreign nations and *among the several states,* and with the Indian tribes, gives that authority.

That the word *among* does not mean between, though by adding qualifying words, it may be made to mean between, as in the case of a devise directing decedent's estate to be equally divided among his children ; but there are no qualifying words, or word, in connection with its use in this paragraph, to give it any other than its own meaning (viz.), "amidst, within."

And that the imperative necessity of authorizing congress to bind the people of the several states to its regulation of commerce with foreign nations and with the Indian tribes, together with the absolute certainty that it was never intended to vest congress with authority to regulate the sale of slaves by citizens of one state to citizens of another state, or the transfer of slaves from one state to another ; conclusively shows that the sole object and function of the power of congress to regulate commerce *among the several states* was intended to give, and does give, the regulation of foreign commerce by the congress force and effect within the states, and was never intended to, and does not, give congress any authority to regulate commerce, or the means of carrying the same, between the states.

However, should the congress find some mode by which it may regulate commerce between the states without conflicting with the second section of article four of the constitution, still it has no constitutional authority to interfere with the means of carrying commerce. It is true, without the means of transportation, commerce could not be carried on. Nor could it be carried on without the factories and farms to produce it, and it may as reasonably be claimed that authority to regulate commerce includes authority to regulate the factories and farms, as to claim that it includes the tramway from a factory to a railroad depot, or a turnpike, railroad, canal or any other means constructed by any state for carrying commerce.

Commerce proper, at the time the constitution was formed and adopted in 1787, was regulated by the *law merchant*, a species of international law which was beyond the control of the municipal authority, and it could not be changed by any one nation alone, however anxious it might be to do so. The high seas being free to all, the navigation thereof was to a limited extent also regulated by international laws, though the main features of navigation were subject to the control of municipal laws. Ships engaged in the carrying of commerce, whether on the high seas or on inland waters, were regulated by the municipal law of the nations to which they belonged ; neither ships, canals, inland rivers, nor roads as means of carrying commerce, were ever regulated by the law merchant, but, on the contrary, they were always controlled by municipal authority.

Since commerce and navigation were regulated not only by different codes of laws, but by different authorities, they could not be considered as parts of each other.

Mr. Blackstone, in speaking of commerce, says: "No municipal laws can be sufficient to order and determine the very extensive and complicated affairs of traffic and merchandise; neither can they have a proper authority for this purpose. For as these are transactions carried on between subjects of independent states, the municipal laws of one will not be regarded by the other. For which reason the affairs of commerce are regulated by a law of their own, called the law merchant, or *lex mercatoria*, which all nations agree in, and take notice of." *

This is accepted by Mr. Jacob and quoted at length in his law dictionary. †

Every civilized nation must have a commerce, for the value of personal property depends on the right to dispose of it, and every industry requires the individual right to dispose of surplus production; without this right no one would produce. As nations occupy different degrees of latitude and produce different articles of commerce, the citizens of each must be enabled to exchange the surplus they produce, or they will seek some nation to live in that will provide them with that convenience; hence, a well-regulated commerce is essential to every nation.

But while every nation is bound to have a commerce, and internal convenience to get that commerce to its ports of entry for exchange, yet every nation is not bound to have ships, for the ships of one may carry the commerce of many nations. Every ship requires the

---

* Blackstone, vol. 1, p. 273, sec. 5.
† Jacob's Law Dict., Commerce, Ships, etc.

protection of some nation, not only against free-booters, and pirates at sea, but to protect them in their rights in the ports of foreign nations ; for this reason merchant ships usually take their charter from a nation able to give them that protection, and they will float and do business under the flag of that nation ; and for the protection it gets, it will owe allegiance to that nation, and will be subject to its control, and may be called on in time of war to do military duty.

The relation between a nation, and the ships that belong to it (which includes all ships that float under its flag), is such that the ship is deemed a part of the territory of the nation whose flag it floats, and this theory is carried so far as to hold infants born on board of a ship to have been born within the nation to which the ship belongs ; however, if the birth does not take place until the ship reaches the home port of the mother, the child will be deemed to have been born within the nation of which its mother is a citizen. *

Although the navigation of the high seas is regulated by international laws, every ship will be under the control of the nation to which it belongs, and regulated by the municipal laws thereof, still, whenever it enters the port of any other nation, it must yield submission to its municipal regulations.   But as soon as it leaves that port and straightens out in the high seas, the municipal authority of its own nation envelops it, and proceeds to control and regulate its business as a carrier of commerce, as far as it can do so without interfering with international law.

Long before the separation of the American states from England, that nation had its navigation laws.†   All

---

* Vattell's Law of Nations, book 1, chap. 19, sec. 216.
† Jacob's Law Dict., Navigation.

questions of navigation were settled according to these laws, instead of international law, by the English courts. Still commerce proper was regulated by the law merchant, and all judicial controversies were determined and settled by the rules of the law merchant, "which all nations agree in, and take notice of;" as said by Mr. Blackstone.

If authority to regulate commerce among the states includes authority to regulate the means of carrying commerce, it must include every means of transportation, and must take into its grasp not only the rivers that lie entirely within a single state, but the canals, railroads, turnpikes and all dirt roads within the state. Though the supreme court has never gone so far in any case that I am aware of ; however, no distinction can be drawn in principle between a river lying entirely within a state and a mountain path lying entirely within a state ; consequently, the position taken by the judiciary will necessarily lead to transferring the control of every public thoroughfare in every state of the Union to the congress of the United States, although there is no authority in the congress to tax the people of one state to construct railroads, canals, turnpike or dirt roads in any other state, or to tax any other state to construct any of said improvements therein, or to compel any state to construct them.

It is conceded by all that any state may construct canals, railroads, turnpikes, dirt roads and bridges within its territorial borders without let or hindrance by congress ; but if congress is authorized to regulate such improvements because they may be designed to be used as channels of commerce, the congress may prevent any state from constructing any such improvements at any time ; yet the congress has no authority to compel any state to construct improvements of any

character whatever and has no authority to spend the
money belonging to the United States for any such purpose, except in the construction of *post-roads* which have
no connection with the convenience of travel or hauling
commerce for the people.

The supreme court further said in said Gibbon-Ogden
case :

"As preliminary to the very able discussion of the
constitution which we have heard from the bar, and as
having some influence on its construction, reference has
been made to the political situation of these states
anterior to the formation of the constitution.

" It has been said that they were sovereign, were completely independent and were connected with each other
by a league.

" This is true.   But when those allied sovereigns converted their league into a government, when they converted their congress of ambassadors, deputed to deliberate
on their common concerns, and to recommend measures
of general utility, into a legislature, empowered to enact
laws on the most interesting subjects, the whole character in which the states appear underwent a change, the
extent of which must be determined by a fair consideration of the instrument by which that change was effected.

" This instrument contains an enumeration of powers
expressly granted by the people to their government.
It has been said that these powers ought to be construed
strictly.

" But why ought they to be so construed? Is there one
sentence in the constitution which gives countenance to
this rule?   In the last of the enumerated powers, that
which grants expressly the means for carrying all others
into execution, congress is authorized to make all laws
which shall be necessary and proper for the purpose.
But this limitation on the means which may be used, is

not extended to the powers which are conferred ; nor is there one sentence in the constitution which has been pointed out by the gentlemen of the bar, or which we have been able to discover that prescribes this rule. We do not, therefore, think ourselves justified in adopting it.''

The tenth amendment to the constitution, which was proposed by the first congress that was elected after the adoption of the constitution, provides as follows ;

'' The powers not delegated to the United States, by the constitution, nor prohibited by it to the states, are reserved to the states respectively, or to the people.''

The constitution being inanimate, it can speak only by its letter. Therefore all powers not delegated by the letter of the constitution to the United States, or prohibited by the letter thereof, to the states, are expressly reserved to the states respectively, or to the people. Suppose A. owned a thousand-acre tract of land, and he should sell to B. five hundred acres of it by metes and bounds, and it should turn out that the survey of land contained fifteen hundred acres instead of only a thousand acres. A. would undoubtedly be entitled to the whole surplus in the land whether he reserved to himself all over and above the five hundred acres he sold to B. or not. Now, the constitution, not only delegates to the United States specifically enumerated powers, but expressly reserves all powers not specifically granted to the United States, to the states respectively, or to the people ; hence, no power can be rightfully accorded to the United States unless it can be found in the letter of the constitution, or may be fairly inferred as a part of a power plainly granted by the letter thereof, which rule requires a strict construction to be complied with.

But that court claims the vesting of congress with authority to enact laws had the effect of converting the

United States into a sovereign nation.   That is equally untenable, for it is not claimed that the congress can go outside of its authority under the constitution to make laws.

It is shown in Chapter III that power to make laws under the limitations of a charter can not have the effect of vesting the corporation with sovereignty, and the constitution of the United States imposes as rigorous restrictions on the making of laws as were imposed by the colonial charters or by the charter of any city ; consequently authority to make laws under the limited authority of the constitution could not of itself alone have given the United States a sovereign government.

However, whether the United States is a sovereign nation, or simply a corporate agent of the people, the congress thereof has, under its authority to regulate commerce, the right to control foreign ships, while they are in the ports of any state within the union, engaged in carrying commerce to or from the United States, and may determine what nation or nations of people the citizens of the United States may trade with, and prescribe the terms and conditions on which that trade and traffic may be carried on.   The congress may also designate the articles of commerce that may be imported or exported, as shown by the embargo acts of 1798–1800 and 1808.   And may regulate American ships and shipping.

Furthermore, as before said, if the congress is authorized to regulate any one of the railroads, canals, turnpikes or dirt-roads constructed by state authority, it must necessarily have control of all of them, and thus the whole police power of the state was transferred to the congress of the United States by said provision, without reference to the police powers of the states.

Justice Miller, of the Supreme Court of the United

States, in discussing this phase of the question in the case of the Wabash, St. Louis and Pacific Railway Co. *v.* The State of Illinois, said that there is a class of cases that the states have exclusive jurisdiction of, but he fails to point them out, and I doubt if he could have done so, as learned and able a jurist as he was, for there is no discernible boundary line between jurisdiction of the congress and that of the state, if the congress has control of any of the means of carrying commerce, which are located entirely in any one state, whether there by the laws of nature, or put there by the state for the convenience of its own citizens and those of its sister states.

Consequently, every effort on the part of congress to interfere with any means of carrying commerce is the exercise of ungranted powers and a stigma upon the union itself, and seriously interferes with the states making other and valuable improvements, as the states will stop making improvements unless they are allowed to control them by state laws.

CHAPTER VI.

GRANT OF POLITICAL POWERS—PROHIBITION OF POWERS TO THE STATES AND TO CONGRESS.

ARTICLE I.

Section 8.

Par. 4. "To establish a uniform rule of naturalization, and uniform laws on the subject of bankruptcies throughout the United States."

The United States having been formed for white races of people only,* and the compact of the union binding each state to extend to the citizens of every other state equal privileges and immunities with its own citizens, being agreed to, prevents any dark races of people from being admitted as citizens; exclusive authority to establish naturalization laws should have been vested in the congress, for privileges and immunities includes the right of marriage and transmitting property by inheritance, as well as by bargain and sale, so that if the states were authorized to enact separate laws of naturalization, and also authorized to pass its own laws relating to marriages, and some of the states should make it lawful for the whites and blacks to intermarry, and other states should prohibit such marriages, and some of the states should naturalize the dark race, and other states should refuse to make the dark race citizens, the law of descent and distribution would necessarily become so entangled as to render it impossible to dispose of the rights of the parties.   But by

---

* Dred Scott case.

vesting the congress with the exclusive right to pass naturalization laws, the congress must adhere to the constitution, and extend the privilege of naturalization to the white races of people only, so that although any state might extend authority to marriages between the white and black races, it could extend no further than that state and would not be entitled to consideration in the other states, under the provision of the constitution requiring each state to extend equal privileges to the citizens of each of the other states.

Any state may extend to persons of African descent, or to emigrants of the white race, the right to vote before they shall have been in the United States long enough to be naturalized under the laws of congress.

The privilege of voting in a state for members of "the most numerous branch of the legislature," will entitle them to vote for members of congress and presidential electors. *

But the right to vote will not of itself make them citizens, or entitle them to equal privileges and immunities in the several states.

The extent of protection due by the United States to naturalized citizens, and to those who have taken the first step towards becoming naturalized, without being in this country long enough to take the final oath, has been rendered somewhat doubtful by treaty alliances.

The English act of 1870 provides for the naturalization of aliens after five years' residence and application to the secretary of state, and also that any British subject who shall voluntarily become naturalized in any foreign country, shall after five years' residence be regarded as alien and no longer a British subject. A treaty was entered into the same year between Great Britian and this

---

* Art. 1, sec. 2, Con.

country providing that aliens, who have complied with the conditions of admission and have been fully naturalized, should be recognized as such by the country of his birth ; but the original allegiance may be recovered by much the same process.   Treaties were also made by the United States in 1868 with Prussia, Bavaria, the Grand Duchy of Baden, Wurtenburg, Grand Duchey of Hess, Belgium and Mexico ; in 1869 with Sweden and Norway ; in 1870 with the Austro-Hungarian empire, and in 1872 with Ecuador and Denmark.   These treaties have the same general stipulations, stating a period of residence, usually five years, after which naturalization is permissible and to be recognized, reserving to the country of original allegiance the right to punish for crimes committed, or to compel the execution of obligations entered into before the change of domicil, and entering into mutual obligation to recognize the rights of each other. The question on which is the greatest likelihood of disagreement under existing laws, arises where an alien comes to this country and becomes duly naturalized and then returns.   Is he then liable to undergo military service or otherwise recognize allegiance to the state of his birth?   Some European nations hold that such a transaction on its face is evidence of an intention to escape natural obligations, but the policy of our government has always been to protect its adopted citizens where the naturalization is not tainted with fraud.*

The right of expatriation lies at the foundation of the American system, and the United States can not afford to surrender that right.

The inhabitants of the colonies were British subjects at the time they severed the tie that bound them to that

---

* International Cyclopedia, vol. 10, p. 339.

kingdom, and constructed charters thereof emanating from themselves.

To have admitted, as may be claimed by reason of the treaties referred to, and as contended by most of the European nations, that the consent of one's native country is necessary to authorize him to sever his allegiance to it, and to be lawfully naturalized in any other country, would have prevented our revolutionary ancestors from becoming citizens of the United States, until sanctioned by the treaty recognizing the independence of the several states of the union. It also surrenders all that the United States gained by the war of 1812 against the right of searching our ships and taking seamen and pressing them into service of their native country.

During the late civil war large numbers came from Germany and elsewhere, and enlisted in the army of the United States and served with distinction, and were naturalized before remaining in this country the five years. If said treaties express what the law was at that time, it was binding on the United States, and every such naturalization was void.

But if it was intended by said treaties to constitute a new rule on the subject, they will prevent the United States from receiving in their navy and army citizens of any friendly nation that has assumed the attitude of neutrality, for no nation can allow its citizens to join the army of either of the belligerant nations and remain neutral, and according to said treaties they will continue to be citizens of their native country for the period of five years, so that if the United States receives them in the army or navy, they, by that act, will violate their obligation to the neutral nation, and subject the citizens thereof enlisting in the army and navy to the punishment indicated by the proclamation of neutrality of their native country.

The reservation of the right to punish for crimes committed in his native country before becoming naturalized must mean extraditable crimes according to international law, so that said treaties do but little more than every extradition treaty ; but as to the character of obligations entered into with his native country before leaving that may be enforced under said treaties, is apt to cause difficulties.   It is a recognized rule, the allegiance to a country includes military service in whatever form the government may prescribe, therefore that service is included in the allegiance transferred to the nation into which he is naturalized ; hence, that can not be the character of the obligation, the right to enforce was intended to be reserved by said treaties.

After a foreign born inhabitant has been fully naturalized, he is entitled to all of the rights, as well as privileges and immunities he would be entitled to if he had been native born, except that of holding certain offices, such as president, etc.

Par. 4. "To establish uniform laws on the subject of bankruptcies throughout the United States."

As no state has jurisdiction beyond its territorial limits, no state could enact a bankrupt law that would protect even its own citizens against the payment of debts to citizens of any other state.

A state might prevent its own courts from giving judgment against its own bankrupt law if they were not prohibited from impairing contracts. still the citizen of any other state would have the right to sue in the federal courts, which could not be controlled by the state laws ; therefore, any bankrupt law enacted by any state could not protect any debtor.   But in addition to this inherent difficulty in the way of a state bankrupt law, it is provided in the tenth section of article one of the constitution, that no state shall pass any law impairing the obli-

gation of a contract ; and every bankrupt law necessarily
impairs the obligation of contracts : it is true this provision in the constitution comes after that which delegates to congress alone authority to pass bankrupt laws,
and is a part of that plan, which was doubtless based on
the difficulty of the states to pass an effective bankrupt
law, to operate alone therein.

The power of congress extends to relief against debts
due to citizens of foreign nations.

However, no bankrupt law can relieve any state
against its liabilities, for that would be interfering with
the sovereignty of the state, and a state may repudiate its debts, since the adoption of the 11th amendment to the constitution, for there is no power to
force a state to pay any debt. Nor can any bankrupt
law relieve any municipal corporation of its debts, for as
long as persons who are solvent live in a municipal-
ity, they would be bound to pay taxes; therefore,
that municipal corporation can not be adjudged a bankrupt.

In addition thereto, under the fundamental principles
of the government, of this country as well as that of England (since the Magna Charter was adopted in that
kingdom), no taxation or scutage can be assessed against
any people without the consent of their representatives ;
hence, no court can order the laying or collecting of
taxes to wind up the debts of any municipal corporation,
or for any other purpose.

Experience of the business of the world shows, that in
the evolution of commerce, some of the best business
men become so deeply involved in debt, as to bind them
in a state of bondage to their creditors, and renders
them valueless as citizens while under that bondage,

who, if they could be released, would make good citizens and valuable agents in the development of the resources of the country ; there ought, therefore, to be some way of releasing them of that thralldom, not only on their own account, but for the benefit of the community in which they live, and they could not be so completely relieved by any state ; hence, the authority was properly vested in congress.

Par. 6. "To provide for the punishment of counterfeiting the securities and current coin of the United States ;"

Par. 7. "To establish post-offices and post-roads ;"

Par. 8. "To promote the progress of science and useful arts, by securing for limited times to authors and inventors the exclusive right to their respective writings and discoveries ;"

These three powers properly belong to what is known as the civil laws, and according to the general plan of the union, they would fall to the state ; but each one of them is necessary to enable the federal authorities to maintain the government thereof, and are necessarily vested in the congress, but they ought not to be augmented by interpretation ; on the contrary they should be strictly construed.

With the exception of laws to punish counterfeiting the securities and currency of national banks, I am not aware of any encroachment on these powers by the federal government even when strictly construed.

But if the congress is authorized to charter banks, authority to create must be accompanied by authority to protect them, and as the laws to punish for counterfeiting bank currency and securities must be the same as laws for punishing the counterfeiting of coin and securities of the United States, no serious inconvenience can flow from the exercise of that power by the congress, particu-

larly as it is held by the supreme court that the states
may pass laws to punish counterfeiting either the coin
or securities of the United States, or the currency or securities of national banks; but it was also held that the
state and federal courts are foreign jurisdictions.* Therefore, a punishment under state statutes in a state court
would not bar a prosecution in a federal court under an
act of congress.

I can not assent to this ruling by the supreme court,
but will not discuss it at this point further than to say
that the government of the United States constitutes a
part of that of each one of the states, and whenever a
citizen is punished by either a state or the federal government, for a crime, they each have jurisdiction of, he should
not again be punished by the other for the same offense;
because it is in conflict with the general principles upon
which the dual form of government of the United States
is based.

The authority to establish post-offices and post-roads
being vested in the congress is so clearly correct that it
needs neither explanation nor comment.

Nor does the provision which authorizes the congress
to secure to authors and inventors the exclusive use of
their writings and discoveries for limited times, call for
explanation or comment, further than there is danger of
the congress renewing useful patents too often, and for
a longer time than they merit.

Par. 9. "To constitute tribunals inferior to the supreme court."

The tribunals intended by this paragraph must be such
as clerks, marshals, bailiffs, commissioners and all other
necessary official aid to the court in executing the laws,

---

* Gordon v. Gillford, 99 U. S.

for article 3, relating to the judiciary, authorizes the establishment of inferior courts, over which the supreme court shall have appellate jurisdiction.

Par. 10. " To define and punish piracies and felonies committed on the high seas and offenses against the law of nations."

Authority to punish piracies and felonies committed on the high seas and offenses against the law of nations must be vested in that division of every government intrusted with the maintenance of the government itself, and as the duty not only to maintain the government of the United States, but of the states also, is lodged in the United States government, it was essentially necessary to vest the congress with said powers. Of course, the felonies committed on the high seas referred to must be felonies committed on ships, whether owned by any one of the states, or by the United States, or by private citizens, provided it shall float under the flag of the United States.

As shown in the discussion of the right of congress to regulate commerce, every ship is regarded as a part of the territory of the nation whose flag it carries ; therefore, every felony committed on its ships must be treated as if it had been committed within the nation itself.

But as ships will always float under the flag of the United States, *not* under the flag of any state, the United States would be responsible, *not* the state, although the ship upon which the felony charged to have been committed may as matter of fact belong to one of the states ; and, as the states are prohibited from owning or keeping ships of war in times of peace, the ship of no state can carry the territory or jurisdiction thereof out into the high seas ; therefore such felonies must always be committed outside the jurisdiction of any state; consequently, it was necessary to give the congress jurisdiction of the felonies committed on the seas.

As to jurisdiction of offenses against the law of nations, since the United States is required not only to protect itself but the states also, the United States alone must be held responsible for all violations of the law of nations committed by a citizen of any of the states, and must have jurisdiction of that class of cases.

Par. 11. "To declare war, grant letters of marque and reprisal, and make rules concerning captures on land and water."

Par. 12. "To raise and support armies, but no appropriation of money to that use shall be for a longer term than two years."

Par. 13. "To provide and maintain a navy."

Par. 14. "To make rules for the government and regulations for the land and naval forces."

Par. 15. "To provide for calling forth the militia to execute the laws of the union, suppress insurrection and repel invasion."

Par. 16. "To provide for organizing, arming and disciplining the militia, and for governing such part of them as may be employed in the service of the United States, reserving to the states, respectively, the appointment of the officers and the authority of training the militia according to the discipline prescribed by congress."

These six paragraphs constitute each a separate part of the authority of making and conducting wars, and each grant is necessary for that purpose. Without authority of the United States to make and maintain wars, the government thereof could neither maintain itself, nor the republican form of government of the respective states. But for the purpose of guarding against unnecessary and useless exercise of these powers, they are divided between the legislative and executive departments, and as they can be better explained by considering the power delegated to each, and in connection with each other, further consideration is postponed until the executive department shall be reached.

Par. 17. "To exercise exclusive legislation in all cases whatsoever over such district (not exceeding ten miles square) as may by cession of particular states, and the acceptance of congress, become the seat of the government of the United States, and to exercise like authority over all places purchased by the consent of the legislature of the state in which the same shall be, for the erection of forts, magazines, arsenals, dock-yards and other needful buildings."

This paragraph granting exclusive legislation to the congress over the seat of government and places purchased to erect forts, arsenals, etc., is a limitation on the congress exercising exclusive legislation anywhere else within any of the states.

The extent to which the congress may go in the exercises of that exclusive legislation seems to be unlimited by the letter of the constitution, but there are serious difficulties in the way of exercising that authority by the congress.

The District of Columbia, the seat of the government, was taken partly from the state of Maryland and partly from the state of Virginia, in accordance with authority granted by this paragraph. If this district constitutes a separate jurisdiction from the states within which the respective parts are situated, it can not be a state with a republican form of government as long as its law-makers are chosen by the states generally and not by the people thereof ; and the language of the paragraph is, " to exercise exclusive legislation in all cases whatsoever over such district." The congress must do the legislation thereof itself, and can not authorize it to be done by any other organ or government.

And this paragraph does not extend the jurisdiction of the congress over any additional objects or subjects of legislation.

The congress can not extend the English common law over said district, as it relates largely to royalty or classes of people, without coming in conflict with the provision of the constitution prohibiting the granting of titles of nobility.

Nor can the congress adopt the common law of any of the states without preventing every other state from changing its own laws in relation thereto. Nor is it possible to compress the laws of the several states relating to marriage, descent and distribution; tenures of title to real estate, evidences of title to personal property; of contracts, the extent contracts shall be guarded by statutes of frauds and perjuries; nor of trade and traffic to be carried on by the citizens thereof.

But a more serious objection to that interpretation of this paragraph arises out of the fact that if said district be entirely separated from the states in which its respective parts are located it will deprive the inhabitants thereof of citizenship, for until the fourteenth amendment to the constitution was adopted no one could be a citizen of the United States unless he was a citizen of some one of the states in the Union; or if the inhabitants thereof could be citizens of the United States, still they would be deprived of voting for any representation in congress, or for any presidential elector.

Consequently, that part of said district taken from the state of Maryland is treated as still in that state and subject to the laws thereof, and the inhabitants entitled to all of the rights as well as the privileges and immunities the inhabitants of any other part of that state enjoy ; and the inhabitants of that part of said district taken from Virginia are entitled to the rights, privileges and immunities of the citizens of that state ; and the same rule applies to the places where the forts, magazines, arsenals, dock-yards, etc., may be situated. But the congress being authorized to "exercise exclusive legislation in all cases whatsoever" over said places by the plain letter of the constitution, that authority in the congress must be regarded by all to the fullest extent it can be exercised under the system of governments established for the United States. Though, as we have seen, the congress being inadequate to the duty of exercising all of the legislation required for the welfare of said places, we are compelled to consider the language therein to have been used in a qualified sense.

Since the language must be considered in a qualified sense, the most reasonable qualification that can be put upon it, is, that jurisdiction to legislate over the places named in the paragraph, should be taken as authority to exercise exclusive legislation upon all subjects the congress was vested with authority to legislate upon, and to exercise exclusive legislation over the land itself within said district, and to appropriate any part thereof, to any governmental use within the scope of the authority of the congress to regulate ; to lay off so much thereof, into lots, streets and alleys, and reserve some lots for the erection of government buildings and sell other lots, and to construct such buildings as to the congress might seem proper ; and to provide for the protection of the same, and to provide for keeping good order in such city, and the whole of said district ; leaving the regulation of the civil rights of the people thereof, under the control and regulation of the state, with all the rights, privileges and immunities of citizens of the state in which that part of said district wherein they resided might be situated. And as this is the only way the inhabitants of said district can be authorized to take part in either congressional elections, or in choosing presidential electors, said district is held to be a part of the state in which its representative parts are situated, and the permanent inhabitants thereof are citizens of the state in which that part of said district in which they reside is situated.

This rule is also made to apply to the places wherein forts, magazines, arsenals, dock-yards and other buildings are erected by the United States.

Par. 18. "To make all laws which shall be necessary and proper for carrying into execution the foregoing powers, and all other powers vested by this constitution in the government of the United States, or in any department or officer thereof."

This paragraph is said to have found its way into the constitution while the draft thereof was before the committee on style; be that as it may, the constitution was but a proposition when it left the convention, and the paragraph was in the constitution, and constituted a part of it when it was submitted to the states, therefore was ratified by the conventions of the several states as a part of that instrument, and is entitled to as much consideration as any other part.

This paragraph is important, for it shows that certain powers were delegated to the United States as an entirety; and that certain powers were delegated to different departments; and certain other powers were delegated to specified officers of the United States.

A close examination of the constitution will show that no power was delegated to the United States except such incidental powers as are necessary to enable the United States to carry into execution a specified duty imposed such as guaranteeing to the states a republican form of government and other like duties and trusts.

The great mass of powers delegated by the constitution is vested *directly* in a distinct department, or a named official of the United States, and are not permitted to pass through the government of the United States to such department or official, enables the several departments to exercise a restraining influence, not only on each other, but on the United States. And this paragraph recognizes that division of the powers granted by the constitution.

With the powers granted to separate departments instead of to the government, it is impossible for the government to be sovereign, yet the supreme court has made use of this paragraph to aid in showing the United States to have a sovereign government.

That part of this paragraph that authorizes congress to make laws which are necessary and proper for carrying into execution the powers delegated to congress was entirely useless, for the delegation of a power to the law making authority carries with it authority to make a law by which the powers can be executed. But it was prudent, if not necessary, to expressly authorize congress to make laws by which powers delegated to another department or officers could be carried into execution.

Hence, that part of this paragraph which recognizes the delegation of powers directly to the departments and officers, that do not pass through the government, was an important provision.

Thus far, we have been considering grants of power to the congress, but now we approach section nine of article one, which contains limitations on the exercise of the powers granted in section eight.

A question may arise as to whether these limitations

on the powers granted shall be strictly construed, as in construing limitations of authority in powers of attorney.

It will be conceded by all that the powers granted by section eight to the congress were granted by the sovereign authority ; and unless the powers were granted by the sovereign authority, the government of the United States must be one of usurpation, which I suppose no American citizen is ready to admit.

Then the universal rule of interpreting grants by the sovereign authority is to construe them strictly ; the grant being strictly construed, it will be a matter of but little importance whether the limitations thereof be strictly interpreted or not.

SECTION 9.

Par. 1. Relates to the importation of African slaves until after 1808, and is now obsolete.

Par. 2. "The privilege of the writ of *habeas corpus* shall not be suspended, unless when in cases of rebellion or invasion the public safety may require it."

Par. 3. "No bill of attainder or *ex post facto* law shall be passed."

Par. 4. "No capitation or other direct tax shall be laid, unless in proportion to the census or enumeration hereinbefore directed to be taken."

Par. 5. "No tax or duty shall be laid on articles exported from any state."

Par. 6. "No preference shall be given by any regulation of commerce or revenue to the ports of one state over those of another ; nor shall vessels bound to, or from one state, be obliged to enter, clear, or pay duties in another."

Par. 7. "No money shall be drawn from the treasury, but in consequence of appropriations made by law ; and a regular statement and account of the receipts and expenditures of all public money shall be published from time to time.''

Par. 8. '' No title of nobility shall be granted by the United States ; and no person holding any office of profit or trust under them, shall, without the consent of the congress, accept of any present, emolument, office, or title of any kind whatever, from any king, prince, or foreign state.''

The unrestrained right to the *writ of habeas corpus* was taken from the British constitution, and has been discussed by the courts and statesmen, both of the United States and of England, and it is useless to say more about it than that, as long as the judges have the courage to discharge their duty and comply with their oath of office, this writ is a complete protection against imprisoning persons for political purposes, and constitutes one of the bulwarks of personal liberty under the English civilization.

Bills of attainder, in brief, are legislative trials and convictions, and although it is elsewhere provided in the constitution that no one shall be deprived of his life, liberty or property, except by due course of law, it was wise to insert this prohibition against the authority of the congress to enact bills of attainder.

The *ex post facto* laws referred to in this paragraph apply to penal and criminal laws only, and the congress by it is prohibited from making any act a crime or penal offense after it shall have been committed. That no one should be made to suffer for doing that which he has a perfect right to do at the time he does it, is so plain to the human mind as to require no comment.

The prohibition against bills of attainder and against *ex post facto* law was also taken from the magna charta of

England, and has received the commendation of statesmen on both sides of the ocean.

The limitation in taxation as well as the power to regulate commerce have been fully considered in treating of the power granted in section eight of the constitution.

As to titles of nobility, they are so repugnant to the free governments of the United States that it is somewhat surprising that the makers of the constitution should have thought it necessary to put that prohibition in the constitution.

But since the United States bonds, together with the interest-bearing bonds of municipalities and states, and the bonds of private corporations, constitute so large a proportion of the property in the United States, that the owners thereof and of stock in favored corporations, having accumulated colossal fortunes to be dissipated and squandered by their heirs, have betrayed a strong inclination to acquire titles, through which to entail those fortunes on their posterity. That inclination is so strong as to have manifested itself in efforts on the parts of the possessors of those fortunes to negotiate marriages between their daughters and titled men from foreign countries.

Those wealthy dealers having control of the money capital of the United States, can furnish the money to carry elections ; therefore they are enabled to exercise a potent influence in elections, and they might cause such changes as to transfer the sovereign authority from the people to a moneyed aristocracy. But before that change can be effected this prohibition against granting titles of nobility will have to be expunged from the constitution, and to change the constitution in relation thereto will require the assent of three-fourths of the states. Not only is

the interest of the people of three-fourths of the states
against such a change, but this provision is so thoroughly
imbedded in the minds and hearts of the American people that it is scarcely possible to amend it out of the
constitution.

Consequently, this is a very important and valuable
provision of the constitution ; and if it is not of sufficient
force to prevent the revolution now being inaugurated, it
will prove a formidable check to it.

The prohibition against public officers accepting presents, etc., or titles from any king, prince or foreign country, is in aid of the prohibition against the granting of
titles of nobility ; but while this provision is limited to
public officers, no one can accept any title of nobility
from any foreign king, prince or foreign nation, except
to the extent he may owe allegiance thereto, and as long
as he may continue to owe allegiance thereto he will be
ineligible to hold any office under the United States.

SECTION 10.

Relates to prohibitions on the powers of the states,
which have been to some extent considered in treating of
the grant of the same powers to the congress, and therefore taken away from the states.   The powers expressly
prohibited to the states are as follows :

Par. 1. " No state shall enter into any treaty, alliance,
or confederation ; grant letters of marque and reprisal ;
coin money ; emit bills of credit ; make any thing but
gold and silver coin a tender in payment of debts ; pass
any bill of attainder ; *ex post facto* law ; or law impairing
the obligation of contracts : or grant any title of nobility."

Par. 2. " No state shall, without the consent of the
congress, lay any imposts or duties on imposts or exports,

except what may be absolutely necessary for executing its inspection laws; and the net produce of all duties and imposts laid by any state on imports or exports shall be for the use of the treasury of the United States; and all such laws shall be subject to the revision and control of the congress.''

Par. 3. '' No state shall, without the consent of congress, lay any duty of tonnage, keep troops or ships of war in time of peace, enter into any agreement or compact with another state, or with a foreign power, or engage in war, unless actually invaded, or in such imminent danger as will not admit of delay.''

The states having entered into the compact of the union under the Articles of Confederation, any other alliance, compact or confederation must necessarily conflict with the compact of the union and the equality of the states; for any compact or agreement between two or more states would be like two or more members of a business firm conspiring against the firm; as no two states would desire to enter into a compact, independent of the union, unless they desired to get an advantage over the other states in the union. If the states could make treaties or compacts with foreign nations, they could by such treaties, not only divest the congress of the power to regulate commerce with foreign nations, but might impair the power of the United States to declare or carry on a war with a nation having a treaty with one or more of the states; hence, it was a wise provision, to take from the states, by express letter of the constitution, authority to make any independent treaties or compacts, either between any two or more states, or with foreign nations.

Since the duty of protecting the states against every foreign force, as well as against each other, is imposed on the United States, and letters of marque and reprisal can be used only as forces of war, it was necessary to prohibit the states from granting them.

The prohibitions against the states coining money or their making any thing but gold and silver coin a tender in payment of debts, have each been discussed in connection with the grant of power to the congress to coin money and to borrow money.

The states being sovereign, they can not be sued without their consent, and have the power to repudiate any debt, and there is no power to force them to pay, though the supreme court of the United States held that they could be sued in the case of Chisholm v. The State of Georgia, but that decision caused an amendment to the constitution denying to the federal courts jurisdiction of actions or proceedings against any state by a citizen of another state, or a citizen of a foreign state or nation ;* but this amendment leaves that court with jurisdiction of actions brought by one state against another, hence no state can repudiate any obligation to a sister state.

Bills of credit could not constitute obligations to a sister state, and from their uses generally, they would pass into the hands of those who are least able to lose their value ; but the controlling motive that caused the states to be prohibited from emitting bills of credit, was the great volume of paper money issued by the states during the Revolutionary War that was of but little value at the time the constitution was being framed, because it was out of the power of the states to redeem it, which aided in depressing the value of the paper obligations of the confederacy ; experience of over a hundred years proves the wisdom of this prohibition against the states.

As the congress is prohibited from passing bills of

---

* 11th Amendment to the Constitution.

attainder or *ex post facto* laws, both of which have been briefly explained, to completely guard the citizens against bills of attainder and *ex post facto* laws, it was also necessary to prohibit the states from doing the same.

But the provision against the states passing any law impairing the obligation of contracts, and against the states granting titles of nobility, are each of American origin, and are each of importance. The latter is in conflict with the principles of government, and it would be useless to prohibit the congress from granting titles of nobility if the states could do so, therefore that prohibition was necessary.

But prohibiting the states from passing laws impairing the obligation of contracts has frequently been before the supreme court of the United States for interpretation, and that court has uniformly construed this provision to include charters granted by a state to private persons, and that said provision was sufficient to prevent the states from amending or repealing such charters, though that interpretation has never been approved of by all the judges thereof.

The great inconvenience that that interpretation has caused the states, together with the fact that it has always been sustained by a divided court, entitles it to a careful consideration.

The United States are required to guarantee to each state a republican form of government, which can not be done as long as the right of the legislature of a state to barter away the power of the state to maintain a republican form of government is upheld by the courts of the United States.

If the legislature of a state can transfer the right of the state to exercise its police powers in any one particular to a private enterprise, another legislature can transfer the right of the state to exercise other police powers

to another private corporation or private individual, and
the different legislatures may continue to grant the powers
thereof until the entire police power of the state is bar-
tered away to private persons or private corporations for
private uses, and the people thereof completely deprived
of their right to govern themselves, or to elect officers
for the government of their state ; for their right to manage their domestic affairs will have been contracted away
to moneyed individuals or to wealthy private corporations, and no possible way to help themselves within
their reach.

To get relief from that bondage, they would be compelled to appeal to the United States to come to their
relief and secure to them a republican form of government, and relieve them from bondage, for the people
would be powerless to relieve themselves from their
bonds, however tyrannically they may be treated by
their masters, whether stockholders in private corporations or individual owners of the police powers that may
have been granted by the different legislatures of that
state.   The constitution of no state authorizes its legislature to barter away the liberties of the people ; but, if
the legislatures of the states are authorized to barter
away the police powers of the state, they are practically
authorized to barter away the right of the people to govern themselves.   The rule of interpreting grants of power
is to so construe the grant as to leave every thing not
expressly granted with the sovereign authority.

No state has as yet granted away its entire police
powers ; but, if a state can, by its legislature, barter
away a part of its police powers by an irrevocable contract, it can the whole by the same sort of contract or
contracts.   And, whenever it reaches that stage in the
drama, it will become the duty of the United States to

take action, under its obligation to guarantee to each
state a republican form of government, and it must
either relieve the state by nullifying those contracts, or
the United States must embark in the revolution started
by the indiscreet action of the legislature thereof, and
uphold the private corporations in the ownership and
control of that state against the will or consent of the
people.

Should the congress declare the transfer of the police powers of that state to the private persons, or corporations, to be void, and by law direct the restoration
of the republican form of government, for the state, as
congress would be in duty bound to do; and the executive proceed to execute that law of the congress, and
the private person claiming to own the whole police
power of that state should apply for an injunction to stop
the proceedings to oust said private person or corporation
of the management and control thereof, what would the
supreme court of the United States do? What could
the supreme court do? All of the writs issued by that
court run in the name of the president; so that, in
the case here hypothecated, there would be an order
issued directly by the president requiring the private
person or corporation to surrender up the police powers
of the state to the state authorities, and the mandate of
the court issued in the name of the president, ordering
said private person or corporation not to surrender to the
state any part of its police powers, and restraining all
persons and officers from interfering with the free exercise and control of the police powers of that state by
such private person or corporation.

For, if it was proper to uphold the legislative grant as to
one police power, it would be equally as obligatory on
that court to uphold legislative grants of all of the police
powers of the state; and if it was lawful to uphold such

grants before the congress should take hold of the matter, it would be lawful to uphold the grant to the private person or corporation even against the power of the congress ; for if the grants were lawful, it would be unlawful for congress to interfere with them ; and it would be the duty of the court to protect the grantee even against the powers of the congress. This is an extreme case, but it is sometimes necessary to resort to extreme cases to bring a question rightfully and clearly before our minds.

Furthermore, the authority of a legislature to sell out its power or ability to legislate for the welfare of the people, is wholly incompatible with a republican form of government ; hence, by recognizing the authority of the legislatures of the states to barter away, by irrevocable contracts, the power to legislate for the people, by the supreme court, of itself, destroys the republican form of government of the states.

The language of the paragraph under consideratoin is : "No state shall . . . pass any bill of attainder, *ex post facto* law ; or *law impairing the obligation of contracts.*" . . .

This can not be construed as a prohibition against a state impairing its own contract, for it is a well-known fact that a state may repudiate its own contracts, and since the adoption of the eleventh article of amendment to the constitution the federal courts have no jurisdiction to force the states to comply with contracts or obligations, unless they be obligations with a sister state.

It was feared, at the time the constitution was being constructed, that some of the states would enact laws obstructing the means of enforcing the collection of debts due to foreigners (which is recognized as the remedy or obligation of contracts), for the states have the right to control the jurisdiction of their own courts and ministerial officers connected with the court. No state could

change any contract without interfering with its citizens
right to make contracts, even for the sale of the products
of their labor, which right is one of the fundamental
principles of freedom ; therefore, no fear was entertained
at that time of any states attempting to change any contract, but the remedy or obligation of all liabilities being
subject to the control of the states ; and this provision of
the constitution recognizing that right, only provides
that the states shall not impair the remedy or obligation
of contracts, in regulating its courts and the jurisdiction
thereof. As there was no remedy, or obligation of any
contract, any state had made, and none likely ever to be
provided, it would have been an utterly idle display to
have attempted to prevent the states from impairing that
which had no existence, and was not likely *ever* to have
any existence.

But, it was intimated by several of the judges of the
supreme court, in the first case in which that court
decided that private corporations chartered by the
states constituted contracts on the part of the state
(which was the celebrated Dartmouth College case), that
the states could protect themselves by reserving in the
charter, or by a general law, the right to amend or repeal the charter, which provision would enter into and
form a part of the contract, as accepted by the corporators, and that being reserved in the contract would be
enforceable in law. Since then all of the states have
amended their respective state constitutions, or enacted a
general statute reserving the right to amend, alter or repeal all grants of franchise or chartered rights, which relieves the states of the greater part of the evils arising
out of that interpretation of the constitution.

But the supreme court of the United States, by *obiter
dictum*, expressed in the argument of several cases, claim
that the courts of last resort of the states, are estopped

from overruling a former decision construing the state
law, or the constitution thereof, if in the opinion of the
federal courts such overruling may perchance impair the
the remedy or obligation. The former decision sustaining rights of contracts under the law of a state
ought to be overruled, if erroneous. The courts of
the state and the ministerial officers connected therewith, constitute the remedy or means provided by law
for obliging the parties to any contract to comply therewith, and all contracts that may be made, are entered
into with that understanding. Whenever the court
of last resort, whether it be a court of a state or the
supreme court of the United States overrules any judgment, it amounts to a decision that the overruled decision never was the law on the subject, and nobody
could acquire any right by reason of the former decision,
unless that decision announced the law on the subject.
Of course the parties to the former case would be estopped by it, but no one who was not a party could acquire any right under it, for the former decision was contrary to the lawful obligations of the party sued ; no
right can be accorded to the payee wrongfully, unless
they are wrongfully imposed on by the payer, and the
payer has a right to make use of all legal defenses in
every suit that may be brought against him. But the
court and its attachments being the remedy through
which the parties are obliged to perform their contracts, because that court decides that it erred in a former decision, can not be held to be an impairing of the
remedy, but rather a strengthening of the remedy, for
the payer is entitled to a lawful compliance with the contract, as well as the payee ; hence, the only question the
supreme court would have a right to inquire into on an
appeal of the case of that sort, is whether the last decision is the law of the case, and it has no right to con-

sider the effect of the former case at all unless it declares the law on the subject ; in that event the supreme court should itself declare the law of the case.

But returning to the prohibition against the states making laws impairing the obligation of contracts, the remedy suggested by some of the judges of the supreme court in the Dartmouth College case, to-wit : of the states reserving the right to alter, amend or repeal charters, leaves serious difficulties in the way of the states exercising their police powers fully, and they must necessarily cause the supreme court great trouble in disposing of the various questions that are to arise under that ruling.

The right to repeal the charter of a private corporation involves the right to prohibit the use of the corporate rights thereof, and in nearly every private corporation the tangible property connected therewith is so changed as to render it valueless for any other purpose ; and to take away from the corporation the use of the corporate franchises would virtually destroy the value of the tangible property connected therewith, consequently, the right not only to impair, but to absolutely destroy, the tangible property used therewith must be included in the right to repeal the charter by its terms.

The constitution of every state contains a clause prohibiting the taking of private property for public use without just compensation being previously paid,* and by the fifth amendment of the federal constitution the United States is prohibited from taking private property without paying for it ; consequently, in the absence of any contract, no state could deprive any one of his private property without previously paying just compensation for it, even if it should be needed for public uses. But, under the contract to repeal, extremely

---

* See Poores' Constitution, etc.

valuable property may be destroyed for public reasons without paying any thing for it. The state may authorize the corporators to change their tangible property so as to be used in conducting the corporate business at great cost at one session of its legislature, and at the session of the next legislature it may destroy it all without any compensation whatever. Whereas, without such a contract no state could enact a law repealing such corporation without repairing all damages caused thereby; for the repeal of the charter would be deemed a taking for public use ; hence there would be no escape from paying for the property so taken if the decision in the Dartmouth College case had never been rendered.

What the supreme court will do with this question remains to be seen ; but the safest and easiest way out of the difficulty appears to be the overruling of the Dartmouth College case and all others sustaining it, and to restore the states to their sovereign right to repeal all laws and charters, whether of a private or public character, that may appear to operate against the public policy of the state ; leaving the protection of the citizens thereof to the state laws, as was intended by the makers of the constitution.

Since the congress was prohibited from laying a tax on any article exported from any state, it was necessary to prohibit the state from laying a tax on exports therefrom, except to the extent it may be necessary to defray the expenses of its inspection laws. But why the states should be authorized to lay such export taxes as the congress may consent to, provided the entire surplus over and above what may be necessary to defray the expenses of the inspection laws of the states shall be held for the United States, and paid into the treasury thereof, is not so clear. For no state is likely to tax its own citizens for the benefit of the United States, unless the

tax would greatly redound to the benefit of the state laying the tax.

Furthermore, no state can lay an export tax further
than may be necessary to defray the expenses of its inspection laws without the consent of the congress, and
the congress is expressly prohibited from laying a tax on
articles exported from any state, and is prohibited from
showing a preference to the ports of one state over those
of another ; therefore should the congress consent that
any number of the states, less than all of them, might
lay that tax, that consent would amount to giving a
preference to the ports of certain states over the ports of
other states.   And should the congress consent that all
of the states might lay an export tax on articles exported
therefrom, that would amount to the congress doing
through the states that which the congress is expressly
prohibited from doing by itself.

This reasoning applies with equal force to all export
taxes.

Should the congress resort to this method of inducing
the states to tax themselves for the use of the United
States, in a way the congress is prohibited from laying
and collecting taxes, the states respectively will have
the power at all times to repeal such taxing laws, without consulting the congress about it.   Suppose, after the
congress had given its consent to any or all of the states
to procure and own ships of war in times of peace, and
after the states had procured ships of war the congress
should conclude that it had acted unwisely, and should
conclude to withdraw its assent therefrom, and the state
or states that owned ships of war desired to continue to
maintain them, what proceedings can the United States
adopt to force a state to give them up?   The duty of

the United States to maintain itself, and to protect all of the states in their equal privileges and rights in the union, is sufficient to justify the United States in coercing any state to give up ships of war.

For, if one state had ships of war to the exclusion of other states, that fact would be regarded with jealousy by the other states, and might be reasonably looked on as a menace against them.

But to cause that state to dispose of its ships, would be equivalent to taking such ships for public use, and the United States would be obliged to pay for them.

The prohibition against the state keeping troops in time of peace, contained in this paragraph, has been so modified by the second article of amendment to the constitution as to amount to nothing more than a prohibition against the states keeping standing armies, leaving the states free to maintain any character of a military force they may choose to keep.

Since the United States are required to protect all of the states alike against each other, as well as against all foreign powers, no state ought to be authorized to enter into any agreement or compact with another state, or with a foreign power, or engage in a war, unless actually invaded, or be in such imminent danger as will not admit of delay.

To enumerate all of the subjects over which the states have concurrent jurisdiction with the United States, would involve a discussion of privileges and immunities not desired to be entered into under the plan of this review. I suppose, however, that it will be conceded that the states have jurisdiction of all necessary powers to conduct the governments thereof, except such as are expressly prohibited to them, including the powers vested in the congress, until the congress shall divest the states thereof, by assuming control of the same.

CHAPTER VII.

ORGANIZATION OF THE EXECUTIVE.

ARTICLE II.

Sec. 1, Par. 1. "The executive power shall be vested in a President of the United States of America. He shall hold his office during the term of four years, and, together with the vice-president, chosen for the same term, be elected as follows : "

Par. 2. "Each state shall appoint, in such manner as the legislature thereof may direct, a number of electors equal to the whole number of senators and representatives to which the state may be entitled in the congress ; but no senator or representative, or person holding an office of trust or profit under the United States, shall be appointed an elector."

Par. 3. "The electors shall meet in their respective states, and vote by ballot for two persons, of whom one at least shall not be an inhabitant of the same state with themselves. And they shall make a list of all the persons voted for, and of the number of votes for each ; which list they shall sign and certify, and transmit sealed to the seat of the government of the United States, directed to the president of the senate. The president of the senate shall, in the presence of the senate and house of representatives, open all the certificates, and the vote shall then be counted. The person having the greatest number of votes shall be the president, if such number be a majority of the whole number of electors appointed ; and if there be more than one who have such majority, and have an equal number of votes, then the house of representatives shall immediately choose, by ballot, one of them for president; and if no person have a majority, then from the five highest on the list the said house shall, in like manner, choose the president. But in chosing the president the vote shall be taken by states, the representation from each state having one vote; a quorum for this purpose shall consist of a member or members from two-thirds of the states, and a majority of all of the states shall be necessary to a choice. In every case, after the choice of the president, the person having the greatest number of votes of the electors shall be the vice-president. But if there should remain two or more who have equal votes, the senate shall choose from them by ballot the vice-president.

"The congress may determine the time of choosing the electors, and the day on which they shall give their votes; which day shall be the same throughout the United States.

"No person except a natural born citizen, or a citizen of the United States at the time of the adoption of this constitution, shall be eligible to the office of president; neither shall any person be eligible to that office who shall not have attained to the age of thirty-five years, and been fourteen years a resident within the United States.

"In case of the removal of the president from office, or of his death, resignation, or inability to discharge the powers and duties of the said office, the same shall devolve on the vice-president, and the congress may by law provide for the case of removal, death, resignation, or inability, both of the president and vice-president, declaring what officer shall then act as president; and such officer shall act accordingly, until the disability be removed, or a president shall be elected.

"The president shall, at stated times, receive for his

services a stated compensation, which shall neither be increased nor diminished during the period for which he shall have been elected, and he shall not receive within that period any other emoluments from the United States, or any of them.

"Before he enter on the execution of his office he shall take the following oath or affirmation : *'I do solemnly swear* (or affirm) *that I will faithfully execute the office of President of the United States, and will, to the best of my ability, preserve, protect and defend the Constitution of the United States.'*"

This is the original plan of electing the president and vice-president of the United States. But Mr. Jefferson and Mr. Burr were of the same school of politics, and they were both voted for by the presidential electors in 1800, and they got the same electoral vote, which was a majority of all of the electoral votes ; therefore, it devolved on the house of representatives to decide which of them should be president. The house of representatives voting by states, *and not individually*, there were as many states for the one as for the other, and it so continued for a great while ; and it was seriously feared that the house of representatives would not come to an agreement.

Had the house of representatives failed to decide between the two candidates, the election would have devolved on the senate to select the president ; as the senate was to elect a vice-president before the 4th of March following, it would then have been the duty of the vice-president to assume the duties of president, and the senate would have to elect a president of the senate *pro tempore*. But this mode of electing the president would have precluded the people from any participation in the selection of president ; and, to avoid a repetition of so embarrassing a contingency, the eighth congress, on the 12th of December, 1803, proposed an amendment, in lieu of the third paragraph of the first section of the second article of the original constitution, which was declared, by proclamation by the secretary of state, to have been adopted by a sufficient number of the states to make it a part of the constitution.

TWELFTH AMENDMENT,

Which is as follows: "The electors shall meet in their respective states and vote by ballot for president and vice-president, one of whom, at least, shall not be an inhabitant of the same state with themselves; they shall name in their ballot the person voted for as president, and in distinct ballots the person voted for as vice-president, and they shall make distinct lists of all persons voted for as president, and of all persons voted for as vice-president, and of the number of votes for each, which list they shall sign and certify, and transmit sealed to the seat of government of the United States, directed to the president of the senate; the president of the senate shall, in the presence of the senate and house of representatives, open all the certificates, and the vote shall then be counted; the person having the greatest number of votes for president shall be the president, if such number be a majority of the whole number of electors appointed, and if no person have such majority, then, from the persons having the highest numbers, not exceeding three, on the list of those voted for as president, the house of representatives shall choose immediately, by ballot, the president. But, in choosing the president, the votes shall be taken by states, the representatives from each state having one vote. A quorum for this purpose shall consist of a member or members from two-thirds of the states, and a majority of all of the states shall be necessary to a choice. And if the house of representatives shall not choose a president whenever the right of choice shall devolve upon them, before the 4th day of March next following; then the vice-president shall act as president, as in the case of the death or other constitutional disability of the president. The person having the greatest number of votes as vice-president shall be the vice-president, if such number be a majority of the whole number of electors appointed; and if no person have a majority, then, from the two highest number on the list, the senate shall choose the vice-president. A quorum for that purpose shall consist of two-thirds of the whole number of senators, and a majority of the whole number shall be necessary to a choice. But no person constitutionally ineligible to the office of president shall be eligible to that of vice-president of the United States."

It will be observed that by the original provision no qualifications were expressly provided for the vice-president, but that was not necessary, for no one could be voted for as vice-president, both being voted for as president; therefore the same qualifications were required of persons to be vice-president as were required for president.

But when persons were authorized to be voted for and selected to the vice-presidency, it became necessary to prescribe qualifications for that office.

It will be borne in mind that each state appoints a number of electors, equal to the number of senators and representatives it is entitled to in the congress, in such manner as the legislature thereof may provide. These electors are required to meet in their own state and vote by ballot for president and vice-president and certify that vote to the seat of the government of the United States, directed to the president of the senate thereof.

So that the electors to choose a president and vice-president are elected by the voters of the states, taken within the state, and they perform the function of their office wholly within their own state, and are commissioned to their office by authority of their own state; consequently, they are officers of their own state. They are, however, limited in casting their votes to but one person who resides in the same state with themselves; that is they may vote for a person for president residing in their own state, provided they vote for a person residing in some other state for vice-president; or they may reverse it, and vote for one of the citizens of their own state for vice-president, provided they vote for a citizen of some other state for president.

This provision is thought to be sufficient to guard against electing a president and vice-president from the same state; but it is addressed to the electors only, and is not made a disqualification to hold the office of either president or vice-president. It being no disqualification where the certificate shows the vote of any state to have been taken in all other respects according to law, ought the vote of such state to be rejected, particularly if rejecting that vote would throw the election in the house of representatives and change the election from one party to another. It must be conceded that the congress must refuse to count the vote of a state in which the electors vote for persons for president and for vice-president both of whom reside in the same state with themselves, unless both houses concur in counting it.

The language of the constitution is: "The certificates shall be opened by the president of the senate in the presence of the senate and house of representatives and the votes shall then be counted." This can not be construed to require the counting of votes, unless they were legally cast. No one will contend that, if by counting the votes, it would elect the Prince of Wales, or any foreign prince, or one who was foreign born, or less than thirty-five years of age, that the votes must be counted however clearly the certificates may show on their face that the vote was taken and certified to in every respect according to law. But, as before shown, the congress being divided into two houses, and each being required to act separately in enacting laws, and in doing all other things, except wherein they may be expressly authorized to act together, the vote of no state appearing on the face thereof to be defective, or informal, can be counted, unless each house shall by separate act concur in counting the vote. Nor can the vote of any state appearing on the face of the certificate thereof, to be formal and valid, be rejected, unless the two houses shall by separate acts concur in rejecting it. The vote of every state appearing to be formal must be counted, unless the two houses agree by separate action not to count it. And, on the contrary, the vote of no state appearing on the face of the certificate thereof to be defective, can lawfully be counted, unless the two houses by separate action concur in counting it.

But the constitutional provision is silent as to how the counting of a defectively certified vote, or votes appearing on the face of the certificate thereof to be formal, shall be rejected or counted.

Any motion to reject or count a vote must be made after the counting begins and before it is concluded, for if it be delayed until the vote shall have been counted, it will be too late, as the counting of the vote amounts to a decision by the congress, from which there is no appeal, nor can the congress itself set aside that judgment and make a new count or change the result of the judgment by the first counting of the vote. The counting of the vote must be in the presence of the senate and house of representatives, and when the votes shall be so counted it must be final ; and the congress must declare the result thereof, which constitutes a final and irrevocable judgment of the congress, and there is no authority for the congress itself to reconsider that count.

It being absolutely necessary to vest somewhere jurisdiction to determine who are elected president and vice-president, the most appropriate tribunal to execute so delicate a trust, is the two houses of congress, one house representing the political organizations of the states, and the other the people thereof. Thus the congress is wisely converted into a court with exclusive jurisdiction to determine this grave question.

Should the congress adopt a rule requiring all motions to be in writing and in form of charges and specifications, and upon the filing of a motion to count a defectively certified vote, or to reject a properly certified vote, the two houses should adjourn and immediately convene in their respective houses and consider the same, or the congress might call through the list of the states to ascertain whether the vote of any other state was objected to or desired to be counted, notwithstanding the informality of the certificate, and vote, and the two houses then adjourn and repair to their respective houses. And as soon as all of the charges and specifications shall have been disposed of by each house separately, the two houses should again come together and proceed with the count of the votes as decided upon in the respective houses and pronounce their judgment thereof. While the congress has exclusive final jurisdiction to determine whether to count the vote of a state upon the face of the certificate of the vote thereof, it has no authority to inquire into the election of the presidential electors of the several states further than to inquire whether the elections were held at the time prescribed by the act of congress. For the constitution provides that :

" Each state shall appoint in such manner as the legislature thereof may direct a number of electors equal to the whole number of senators and representatives to which the state may be entitled in the congress ; but no senator or representative or person holding an office of trust or profit under the United States shall be appointed an elector.

" The congress may determine the time of choosing the electors and the day on which they shall give their votes, which shall be the same throughout the United States."

The congress has provided by law that the electors shall be elected on the Tuesday after the first Monday in November in each state, and that the electors shall meet at the seat of government of their respective states on the second Monday in the January following their election, and then and there cast their votes for president and vice-president, and this is all the power the congress has over the subject under the constitution ; but, having jurisdiction to enact this law, it has jurisdiction to determine whether it has been complied with, but can go no further in its inquiry about choosing the electors. For the mode and manner of appointing the presidential electors is expressly vested in the states respectively, and neither the mode nor the manner of electing them can be interfered with by the congress without usurping power vested in the states by the plain letter of the constitution.

The congress is, therefore, bound to accept the certificate of the state authorities as to the regularity and validity of the choosing of the presidential electors.

However, in 1876, the congress decided that it had the right to go behind the returns and certificates of the state officials, and to declare a different set of electors had been chosen by the popular vote of the state than those certified to have been elected by the executive authority of the state. But that action of that congress was condemned by the people at the ballot-box at the next ensuing election by electing a congress with a decided majority on the other side of the political question.

Hence, as the congress has no authority to interpret the constitution (as will be shown in considering the judiciary department), the act of that congress in going behind the returns and certificates of the state officials can have no effect or influence on the powers of congress in the future, even as precedent to be followed.

The congress, however, if both houses could be induced to concur therein, could refuse to count the vote of a state, and in that way defeat an election. Or, should both houses of congress concur in so doing, may count the vote of a state defectively certified to, or not given at the time prescribed by the act of congress ; but the congress has no power to count the vote of a state for any one, unless that state actually voted for such person.

Consequently, the congress may count out those who may have been elected, and throw the election into the house of representatives. But it can in no event constitutionally count persons into the offices of president and vice-president, who were not elected thereto.

The congress being itself elected every two years, is not likely to resort to such extreme measures as to count out one elected by the people, unless under a high state of political excitement. And such excitements usually arise from efforts on the part of one political party to change the policy of the government, and an equally zealous effort of the other party to hold on to the existing policy.

The probability is, that the party that elects the president and vice-president will also elect the new house of representatives.   But the counting will have to be by the congress elected the two years before the election of the president and vice-president, and the senators to act on the counting will all have been elected before the president and vice-president whose election is to be passed on by the congress.

Should the congress called on to count the votes, be corrupt enough to refuse to count the votes fairly, and throw the election in the house of representatives, where the vote would have to be taken by states, it might be that enough of the representatives of the smaller states would follow the expressed will of the people thereof to still elect the same person that had been elected by the people of the United States.   However, if they should continue subject to the political lash, and vote to defeat the will of the people, there is no remedy as to that decision.   But the people would hold their members in each house in remembrance, and having been misrepresented by them once, would not give them another opportunity.

Unless a majority of the states should be with the defeated party, the rejection of enough of the electoral vote to throw the election in the house of representatives would be an idle act, and would not likely be resorted to, as it could not avail anything to the party resorting to such extreme schemes as to throw out votes without cause. Therefore, no serious evils need be apprehended from that source.   Since the custom of buying the vote of states appeared in the presidential election, the wisdom of authorizing the congress to fix the same day for choosing the electors, and the same day for the electors to meet at the seat of government of their own state, to vote for president and vice-president throughout the United States, has become manifest ; for it is much more difficult to buy the vote of states when the elections are held on the same day in each of the states, as the voters who were usually carried from one state to another to vote before this act of congress, are required to stay in their own states and vote to aid in carrying their own election ; and as the jurisdiction of no state extends beyond its boundaries, and the states are prohibited from forming any agreements or compacts with each other, the congress is the only authority that has jurisdiction to enact such a law, and the United States alone can enforce it.

Authority in congress to provide for cases in which neither the president nor the vice-president can act, is manifestly to avoid the possibility of a vacancy in the office of the chief executive of the United States.

With no provision in the constitution extending further than the vice-president, a vacancy might occur during a session of the congress, and as no bill can become a law without the approval of the president, or being passed over his veto, a vacancy in the office of president would stop the running of the governmental machinery and all possible legislation.

The congress, being impressed with what a dire calamity a vacancy in that office would be, at an early day discharged that duty, and provided that in the absence of the president and the vice-president, or the inability of either one of them to act, the duties of the office of president shall first devolve on the president of the senate ; if there be none, then on the speaker of the house of representatives to act until the inability be removed, or a president be elected.

Sec. 147. "Whenever the offices of president and vice-president both become vacant, the secretary of state shall forthwith cause a notification thereof to be made to the executive of every state, and shall also cause the same to be published in at least one of the newspapers printed in each state."

Sec. 148. "The notification shall specify that electors

of a president and vice-president of the United States
shall be appointed or chosen in the several states as
follows :

" 1st. If there shall be the space of two months yet
to ensue between the date of such notification and the
first Wednesday in December next ensuing, such notification shall specify that the electors shall be appointed or
chosen within thirty-four days preceding such first
Wednesday in December.

" 2d. If there shall not be the space of two months
between the date of such notification and such first
Wednesday in December, and if the term for which the
president and vice-president last in office were elected
will not expire on the third day of March next ensuing,
the notification shall specify that the electors shall be
appointed within thirty-four days preceding the first
Wednesday in December in the year next ensuing.   But
if there shall not be the space of two months between
the date of such notification and the first Wednesday in
December then next ensuing, and if the term for which
the president and vice-president last in office were elected
will expire on the third day of March next ensuing, the
notification shall not specify that electors are to be appointed or chosen."

Sec. 149. " Electors appointed or chosen upon the notification prescribed by the preceding section shall meet and
give their votes upon the first Wednesday in December
specified in the notification."

Sec. 150. " The provisions of this title relating to the
quadrennial election of president and vice-president, shall
apply with respect to any election to fill vacancies in the
office of president and vice-president, held upon a notification given when both offices become vacant." *

---

* Revised Statutes of United States, Title 3.

The former quadrennial elections of president and vice-president required the electors to meet in their respective states on the first Wednesday in December ensuing the choosing of the electors to cast their votes. But the law now requires them to meet on the second Monday in January, following the election of the electors, to cast their vote for president and vice-president. Whether the change in the time for the electors to meet to cast their vote will have any effect on the foregoing provision, is not necessary to inquire into in this review.

The salary of the president being subject to no increase or diminution during his term of office, was thought sufficient and proper to avoid any bargaining between the president and congress, and to relieve the president from the control of the congress ; but the modern use of the appointing power of the president, to control legislation, shows that it is inadequate to produce so desirable an effect, though it relieves the president of any inducement to court the congress on account of his salary. It also removes every means of forcing the president to discharge his duty, except in so far as he may feel bound by his oath, or fear of impeachment (and it is puerile to expect to bind ambitious officials by oaths), and as hereinbefore shown he may so use his appointing power as to defeat an impeachment. Hence, the congress should be cautious about augmenting his power by increasing his salary, particularly, as he can excuse himself for vetoing a reduction, on the plea of delicacy, as it could not apply to himself, therefore it will be extremely difficult to reduce the same. The president should be paid an amount adequate to maintain the dignity of his office, and no objection can be made to the salary, however high it may be, provided it is not put so high as to attract venal aspirants to seek the office for the pay it carries, who will anticipate it to bribe his way into that office.

Sec. 2. "The president shall be commander in chief of the army and navy of the United States, and of the militia of the several states when called into the actual service of the United States ; he may require the opinion, in writing, of the principal officer in each of the executive departments, upon any subject relating to the duties of their respective offices, and he shall have power to grant reprieves and pardons for offenses against the United States, except in cases of impeachment.

"He shall have power, by and with the advice and consent of the senate, to make treaties, provided two-thirds of the senators present concur ; and he shall nominate, and by and with the advice and consent of the senate, shall appoint ambassadors, other public ministers and consuls, judges of the supreme court, and all other officers of the United States, whose appointments are not herein otherwise provided for, and which shall be established by law.   But the congress may by law vest the appointment of such inferior officers, as they think proper, in the president alone, in the courts of law, or in the heads of departments.

"The president shall have power to fill up all vacancies that may happen during the recess of the senate, by granting commissions which shall expire at the end of their next session."

Sec. 3. "He shall from time to time give to the congress information of the state of the union, and recommend to their consideration such measures as he shall judge necessary and expedient : he may, on extraordinary occasions, convene both houses of congress, or either of them, and in case of disagreement between them, with respect to the time of adjournment, he may adjourn them to such time as he shall think proper ; he shall receive ambassadors and other public ministers; he shall take care that

the laws be faithfully executed, and shall commission all
the officers of the United States.''

Sec. 4. ''The president, vice-president, and all civil
officers of the United States shall be removed from office
on impeachment for, and conviction of, treason, bribery,
or other high crimes and misdemeanors.''

The making of the president commander-in-chief of
the army and navy of the United States, and of the
militia of the several states when called into actual service of the United States, does not mean that he is to
command either in person; since, as commander-in-
chief of both the army and navy practically precludes
the president from commanding either of said arms of
war in person, this section could not have been intended to vest him with that authority, hence the president cannot command either the army or navy in
person while in active service without violating this
section.

The co-operation of the army and navy must be
obtainable to enable a nation to use all of its forces in its
wars; this co-operation requires that both of these
arms of war be subject to the control of one common authority, to make reports to, and receive orders from.
The president is vested with this common authority,
and the exercise of it requires him to keep himself in
convenient communication with each. He therefore
cannot possibly in person command either while in active
motion, and at the same time keep himself in convenient
communication with the other. Therefore, as commander-in-chief of both, he is practically precluded
from in person commanding either, while it is in active
service. As commander of the militia of the several
states, he may order it to do duty in any part of the
army of the United States. This authority may have

been thought necessary, because no state is authorized to send its militia or armed men into any other state without the consent of that state into which they may be sent ; but it is also necessary to enable the proper officers of the army to assign the militia to such regiments, brigades, and divisions as a complete organization of the army may require, as all orders of any officer of the army or navy, lawful in character, would be regarded as being given by the president as commander-in-chief.

Authority to require the opinion in writing from the head of executive departments greatly strengthens the president's control over the subdivisions of the executive department of the United States, he being the chief executive officer thereof.

But it is of greater importance to have advisers to consult with in private conversations on questions of great interest to the welfare of the United States.   So, the cabinet officers, each of whom is at the head of some bureau under the jurisdiction of the president, constitute his advisers.   The president has a right to call them together at will, and confer with them in a body about any matter relating to state affairs, and may require any one of them to give his opinion in writing about any matter relating to his bureau.

The authority of the president, with the advice and by the consent of the senate, to make treaties, appoint ambassadors and other public ministers and consuls to foreign nations, seems to be sufficiently guarded, though it was the cause of much contention during the time the constitution was before the states for adoption, but the president can do nothing without the senate, and as the senators are the representatives of the several states in their organized capacity, that ought to be held as a sufficient guard against the mal-exercise of this power.

But the duty imposed on the president to *receive* ambassadors and other public ministers and consuls was so magnified by Mr. Washington, and his secretary of state, Mr. Hamilton, that it deserves more than a passing notice.

It will be remembered that France aided the United States in winning their freedom and independence. And in 1793, ten years after the war of the revolution ended, France became involved in a state of war with nearly the whole of Europe, and the American people generally sympathized with her, particularly as she had adopted a republican form of government. There was danger of the citizens of the United States doing something that would involve the United States in hostilities to some of the enemies of France.

To avoid all danger of a war being brought on by the conduct of indiscreet citizens, Mr. Washington, who was then president of the United States, · issued his proclamation of neutrality ; though many of the best informed citizens thought that the treaty with France required the United States to aid that nation in its struggle to maintain its republican form of government, as well as being in strong sympathy with the new republic. Consequently, that proclamation was highly censured and the president himself was not spared from their criticisms.

The proclamation having been issued without consulting the senate, the senators felt their dignity had been overlooked by the president, and some of them openly condemned the issuing of said proclamation. The friends of France constituted a large per cent of the American people.

So formidable was the opposition that Mr. Hamilton wrote a series of articles in defense of said proclamation, claiming that the president was authorized to interpret treaties, and to decide whether to receive ambassadors, ministers, consuls, etc., which letters were published as an addenda to the Federalist, under the title of *Pacificus*.

Mr. James Madison answered each of Mr. Hamilton's letters, which were published in the same book (the Federalist) under the title of *Helvidius*.

The authority of the president of the United States to exercise his discretion in receiving or refusing to receive ambassadors, ministers and consuls was discussed by those two great men with distinguished ability and minuteness. Although Mr. Hamilton thought it necessary to shift his position during that discussion, it by no means shows Mr. Madison to have been his intellectual superior, for Mr. Hamilton not only exhibited great mental power, but a wonderful elasticity and ready grasp of resources in debate, but he was hampered by his previous letters in defense of the constitution, while it was before the states for adoption, which were frequently quoted on him by Mr. Madison.

Mr. Hamilton, drawing from a difference in the language used in the delegation of the legislative authority from that used in the delegation of the executive authority—the language used in the former being: "*all legislative power herein granted shall be vested in a congress,*" etc., while the language used in the latter is: "*The executive power shall be vested in a president,*" etc.— claimed that by this language all executive authority was granted to the president, that therefore the president was vested with all executive powers that belonged to the executive authority of nations, except such powers as may have been taken away from him by express limitation in the constitution; and contended that under the law every limitation must be construed strictly. He admitted that the power to declare war, and the power to grant letters of marque and reprisal, being expressly granted to congress, the president was, by that delegation to congress, ousted of that executive authority. And the concurrence of the senate being required to all treaties and the appointment of public officers by express provision of the constitution, he admitted, deprived the president of that executive power also, but he claimed that these powers were taken out of the grant of powers to the executive, and that they must be strictly construed. His own language is:

"The general doctrine of our constitution then is that the *executive power* of the nation is vested in the president; subject only to the *exceptions* and *qualifications* which are expressed in the instrument.

"Two of these have already been noticed : the participation of the senate in the appointment of officers, and the making of treaties.

"A third remains to be mentioned : the right of the legislature to declare war and grant letters of marque and reprisal.

"With these exceptions, the executive power of the United States is completely lodged in the president. . . . It may be said that this inference would be just if the power of declaring war had not been vested in the legislature; but that this power naturally includes the right of judging whether the nation is or is not under obligations to make war.

"The answer is, that however true this position may be, it will not follow that the executive is in any case excluded from a similar right of judging in the execution of its functions."

Passing by the claim of Mr. Hamilton as to the powers that inherently belong to the executive, for the present (which, however, is disputed on high authority), he has fallen into several other grave errors, that should be noticed.

The United States was always limited to one of the grand objects of government, therefore is not and never was a complete government ; all of the powers they have or can have must be delegated to them.

The reservation of sovereignty in the people of the respective states made the United States a federal republic, and prevented them from constituting a nation in a technical sense.

Now, granting Mr. Hamilton's interpretation of the language, "*The executive power shall be vested in a president,*" etc. What executive power was vested in the president?   Of course, it must be the executive power of the United States, and can not possibly be any other executive power ; then what belongs to the United States? There can be but one answer to that inquiry, which is, nothing but delegated powers, as defined by the constitution ; hence, the delegation of *the executive power* simply means, the executive powers granted by the constitution shall be vested in a president.   Therefore, although the power to declare war, make treaties, appoint ambassadors, etc., may belong to a royal prince, it by no means follows that these powers were vested in the president of the United States by the language quoted, and there is no practical difference between the language in the delegation of the executive powers and the delegation of the legislative powers.

The grant of authority to the congress to declare war necessarily carries with it absolute and exclusive discretion to decide when the United States has a cause for going to war, and that discretion can not reside in the president and in the congress at the same time.

After the congress shall have declared war, the congress has no further control over it, except to vote the means to carry it on; the power of making treaties being vested in the president and the senate, they alone can end the war. However, the congress may, by refusing to vote the means of carrying it on, force the president and the senate to conclude the war by a treaty of peace, and every treaty is declared to be a part of the supreme law of the United States by the constitution.

But Mr. Hamilton further says: "Hence, in the instance stated, treaties can only be made by the president and senate jointly; but their activity may be continued or suspended by the president alone."

It being the duty of the president to see that all laws are faithfully executed, and all treaties being expressly declared to be part of the supreme law of the land by the constitution, how can the president suspend it without violating his oath of office and laying himself liable to impeachment?

If we concede the authority of the president to give greater activity to one treaty than another or to suspend a treaty, we must concede to him the power of giving cause of war and of bringing it on; for, what can be a more fruitful cause of war than bad faith in keeping or complying with treaties? By a faithless compliance with a treaty, the nation having rights under it may by retaliation so act as to force the congress to declare war practically brought on by the president.

Mr. Hamilton, in advocating the adoption of the constitution by the states, said :

" However proper or safe it may be in a government where the executive magistrate is a hereditary monarch to commit to him the entire power of making treaties, it would be utterly unsafe and improper to intrust that power to an executive magistrate of four years' duration. It has been remarked, upon another occasion, and the remark is unquestionably just, that a hereditary monarch, though often the oppressor of his people, has personally too much at stake in the government to be in any material danger of being corrupted by foreign powers; but that a man raised from the station of private citizen to the rank of chief magistrate, possessed of but a slender or moderate fortune, looking forward to a period not very remote, when he may probably be obliged to return to the station from which he was taken, might sometimes be under temptation to sacrifice duty to interest, which it would require superlative virtue to withstand. An avaricious man might be tempted to betray the interests of the states for the acquisition of wealth. An ambitious man might make his own aggrandisement by the aid of a foreign power, the price of his treachery to his constituents. The history of human conduct does not warrant that exalted opinion of human virtue, which would make it wise in a nation to commit interests of so delicate and momentous a kind as *those which concern its intercourse* with the rest of the world, to the *sole* disposal of a magistrate created and circumstanced as would be a president of the United States." *

If the president can suspend treaties or give greater activity to some than to others, what will prevent him from using that power to increase his fortune or gratifying his ambitions by the aid of foreign powers should he be inclined to do so?

Mr. Hamilton claims that the authority of the president to receive ambassadors and other public min-

---

* Letter 75, p. 344. Federalist.

isters and officers, vests the president with a discretion
to receive them or not when defending President Washington's neutrality proclamation, but when he was anxious
for the states to adopt the constitution, he thought differ-
ently. He said :

" The president is also to be authorized to receive ambassadors and other public ministers. This, though it
has been a rich theme of declamation, is more a matter of
dignity than of authority. It is a circumstance which
will be *without consequence* in the administration of the
government, and it is far more convenient that it should
be arranged in this manner than that there should be a
necessity for convening the legislature or one of its
branches upon every arrival of a foreign minister,
though it were merely to take the place of a departed
predecessor." *

The authority to receive ambassadors and other public
ministers makes the president the usher or an officer to
receive strangers at the door and to conduct them into
the court, and to point out to them their proper places,
which court consists of the president combined with the
senate ; and until the president convenes himself with
the senate, he has no more authority than an ordinary
bailiff or sheriff has to render judgment in any case before the court.

The authority to make wars must be lodged in but one
department of the government to prevent the clashing of
judgment, and to secure the energetic participation of the
whole people, and of every department in conducting the
same. For if the president can make war and the congress can also make war, they will each seek to go ahead
of the other in bringing on a popular war, and the de-

* Letter 69, p. 319, Federalist.

partment left behind may, out of a spirit of jealousy, decry the war as not necessary or proper, and without actually opposing it, may to some extent weaken the power of prosecuting it with vigor and the full force of the nation ; and it is more than likely the president would act during the adjournment of the congress in bringing on a popular war, and fail to call the congress together, in extraordinary session, until the war had begun, and he would then convene the congress to vote the means of carrying it on, or he might by withholding information on a plea of prudential reasons, prevent the congress from taking steps before the end of the session, and then bring on a war.

No one can dispute the authority of congress to declare war by express letter of the constitution, and the only claim that can be made that the president has power to bring on a war, must be based on his duty to act as usher in receiving ambassadors and other public ministers ; though the exaltation of the office and powers of the president has advanced so far as to create some doubt whether he is authorized to bring on a war without a formal declaration thereof by the congress. No one can dispute the exclusive authority of the congress to grant letters of marque and reprisal ; to raise and maintain armies ; to provide and maintain a navy ; to make rules for the government of the land and naval forces ; to provide for calling forth the militia. Consequently, the congress alone is the power to determine first, whether war shall be declared ; second, whether after a war has begun, it shall be prosecuted with vigor ; therefore, the greatest harmony should prevail between the executive and legislative departments, but if one disputes the authority of the other and refuses to respect its claims or authority, they each are provided with a check on the other.

The country may suffer by such disputes, but it can

not suffer more by them than it would by letting either of
those departments usurp powers that were never granted
to it, to be used as a precedent for further encroachments
on the reserved rights of the people on which to base a
revolution.

While the congress alone is authorized to declare war,
and to put the country on a war basis, and to declare
martial law, the president and senate conjointly must
agree to any treaty of peace ; for neither the president
alone, nor the senate alone, can form a treaty to end a
war after it has been declared ; but the president and the
senate must concur in concluding to end a war by forming a treaty of peace.

Authority to appoint ambassadors, consuls and other
public ministers, through whom this country communi-
cates with every other nation, and through whom treaties
are generally conducted, under the direction of the president, is also intrusted to the president and the senate, *not*
to the president alone, nor to the senate alone, but to the
concurring action of both.

The ambassadors, consuls, and other public ministers,
constitute officers and agents of the United States
whenever they are properly appointed and commissioned ;
not agents and officers of the president or the senate, and
every act or agreement they may enter into or perform
officially, are acts and *agreements* of the United States,
when properly ratified, and bind the United States, *not
the president or senate*, further than they are bound as departments or agents of the United States, to observe
them as a part of the supreme law of the land.

Going back to the duty of the president to receive
ambassadors and other public ministers. If imposing on
the president that duty has the effect of vesting him with
authority to refuse to receive them, then all of the foregoing checks and limitations on his power were practi-

cally nullified thereby ; to illustrate take the case discussed between Messrs. Hamilton and Madison. France
had thrown off its regal government and constructed
a republic in its stead, and the United States had its
representative at the court of the republic, at the time
President Washington issued and published his neutrality
proclamation. Mr. Madison demonstrates the fallacy of
Mr. Hamilton's argument by giving a supposed proclamation to suit the case, which is as follows :

" Whereas a treaty was conducted on —— day of ——
between the United States and the French nation,
through the kingly government which was then the
organ of its will, and whereas the said nation hath exercised its right (no wise abridged by the said treaty) of
changing the organs of its will by abolishing the said
kingly government as inconsistent with the rights and
happiness of the people, and establishing a republican
government in lieu thereof, as most favorable to the public happiness and best suited to the genius of a people
become sensible of their rights and ashamed of their
chains, and whereas by the Constitution of the United
States the executive is authorized to receive ambassadors,
other public ministers and consuls, and whereas a public
minister duly appointed and commissioned by the new
republic of France hath arrived and presented himself to
the executive, in order to be received in his proper character, now be it known that by virtue of said right
vested in the executive to receive ambassadors, other
public ministers and consuls, and of the rights included
therein, the executive hath refused to receive the said
minister from said republic, and hath thereby caused the
activity and operation of all treaties with the French
nation, *hitherto in force as the supreme law of the land*, to
be suspended until the executive, by taking off the said

suspension, shall receive the same; of which all persons concerned are to take notice.*

This piece of satire shows the absurdity of the claims of that power for the executive.

But, as absurd as Mr. Madison made that claim of power in the executive to appear, Mr. Washington declining to make another race for president, deprived the people of an opportunity to express themselves, about that assumption of power.

The neutrality message by which that power was assumed was obeyed, and no public condemnation by a vote of the whole people was had, although many openly and publicly condemned it. That assumption of power stands as a precedent to be followed by other presidents, which has not only been followed but expanded until it is a matter of doubt whether the war making power resides exclusively in the congress or not.

Of course the executive authority can not exercise any war making power as long as the congress continues alive to its duties and trusts, and ordinarily mankind loves power and is slow to surrender it; and with this natural inclination the congress could be safely intrusted with the war making power as long as no other conflicting forces can be made to bear on the members of the congress.

But unfortunately there are three forces that are utilized by the executive to overcome the pride of the legislative powers of the congress.

The first and most potent of these forces was made by the congress itself, which arises out of the patronage of the president, or his power of appointing to ministerial offices persons in every congressional district in the

---

* Letter No. 3, page 447, Federalist.

union, and by appointing persons to fill those offices who are recommended by the members whose votes the president may desire to secure, such members may be induced to vote on measures before the congress as the president dictates.

The second of said forces, arises out of a natural disinclination to make, what appears to be an unsuccessful contest with the president of their own party, by those members who remain true to their constituents, however severely they may condemn such proceedings ; and should a considerable number of the members have been influenced by the president's giving them the use of his power to appoint their friends to office, it will always appear at least doubtful whether a conviction could be accomplished, with the strongest outside evidence, particularly as a criminal intent must be shown to overcome the custom of appointing on the recommendation of the members of each house of the congress.

The third of said forces arises out of a natural inclination to avoid doing any apparently unnecessary labor, or taking any trouble on themselves, and to avoid the same the congress has attempted to vest the executive department and its horde of ministerial agents with powers and trusts that were reposed exclusively in the personal judgment and discretion of the congress while in actual session.

Among said attempts to delegate its powers the congress passed an act to vest the secretary of the treasury with power to issue and sell bonds of the United States whenever he should find it necessary to do so, to enable him to redeem the legal tender notes of the United States.

The part of said act relating to vesting the secretary of the treasury with that discretionary power to issue and sell bonds reads as follows :

"And to enable the secretary of the treasury to pre-

pare and provide for the redemption in this act authorized or required, he is authorized to use any surplus
revenue, from time to time, in the treasury not otherwise appropriated, and to issue, sell and dispose of at
not less than par, in coin, either of the description of
bonds of the United States described in the act of congress approved July fourteenth, eighteen hundred and
seventy, entitled ' an act to authorize the refunding of
the national debt,' with like qualities, privileges, and
exemptions to the extent necessary to carry this act into
full effect, and to use the proceeds thereof for the purposes aforesaid.''   .   .   .

Under this act, during the administration of President
Cleveland, bonds to the extent of two hundred and sixty-
two millions of dollars were issued and sold by the then
secretary of the treasury ; although his authority to
issue and sell bonds was limited to one object or purpose, yet if he had authority to issue and sell the
bonds of the United States for any purpose, the pre-
sumption of the law is that they were issued for that
purpose, and therefore legal and binding, whatever
may have been the real purpose of issuing and selling
them.

If the secretary of the treasury can be vested with authority to issue and sell bonds of the United States at
his discretion as to when they may be needed, when the
bonds are sold and the proceeds thereof is in the treasury, he may use the money they sold for, in the same
way that any other money in the treasury can be used,
even to the maintaining of an army contrary to the will
of the congress.

With a doubt as to whether the power of making wars
is in the president or in the congress, coupled with the
power to raise money to carry on a war, through his secretary of the treasury, the president can soon settle the

question as to where the war making power resides, by usurping that power to himself.

But if any one provision of the constitution is placed beyond all equivocation and doubt, it is that the congress alone is authorized to put the United States in debt or to appropriate any money that belongs to the United States, and the congress must exercise its own discretion and judgment in each case, and it has no authority to delegate this discretion and judgment to any other tribunal or agent ; therefore, that part of said act that attempts to vest the secretary of the treasury with the discretion of determining when to issue said bonds, and to what extent to issue and sell them, is clearly unconstitutional and void.

I admit that the congress must issue and sell whatever bonds of the United States they desire to sell, through some sort of an agency, and that the secretary of the treasury is the most appropriate agent the congress can adopt for that purpose ; however, not only the character of the bonds must be specified, but the number or extent to which and the time when they are to be issued and sold, must be fixed by the congress itself. If authority to determine when to issue and sell them, or authority to determine the extent they may be issued and sold, be reposed in any other tribunal, officer or person, than the congress itself. the issue and sale of them would be unconstitutional and void.

CHAPTER VIII.

ORGANIZATION OF THE JUDICIARY DEPARTMENT.

ARTICLE III.

Sec. 1. " The judicial power of the United States shall be vested in one supreme court and in such inferior courts as the congress may from time to time ordain and establish.   The judges, both of the supreme and inferior courts, shall hold their offices during good behavior, and shall, at stated times, receive for their services a compensation which shall not be diminished during their continuance in office."

Sec. 2. "The judicial power shall extend to all cases in law and equity, arising under this constitution, the laws of the United States, and the treaties made, or which shall be made, under their authority ; to all cases affecting ambassadors, other public ministers and consuls ; to all cases of admiralty and maritime jurisdiction ; to controversies to which the United States shall be a party ; to controversies between two or more states ; between a state and citizens of another state ; between citizens of different states ; between citizens of the same state, claiming lands under grants of different states, and between a state or the citizens thereof, and foreign states, citizens or subjects. In all cases affecting ambassadors, other public ministers and consuls, and those in which a state shall be a party, the supreme court shall have original jurisdiction.   In all the other cases before mentioned, the supreme court shall have appellate jurisdiction, both as to law and fact, with such exceptions and under such regulations as the congress shall make.

"The trial of all crimes, except in cases of impeachment, shall be by jury ; and such trial shall be held in the state where the said crime shall have been committed ; but when not committed within any state, the trial shall be at such place or places as the congress may have by law directed."

Sec. 3. "Treason against the United States shall consist only in levying war against them, or in adhering to their enemies, giving them aid and comfort. No person shall be convicted of treason unless on the testimony of two witnesses to the same overt act, or on confession in open court.

"The congress shall have power to declare the punishment of treason, but no attainder of treason shall work corruption of blood, or forfeiture except during the life of the person attainted."

The acts necessary to constitute treason having been so plainly defined, and the provision that the testimony of two witnesses to the same overt act, or a confession in open court, to convict any one of treason, no great evil can arise out of authorizing the congress to prescribe the punishment thereof. The congress is, however, limited in prescribing the punishment of treason by the last paragraph, for any punishment that would include the working of the corruption of blood that might be provided by congress, would be absolutely void, and ought to be ; for, by the corruption of the blood of those convicted not only inflicts punishment on the offender, but also punishes his family. Nor can the congress make the forfeiture of the estate of any one convicted of treason extend beyond the lifetime of the offender.

"The judicial power of the United States," as used in the first section of this article, includes the whole judi-

cial authority vested in either of the departments of
the United States, for all powers to be used for the
United States were granted to the three several departments respectively, and neither department, either singly
or as a whole, has any power except such as was delegated by the constitution. ''The judicial powers of the
United States'' include the powers granted, and no more,
and the judges of the courts of the United States should
always ascertain whether the power has been granted before taking jurisdiction of every case or exercising judicial control over it.

The second section of this article defines the subjects,
interests, and rights over which the supreme court is to
have jurisdiction, which appears to include every subject that is in any way connected with the powers granted
or duties imposed on the union or any of the departments or officers thereof, yet that jurisdiction is necessarily
limited by the limitations imposed on the several grants
of powers to the respective departments or to the union
as a whole ; notably among this class of limitations are
actions arising under acts of congress. Before considering such cases the court should ascertain whether
the congress was authorized to pass the act ; and if it be
found that the congress had no authority to enact the
law under which the claim arises, the federal court would
not have jurisdiction of the case, and should dismiss it
and remit the parties to the action to a state court having jurisdiction of the common law and the remedies
thereof.

There is nothing in the language of this article that expresses exclusive jurisdiction of any of the subjects named
therein ; but from the character of all cases between two
or more states, the jurisdiction ought to lie exclusively
in the federal judiciary, for the judiciary of neither of
the states that are parties to the action would be regarded

by the other state or states, parties thereto, as prepared to render impartial justice between them. However, any state may sue any other state, and has its option to bring its suit in the supreme court of the United States directly or in the state court.

Article 6 of the constitution conclusively shows that the jurisdiction of the federal judiciary is not exclusive as to any subject committed to it, unless as to controversies between states and those relating to ambassadors.

Said Article 6 is as follows: "This constitution, and the laws of the United States which shall be made in pursuance thereof; and all treaties made, or which shall be made, under the authority of the United States, shall be the supreme law of the land; and the judges in every state shall be bound thereby, any thing in the constitution or laws of any state to the contrary notwithstanding."

It will be seen that the judges of the states are mentioned in their official capacity, and they are to be bound in their official capacity, and are therefore vested with a judicial discretion to ascertain and determine what act of the congress shall have been made in pursuance of the constitution, and whether that which is claimed to be a treaty was made "under the authority of the United States," and, to determine either of these questions, they must necessarily have authority to inquire into the meaning of the constitution in relation thereto.

But, as the supreme court has appellate jurisdiction of all cases named in said second section (except the cases of which it has original jurisdiction), whether the case originates in a state court or in an inferior federal court. The supreme court necessarily constitutes the only tribunal of the United States vested with authority to finally interpret the constitution and laws of the United States. The convention itself did not intend to vest it with that authority, for, when the constitution was turned over to the committee on style, it was as follows :

Art. 11, Sec. 1. "The judicial power of the United States shall be vested in one supreme court, and in such inferior courts as shall, when necessary, from time to time, be constituted by the legislature of the United States."

Sec. 2. Provides for paying the judges.

Sec. 3. "The jurisdiction of the supreme court shall extend to all cases arising under laws passed by the legislature of the United States ; to all cases affecting ambassadors, other public ministers and consuls ; to the trial of impeachment of officers of the United States ; to all cases of admiralty and maritime jurisdiction ; to controversies between two or more states, except such as shall regard territory or jurisdiction ; between a state and citizens of another state ; between citizens of different states ; and between a state or citizens thereof and foreign states, citizens or subjects. In cases of impeachment, cases affecting ambassadors, other public ministers and consuls, and those in which a state shall be a party, this jurisdiction shall be original. In all the other cases before mentioned, it shall be appellate, with such exceptions and under such regulations as the legislature shall make. The legislature may assign any part of the jurisdiction above mentioned (except the trial of the president of the United States), in the manner, and under the limitations, which it shall think proper, to such inferior courts as it shall constitute from time to time." *

It will be observed that this draft of the constitution

---

* Elliott's Debates, vol. 1, pp. 228, 229.

did not vest the judiciary with jurisdiction of cases *arising under the constitution.*

But, when it was put into the hands of the committee on style, it was changed. The Hon. Gouverneur Morris claims the credit of changing it. He says in a letter to the Hon. Timothy Pickering, written from Morrisania, December 22, 1814:

"My Dear Sir—What can a history of the constitution avail toward interpreting its provisions? This must be done by comparing the plain import of the words with the general tenor and object of the instrument. That instrument was written by the fingers which write this letter. Having rejected redundant and equivocal terms, I believed it to be as clear as our language would permit, excepting, nevertheless, a part of what relates to the judiciary. On that subject, conflicting opinions had been maintained with so much professional astuteness that it became necessary to select phrases which, expressing my own notions, would not alarm others, nor shock their self-love ; and, to the best of my recollection, this was the only part which passed without cavil.

"But, after all, what does it signify that men should have a written constitution, containing unequivocal provisions and limitations? The legislative lion will not be entangled in the meshes of a logical net. The legislature will always make the power which it wishes to exercise, unless it be so organized as to contain within itself the sufficient check. Attempting to restrain it from outrage, by other means, will only render it more outrageous. The idea of binding legislators by oath is puerile. Having sworn to exercise the power granted according to their true intent and meaning, they will, when they feel a desire to go farther, avoid the shame, if not the guilt, of perjury, by swearing the true intent and meaning to be, according to their comprehension, that which suits their purpose."*

If the legislative department can not be entangled in logical nets, how can a judiciary clothed with autocratic powers be expected to be controlled thereby?

This letter shows that the able writer of it greatly desired to change the organization of the judiciary department so as to make it agree with his own notion, against which conflicting opinions had been maintained with professional astuteness in the convention, consequently the change was so skillfully drafted as to escape the attention of those who opposed his notions with such professional astuteness, for if their attention had been drawn to the changes, they could with the same professional astuteness defeat the ingrafting of his notions in the judiciary department, though, as an appointee of the convention, to correct the style only, he was in duty bound to have called the attention of the convention to any and every change made in any part of the instrument by his committee ; but, having admitted in this letter that he was willing to ingraft his notions in the organization of the judiciary by phrases that "would not alarm others nor shock their self-love," his moral sentiment was no spur to the discharge of that duty, and he was a man of too much mental capacity to invite the attention of the convention to the changes made, as it would not only defeat his scheme, but expose his shame, and thereby destroy his ability to lead the convention into any of his measures.

What changes the Hon. Mr. Morris so earnestly desired to ingraft on the judiciary, he does not state.   But by comparing the draft of the constitution as it was when it was put into the hands of the committee on

---

* Elliott's Debates, vol. 1, pp. 506, 507.

style with what it was when returned to the convention, the desired change must have been to give jurisdiction in cases arising under the constitution.   The draft of the constitution as agreed to by the committee on detail was reported to the convention on the 6th of August, and was debated by the committee of the whole and the convention until the 12th of September, during which time some minor changes were made by the convention itself, among which was that of making the senate a court to try impeachment of the officers of the United States.

But the important changes made by the committee, to which I desire to call attention in this connection, is, that of extending jurisdiction of the judiciary " *to all cases . . . arising under the constitution,*" which, from the proceedings in the convention, as well as the original draft of the constitution as it was when turned over to the committee on style, must have been the change necessary to put that instrument in accord with Hon. G. Morris's notions referred to in his letter to the Hon. Mr. Pickering. But whatever the change so earnestly desired may have been, the Hon. Mr. Morris doubtless believed it was necessary to perfect the character of the government, else he would not have given publicity to his double dealing with his associates in the convention.

The committee on style was appointed by ballot on the 8th of September, consisting of Messrs. Johnson, Hamilton, G. Morris, Madison and King, and they reported back to the convention on the 12th of said month ; and on the 17th thereof, the engrossed constitution was read and adopted by the convention and ordered reported to the congress.

Letters of Mr. Hamilton (published in the Federalist), in defense of the constitution while it was before the states for adoption, show that he, in glowing terms, approved of the organization of the judiciary in every particular as changed and adopted by the convention.

He also approved of dispensing with the English rule of removing the judges by address of the legislative department, and urged as a reason thereof that the judiciary should be entirely free from the control of either of the other departments to enable it to protect the people against oppressions from either of them, and to protect the weak against the strong.

It is true, had the judges been made removable by the legislative, it would have weakened the judiciary, and it may have required a clear case of usurpation by the congress to induce the courts to decide any act to be unconstitutional.

Judge Tucker, in notes to his edition of Blackstone's Commentaries, also expressed his approval of giving the judiciary jurisdiction of cases arising under the constitution, and of dispensing with the English rule of removing the judges by address of the legislative department.

Judge Tucker, Mr. Hamilton and Mr. G. Morris were each learned lawyers of recognized ability ; but as patriots, it probably did not occur to them, that exclusive authority to interpret the constitution carried with it the power to change the constitution at will, which, coupled with life tenure in office, tended to make aristrocrats of the judges, and cause them to lean to an aristocracy in their rulings and construction of the powers under the constitution.

The history of governments shows that the judiciary is as much inclined to augment the powers of their government as the officers of any other department thereof.

But that is a natural weakness of human nature, for the greater the powers of the government, the greater the powers of the judiciary must be ; and the greater their powers, the more resplendent their official position is made, and it is quite natural for them to grasp after power and position,

Without intending any reflection on the personal character of the judges of the supreme court of the United States, for they have always been gentlemen of such high character, and recognized patriotism, that any reflection on them, would recoil on their assailant, yet the history of adjudications in the United States shows that they were not strangers to this human weakness, and that on several occasions they have shown a disposition to augment the powers of the United States, which will be pointed out in a subsequent part of this chapter.

While the language of the second section of article three seems to vest the supreme court with exclusive jurisdiction to interpret the constitution, it must be conceded that this language is the work of the skillful pen of the Hon. Gouverneur Morris. That seeming jurisdiction is in conflict with the organization of the three grand departments, legislative, executive and judiciary. And is in conflict with article six of the constitution.

The United States being merely a name to indicate the several states united, and not a government to be divided into departments, as is the case with the states; and as shown by the preamble to the constitution, *the constitution alone* was ordained and established by the convention. Under that instrument no power was granted to the United States in that name; but all powers that were granted by that instrument were granted directly to each department separately. By the sixth article the officials of each department are required to take an oath to support the constitution, and the judges of the courts of the several states are also required to take an oath to support the constitution, and as judicial officers are bound to enforce the constitution ; the laws made in pursuance thereof, and all treaties made and those to be made under authority of the United States.

The several departments of the United States and the judiciary of the several states being equally bound to support the constitution, they must be authorized to construe it.   If the legislative and executive departments of the United States, and the judiciary of the several states, are bound to support the constitution as it may be interpreted by the supreme court, they may be required to support it in one way to-day, another to-morrow, and still a different way the day after to-morrow, even if contrary to their conscientious belief.

The state judges being authorized to exercise a judicial discretion, they are necessarily authorized to interpret the constitution in the administration of their judicial duties.   Then, suppose the supreme court should decide that the constitution, rightly interpreted, authorizes the president to suspend the *writ of habeas corpus*, and the president should by proclamation attempt to suspend that writ, and a citizen of a state was in prison without a trial by due course of law, and a state judge should be called on to issue that writ, can there be a doubt of the duty of the state judge to issue it?   Or, suppose the congress should by a bill of attainder deprive a citizen of a state of his right to hold the title to his property, and the supreme court should hold that a proper interpretation of the constitution authorized such bills of attainder, can there be a doubt in the mind of any one as to the duty of the state courts to refuse to enforce such attainders?   These, it is true, are strong cases, but it often requires strong cases to carry a principle clearly to the mind, and it will be shown by the adjudications of the supreme court that the use of strong cases to illustrate principles are at least excusable.

Furthermore, the fact that the powers granted by the constitution were vested in each department separately, clearly shows that the makers of the constitution intended that the three departments should be co-ordinate, and that each department should be supreme to the extent of the powers vested in it, and that neither one should be superior to the other. If the legislative and executive departments are required to accept the constitution as it may be interpreted by the supreme court, they are, each, subordinate to that court, or that court may, by interpretation, change the powers of each of said departments.

And whenever that court enlarges the powers of either the legislative or executive, or its own, such additional powers must be taken from the states, or from the people, or from the other departments, for they could not be taken from any other source ; and whenever that court takes away from either the legislative or executive departments any powers by interpretation, the powers so taken would fall back to the states or to the people, unless otherwise appropriated by that court. If the change made by the committee on style had the effect of giving the supreme court exclusive jurisdiction to interpret the constitution, that court was converted into an oligarchy instead of a co-ordinate department of a republican form of government. Still the freedom of the states will be in the way of that department exercising its unlimited powers ; the government must therefore be first converted into an empire, by breaking down the independence of the states and reducing them to provinces ; to do which, the aid of both the legislative and executive departments will be needed ; but as soon as the states can be reduced to provinces the supreme court can assert its unlimited authority over the legislative and executive departments with impunity. And our constitutional fathers gave us the most autocratic oligarchy the world has ever known, instead of the federal republic boasted of by American statesmen and politicians.

This jurisdiction is too great and far reaching to be reposed in any human authority, except the sovereign people themselves. And Mr. Jefferson when a candidate for president in 1800; President Jackson while a candidate for re-election to the office of president in 1832; and Mr. Lincoln while a candidate for president in 1860 : each denied the supreme court was vested with that jurisdiction.

While the *alien and sedition* act of congress was never acted on by the whole court, enough of the judges of that court sustained the validity of it, while on the circuit court bench, to show that it would be sustained by the supreme court. And Mr. Jefferson denied the constitutionality of that act, which was discussed as an issue in his election in 1800, and the people sustained Mr. Jefferson by electing him by a large majority.

President Jackson during his first term vetoed what was known as the recharter of the United States bank, on the ground that the congress had no authority to charter banks, although the supreme court had decided the original charter thereof to be constitutional. President Jackson contending that it was his duty to decide upon the constitutionality of the charter for himself, and refused to follow the interpretation of the supreme court; and went before the people on that issue and they sustained him by electing him by a large majority.

Mr. Lincoln denied the validity of the decision of the supreme court in the celebrated case known as the Dred Scott case, in which that court held that negroes were not citizens, and could not be made such, so as to entitle them to the privileges and immunities of citizens in all of the states, and the people sustained him, by electing him by a large majority.

But there being no provision of the constitution authorizing appeals of such cases to the people, the action of the people in neither of said cases amounted to any thing, except Mr. Lincoln's appeal, which resulted in manumitting slavery in the United States, and making native-born negroes wards of the United States and of the state wherein they reside, with the right to vote in elections, and to buy, own and pass the title to every character of property.

As able and patriotic as the judges of the supreme court have always been, they have betrayed a disposition to augment the powers of the judiciary by defining the character of the United States government and holding the same to be vested with sovereign powers. While the preamble thereof shows that nothing was ordained or established except the constitution; and the constitution shows that every power granted by it was granted directly to one or the other of the three departments, to-wit: legislative, executive and judiciary, and that no power was granted to the United States as a government, though specific duties were imposed on the states united, in that name; hence, the United States government can not be sovereign in any sense whatever, but is simply an agent and representative of the several states in the union.

Among the cases that court so held, are the cases of Chisholm *v.* the State of Georgia, decided in 1792 ;* that of Martin *v.* Hunter's Lessee ;† that of McCollough *v.* the State of Maryland ;‡ that of Gibbons *v.* Ogden ;‖

---

* Reported in 2 Dall. 419. † 1 Wheat. 304. ‡ 4 id. 316. ‖ 9 id. 1.

and that of the Dartmouth College.* It is true, that court recognizes the right of the people to recover sovereign control at any time ; but, as shown in the first chapter of this review, that right can not benefit the people, for, if the sovereignty is in the government, the government holds it as trustee, and is in duty bound to hold on to it, unless it be lawfully demanded, so that unless the constitution provides for the exercise of that authority by the people without assigning any cause, a cause must be assigned to authorize the officials to surrender it, and if the government is sovereign, it alone has the right to decide whether the assigned cause be well founded ; and any cause that could be assigned must involve the good faith of the government officials, as trustees thereof, and they would not be likely to admit their guilt.

The decision of Chisholm *v.* The State of Georgia in 1792, together with several other cases of similar character in the United States circuit courts, brought by foreign creditors against different states, caused the eleventh article of amendment to the constitution to be adopted, which provides that the constitution shall not be so construed as to give to the federal courts jurisdiction of actions against any state by citizens of another state, or by citizens or subjects of any foreign nation or state.

Notwithstanding this amendment the supreme court did take jurisdiction of the action of McCulloch *v.* The State of Maryland, and on the theory that the government of the United States was sovereign, decided that the congress was authorized to charter banks as a necessary power to the sovereignty of the government of the United States, although no such authority could be found in the letter of the constitution.

* 4 Wheat. 518.

Yet notwithstanding said eleventh amendment, the supreme court has uniformly taken jurisdiction of actions to prevent any state from amending or repealing a charter of a private corporation created by the state, on the ground that such charters are contracts between the state and the corporators, ever since the celebrated case of Dartmouth College, until the states relieved themselves of that interference by providing by general statutes or amendments to their respective constitutions, making such charters subject to repeal or amendment as a part of the contract indicated by the charter.

Since the Ogden-Gibbon case, reported in 9th Wheaton, page 1, the federal courts have taken jurisdiction of cases relating to commerce between states, notwithstanding the fourth article of the constitution, which of itself regulates commerce and all intercourse between the states as the basis of the union, in such a clear and concise manner as to leave no room for the regulation of commerce between the states by the congress, which has been shown in considering the delegation of authority to congress to regulate commerce with foreign nations and among the several states.

The supreme court applies an act of congress, passed to enable the president to enforce the constitution in states standing in rebellion to the union and the constitution by state legislative acts prohibiting the enforcement of the constitution therein, and the fugitive slave acts of congress; to states in entire harmony and accord with the union and constitution, notably is the case of Neagle, of California.

As this question has not been discussed elsewhere in this review, I will consider it fully here. This case arose in San Joaquin county, California, in 1889. Ex-Chief-justice Terry of the supreme court of that state took offense at the manner and ruling of Justice Field, of the supreme court of the United States, while sitting in the circuit court of the United States, in that state. And Justice Field conceiving it to be his duty to return to California to again aid in holding the circuit court of the United States, the attorney-general; fearing harm might overtake him (Field) at the hand of ex-Chief-justice Terry, telegraphed the United States marshal of that state to furnish a deputy to go with Justice Field to protect him, and Mr. Neagle was deputed for that purpose, being a fearless and resolute man.

When ex-Chief-Justice Terry and Justice Field met in California, Neagle thinking the apprehended collision was about to take place, thereupon shot and killed ex-Chief-Justice Terry. The state authorities instituted proceedings to try him, but the circuit judge of the United States circuit court, embracing the northern district of that state, by writ of *habeas corpus*, took Neagle out of the custody of the state officials, and discharged him without a trial by jury.

An appeal was taken by the state of California to the supreme court of the United States, and by a divided court, the ruling of the circuit judge on the writ of *habeas corpus* was sustained, Chief-Justice Fuller and Justice LaMar dissenting.*

If the state of California had been in rebellion (as the states that passed acts against the enforcement of the fugitive slave laws were), and Neagle had been on military duty, and had committed that crime in the discharge of that duty, he could have been tried under the laws of the United States, and shielding him from a public fair trial under the state laws, would not have been so severe a blow against the safeguards of life, liberty and property. But the state of California was in absolute

* 315 U. S. Reports, p. 1.

subordination to the United States at the time, and had full control of the police and peace laws of the state, and could have furnished better protection to Justice Field than the United States authorities could. The attorney-general of the United States, however, must have thought otherwise, else he would not have ordered the United States marshal to disregard and nullify the rightful police authority of the State of California. In the execution of that usurped authority, the crime was committed.

The supreme court admitted that there was no authority to try said Neagle by a jury under the laws of the United States. But a majority of said court claimed that he could be tried without a jury by the federal courts. It is provided by the federal constitution that :

"In all criminal prosecutions the accused shall enjoy the right to a speedy and public trial, by an impartial jury of the state and district wherein the crime shall have been committed. . . ." *

The majority of the court may have acted on the theory that this provision applies alone to the accused, and that no right is guaranteed to society by it.

In every prosecution there must be two parties, the representative of society as prosecutor, and the accused who is being prosecuted, and each party is entitled to a speedy public trial, by an impartial jury of the state and district wherein the crime was committed. If this provision applies to the accused alone, no guilty man would ever be ready to demand that right, and no guilty man would ever be tried and punished.

The only protection society can possibly derive from any government, must necessarily arise out of the power to punish those who commit crimes ; for it is by punishing criminals that others are deterred from committing

* Art. 6 of Amendment to Con.

similar crimes, so that society has as much interest in the just and impartial execution of the criminal law as any criminal can possibly have.

That ruling not only lays the foundation for depriving any state from protecting the society thereof, by executing the penal and criminal laws of the state, but it establishes a precedent for shielding a favored class from responsibility to the penal and criminal laws of the state, and thereby establishes grades of society in the states more obnoxious to the spirit of freemen than the distinction between the patricians and plebeians of Rome, or the distinction between the aristocracy and the common people of England.

The claim that Neagle was obeying orders of the president in going with Justice Field to protect him, concedes that he was in the act of violating that provision of the constitution that requires the United States to guarantee to the *states* republican forms of government and the exercise of *their police powers.*

If the president is authorized to send civil officers into a state, in entire subordination to the United States, to take the life of an honored citizen, against whom no charge has been made, and to shield such officers from a public fair trial for his crime, the safeguards incorporated in the constitution for the protection of life, liberty, and property amount to nothing but a snare and delusion.

If the president has this power, what would prevent him from sending an officer into any state to take the life of any formidable adversary, and shield the culprit, who committed the crime, from a trial?

Equally as dangerous an invasion of the safeguards to life, liberty, and property, incorporated in the constitution, arises out of the modern use of injunction in apprehended trespass cases by the federal courts.

Injunctions are but aids to courts of equity in protecting the particular property or property rights involved in the action ; as they are merely aids in chancery practice, they can never be used to give courts of equity jurisdiction ; the court of equity must have jurisdiction independently of any injunction to authorize it to issue a writ of injunction. Having jurisdiction of the action, it may issue a writ of injunction only to protect the property involved in the action.

The great commentator, Mr. Blackstone, after summing up the jurisdiction of courts of chancery, says :

" This is the business of our courts of equity, which, however, are only conversant with matters of property. For the freedom of our constitution will not permit that in criminal cases a power should be lodged in any judge to construe the law otherwise than according to the letter. This caution, while it admirably protects the public liberty, can never bear hard on individuals." . . .*

The same author again says :

" Not only the substantial part or judicial decisions of the law, but also the formal part or method of proceeding, cannot be altered but by parliament ; for, if once those outworks were demolished, there would be an inlet to all manner of innovation in the body of the law itself." . . .†

Life, liberty and property are better guarded in the United States, because the outworks, as Mr. Blackstone calls them, or the safeguards (as they are called by the supreme court in the Milliken case), are incorporated in the constitution, and cannot be changed by any department of the United States.

" No person shall be held to answer for a capital or otherwise infamous crime, unless on a presentment or indictment of a grand jury." . . .

---

* Bl. Com., vol. 1, p. 92.   † Id., p. 142.

"Nor be deprived of life, liberty, or property, without due process of law. . . . Nor be twice put in jeopardy of his life and limb. . . .

"In all criminal prosecutions, the accused shall enjoy the right to a speedy and public trial by an impartial jury of the state and district wherein the crime shall have been committed, which district shall have been previously ascertained by law." *

"No bill of attainder or *ex post facto* law shall be passed." †

"In suits at common law, where the value in controversy exceeds twenty dollars, the right of trial by jury shall be preserved." ‡

The right of trial by jury applies to every one accused of crime who is not attached to the army or navy or militia in actual service.

"Neither the president nor the congress nor the judiciary can disturb any one of the safeguards of civil liberty incorporated in the constitution, except so far as the right to suspend in certain cases the privileges of the *writ* of *habeas corpus*." ||

It may be said with equal force that neither the president nor the congress nor the judiciary can deny to either party to a case at common law, where the value in controversy exceeds twenty dollars, a trial by jury.

Trespass is an indictable offense and a violation of the criminal law under the common law; still the party injured may bring a civil action for the injury he may have suffered by reason of the trespass; but the party sued would be entitled to have the action tried by a jury.

Trespass being an indictable offense punishable by im-

---

* Amendments to Constitution, 5 and 6.
† Art. 1, sec. 9, Con.   ‡ Art. 7 of Amendment.
|| Ex parte Milliken, 4 Wall., p. 2.

prisonment, it comes under the classification of "*otherwise infamous crimes*," which no one can be held to answer for unless upon information or indictment of a grand jury.

But suppose the trespassers be proceeded against in a civil action, and without regard to its being an indictable offense, still it is an action at common law, and the defendant would be entitled to a trial by jury if the value sued for exceeded twenty dollars ; and courts of equity could not take jurisdiction of the trespass for that reason alone ; and as courts of equity are only conversant with property and property rights, while every action of trespass is a punishment in damages against the person of the offender for violating the penal laws of the country, for if there was no law against the act done by the defendant his acts would not amount to a trespass, and no damages could be adjudged against him.

But as some of the states have enacted statutes authorizing injunctions in cases of trespass to realty to prevent waste or injury to the land sued for, while the suit is pending, it may be contended that the federal courts could avail themselves of such state statutes and order writs of injunction to issue.

The states cannot give jurisdiction to the federal courts, though the states may create legal rights which the federal courts may take hold and dispose of, provided they are of a character to pass under the jurisdiction of the federal courts as prescribed by the constitution.

That class of cases that belonged to the exclusive jurisdiction of courts of law, at the time the constitution was made and adopted, must remain of exclusive jurisdiction in courts of law, and neither the congress nor any legislature can change it.

"In suits at common law, where the value in controversy shall exceed twenty dollars, the right of trial by jury shall be preserved ; and no fact tried by a jury shall be otherwise re-examined in any court of the United States than according to the rules of the common law." *

The rules of the common law existing at that time must be taken as the rules thereof referred to.   For if the rules of the common law could be changed from what they were recognized to be at that time, that article of amendment would not have provided any limitation, and its adoption would amount to an idle act ; hence the distinction between the rules of the common law and equity practice existing at that time must continue to prevail, for the purposes of interpreting that article of amendment.

Courts of equity in England never had jurisdiction of criminal or penal cases ; nor of actions sounding in damages.   They could, however, always require the parties to an action to pay over the rents and profits of property involved in the action, which was sometimes erroneously spoken of as damages.   But in actions sounding in damages, the cause of action arises out of a wrongful act or acts, for which the wrongdoer may be punished, by paying in damages, the amount of the injury suffered by the party suing for the same.   But no such suit could be brought until after the law had been violated, and the wrongful acts complained of had been fully enacted, and it would be farcical to grant a writ of injunction to restrain one from doing that which he had already done.   And to grant that writ to prevent the wrongful acts from being committed, before any act violating the law had been committed, must be based alone on an *apprehension* that the party enjoined would commit the dreaded trespass.   Under that state of case no cause of

* Seventh Article of Amendment to the Constitution.

action, either in equity, or at law, would exist ; but not-withstanding the total failure of a cause of action, the injunction would not only deprive the person enjoined of his personal liberty, but of the free use of property he had in possession claiming as his own without a trial, and without due course of law as guaranteed by the constitution.

Furthermore, the fine for contempt in violating an injunction is a criminal judgment. The supreme court says :

"Contempt of court is a specific criminal offense. The imposition of the fine was a judgment in a criminal case. That part of the decree is as distinct from the residue as if it were a judgment upon an indictment for perjury committed in a deposition read at the hearing. This court can not take cognizance of a criminal case only upon a certificate of division of opinion." . . .*

This was a case wherein an action was pending by the steamship company to enforce a contract entered into for the lease of a certain part of the wharf of the city of New Orleans, in the circuit court of the United States, and the mayor of that city caused an action to be instituted in the state court to settle the same matters that were involved in the case in the United States court. The offense having been completely committed, the fine was clearly a judgment in a criminal case, and the mayor was entitled to an indictment or presentment by a grand jury and a verdict of a petit jury.

There is, however, a class of contempts that the courts of justice must have jurisdiction to dispose of without an indictment of a grand jury or the verdict of a petit jury. This class of contempts has been provided against by act of congress in the following language :

---

* 20th Wall. 387, New Orleans v. Steamship Co.

Sec. 725. " The said courts shall have power to impose
and administer all necessary oaths, and to punish, by fine
or imprisonment, at the discretion of the court, contempts
of their authority ; *provided*, that such power to punish
contempts shall not be construed to extend to any cases
except misbehavior of any person in their presence, or so
near thereto as to obstruct the administration of justice,
the misbehavior of any of the officers of said courts in
their official transactions, and the disobedience or resistance by any such officer, or by any party, juror, witness,
or other person, to any lawful writ, process, order, rule,
decree, or command of the said court." *

If this provision of congress be construed to apply to
present and continuing contempts committed in the presence of the court, or contempts of jurors, witnesses, and
the officers of the court in refusing to obey the rules
and orders of court during its sesssions, the entering of
fines or orders of imprisonment until the offender con-
sents to purge himself of the contempt, is the only
means of maintaining the courts in the discharge of
their respective duties within their jurisdiction.   Such
acts of contempt would amount to assaults on the dignity
and proceedings of the court, the judge, by imposing a
fine or ordering the offender to prison until he purge himself of the contempt and surrender to every lawful order
of the court, would simply be maintaining the court
by the only means within the power of the court to protect itself.   This power of self-protection is inherent in
the courts, and must be a part of the institution of every
court ; furthermore, such contempts are always committed
within the personal knowledge of the judge, and need
no evidence.

* Revised Statutes U. S., Sec. 725.

But, if said act of congress be construed to apply to contempts that have already been completely committed, unless committed in the presence of the court, that act invades the execution of the criminal and penal laws, and is in conflict with the safeguards of the constitution for the protection of life, liberty and property ; therefore, they must be held to be unconstitutional.

Injunctions as aids to courts of equity, in equity cases are regulated by positive law. But, as they are fordidden by the constitution of England as well as by the constitution of the United States, in penal or criminal cases, or in civil cases sounding in damages, they can not be regulated by any positive law ; therefore, whenever they are issued in this class of cases, the judge who grants them necessarily makes the law for granting them with the expectation of executing the law of his own making, and must necessarily reserve to himself the right to prescribe the punishment for disobeying his injunction, which must always be held back until after the offense of disobedience has been heard by him, thereby making the punishment *ex post facto*. Therefore, injunctions in this class of cases, not only abnegates the safeguards of the constitution for the protection of life, liberty and property, but they disregard and nullify the greatest and most valuable principle of the common law, and of the English civilization ; that of separating the law making jurisdiction from the law executing jurisdiction. Which is the primary principle of both individual and popular liberty. It is the fountain from which popular government under the English civilization flows. Without this fountain, every channel that nourishes free government would dry up, and all would become slaves to the magistrate having jurisdiction to make and execute whatever laws his whims may prompt. So that the purer the fountain is kept, the freer the people are bound to continue. And, the several safe-guards to life, liberty and property being branches flow-ing from this fountain to irrigate and nourish civil lib-erty, they must be kept pure also to maintain the free-dom of the people. These principles can not be too crit-ically or clearly guarded by the great body of the people themselves.

The objections to injunctions in this class of cases ap-ply with equal force to punishments without a verdict of a jury, in trespass to property in the custody of a re-ceiver of a court in an equity case. And in cases with a broad-spread injunction, commonly called blanket injunc-tions, in suits properly brought in equity.

These encroachments on the safeguards of life, liberty and property are the outgrowth of the theory that the supreme court is vested with exclusive jurisdiction to in-terpret the constitution, which necessarily includes power to change the constitution by interpretation. And there are but few if any who can resist the intoxicating influ-ence of such oligarchic powers. Hence, these encroach-ments on the rights of the states and of the people, and on the several departments of the United States, by the judiciary, are ascribable to a natural weakness of man-kind under a bad system, and not to a bad motive on the part of the judges of the supreme court.

No government can be stable or rest on fixed constitu-tional principles as long as it can be changed by the judi-ciary thereof, by interpretation; for the judges them-selves are liable to change, and no judge or set of judges can hold office always, even where they are selected for life, as all must die sooner or later, and whenever a new man is installed in office as judge he carries his political notions with him, and they will, to some extent, give coloring to his judicial views; and as every case arising under the constitution or an act of congress in the United States necessarily partakes of a political character, the constitution will be changed from time to time to make it correspond with the political views of the judges who may be on the bench at the time the court is called on to interpret that instrument.

The supreme court upon two notable occasions so changed its rulings as to sustain the views of one political party over the views of the opposing political party. One of said cases related to treasury notes, commonly called greenbacks, in which that court first decided that the legal-tender feature was unconstitutional, and in a short time thereafter the legal-tender feature was held to be constitutional and valid. The other case related to the power of congress to lay an income tax. The court had adhered to the power of congress to lay that tax on excise principles for over a half century, and at one session of that court held the income tax valid, but granted a rehearing and re-argument, and at the next session of the court overruled its former ruling, and held that income tax to be a direct tax, and that it must be laid by apportioning it among the states according to enumerations under acts of congress.*

I do not complain of that court exercising the inherent right of all courts to overrule its former decisions, to correct its own errors ; nor do I intend to intimate an opinion as to which ruling was correct, the first or second, in said cases, but refer to these two cases out of quite a number because they are probably the most public cases that have been overruled by that court, wherein any of the provisions of the constitution have been changed.

Pollock v. Loan, etc., Co., 157 U. S. 429.

Courts ought always to correct their own errors, whenever they discover them, without hesitation; but no court has, or ought to have, authority to change the supreme law of the land, even for the purpose of correcting its errors, or for any other purpose: though courts may develop new principles of the common law, provided such new principles do not conflict with the letter of the fundamental principles of freedom and the safeguards of life, liberty and property, under the organic law.

The constitution is the only authority for the existence of either of the departments of the United States; it was by that instrument *each of them* was ordained, and neither one of them is authorized to exercise any power not expressly granted to it by that instrument, and that instrument expressly reserves to the people of the states the right to alter or amend the same at will.*

This article five shows a compact between the people of the states; but neither the United States, nor either of the departments thereof, nor any officer thereof, can possibly have been parties to that compact, for neither one of them had any existence until the compact was completed and ratified, and every power granted by the constitution to either of the departments or officers of the United States, was a gratuity, and may be revoked at will by those who granted them.

But if exclusive authority to interpret the grant of powers by the constitution be vested in either or all of the three several departments, the people of the states are excluded from exercising that authority, and they can not alter or amend that instrument without the assent of the tribunal having exclusive authority to interpret the

* Art. 5, Con.

same, and the sovereignty would necessarily reside in that authority and not in the people.

All judicial powers, as well all other powers of government, emanate from the people, and they have as much right to regulate their judiciary organization as they have to regulate their legislative or executive organizations.

" The original power of judicature, by the fundamental principles of society is lodged in the society at large." *

And the people must retain exclusive authority to interpret for themselves every grant of power they may make, or they will be compelled to surrender their sovereignty and freedom to the tribunal they vest with exclusive authority to interpret the same.

If the constitution had not been changed by the committee on style, not only each department of the United States, but the courts of last resort of the states, having appellate jurisdiction of actions in the states, would have been vested with equal authority to interpret the constitution ; but as neither of them had a right to bind any other department or court to its own interpretation, the courts of last resort of the several states, and the supreme court of the United States, would have tried to come together, and to agree to the true and proper meaning of every provision in the constitution, as was intended by the convention that ordained it, and as the people of the states understood them when they were ratified by conventions of the states, which would have given the benefit of all of the judiciary authority, both state and federal, to interpret that instrument.

It is true that the courts of last resort of the several states are vested with appellate jurisdiction of all cases arising under the constitution of their respective states ;

* Bl. Com., vol. 1. p. 267.

but the constitutions of the respective states are limited by that of the United States, and to the extent of the limitations named therein, the state constitutions are subordinate to that of the United States. The judges of the several states are elected or appointed for limited terms, and are removable by address of the legislative department thereof, hence, should the judges of any state betray an inclination to disregard the reserved powers of the people, the people would defeat their re-election or re-appointment, and should their rulings be deemed dangerous to their liberties, the people then could elect a legislature that would remove them by address.

But some may share the Hon. Governeur Morris' fears of the " legislative lion " of the states; those fears, however, are groundless, for the congress is authorized to enact laws relating to every subject of government vested in either of the departments of the United States, so that in every case where a state legislature should attempt to invade any authority of the United States by state legislation, the congress could check it by an act of congress on the subject, which would give the supreme court of the United States appellate jurisdiction of all cases under such acts.

All laws that may be enacted must be in conformity with the constitution, else the acts would be no law at all, and each department must constitute a part of each of the other two departments, and a part of the government of the United States, and each is vested with separate functions; hence, the judiciary must have jurisdiction of all laws enacted by the congress, as all acts of the congress are acts of the government as agent of the sovereign authority. But the constitution was ordained by a higher authority, and is the charter of each department and of the government itself, and is above the government and all connected therewith, and to give to either department thereof, or to all of them combined, sole au-authority to interpret the constitution, necessarily involves authority to change or to destroy the same, which was never contemplated by the makers of that instrument.

By the provisions of article five of the constitution, any mischief that may be done by the supreme court or either of the departments, may be repaired by a convention of the United States, and the ratification thereof by conventions in three-fourths of the states.

Or, if Justice Story correctly interprets said article five in his "Commentaries on the Constitution," any mischief the judiciary may do may be remedied by amendments proposed by the congress and ratified by the legislatures of three-fourths of the states.

CHAPTER IX.

INTERCOURSE AND TRADE BETWEEN THE STATES, AND
POWER OF CONGRESS TO ADMIT NEW STATES.

ARTICLE IV.

Section 1.

Par. 1. "Full faith and credit shall be given in each
state to the public acts, records and judicial proceedings
of every other state. And the congress may by general
laws prescribe the manner in which such acts, records
and proceedings shall be proved and the effect thereof."

The union of the states would be incomplete and extremely cumbersome without faith and credit being given
by the authorities of each state to the public acts, records
and judicial proceedings of every other state in the union ;
the first clause of this paragraph may, therefore, be said
to constitute one of the most valuable provisions of the
constitution in support of the union.

But the second clause tends to weaken the union, and
it can not be enforced without depriving the states of the
right to exercise eminent domain over the territory within
their respective borders ; and to prescribe their own rules
of evidence, to prove their public acts, records and judicial proceedings ; though the congress acting on this latter
provision did at an early day enact a general law on the
subject. Yet the rules of evidence, and the evidence
required by the respective states to establish the title to
real estate or prove their public acts, records and pro-

ceedings of the courts thereof, are recognized by the courts of the several states and by the courts of the United States, as the paramount law on the subject, notwithstanding the provision of the constitution making all laws passed in pursuance of the constitution the supreme law of the land.

However, this clause does not require, nor is it necessary for the congress to pass any law on the subject to aid in putting the constitution into operation; therefore, while the congress is authorized to enact a general law on the subject, such a law would not be in pursuance of the constitution, and under a strict construction is not the supreme law. This clause was not in the draft of the constitution as it was when turned over to the committee on style, and after it was reported back to the convention by that committee, the journal of the convention fails to show any discussion or mention of it in any way. Why that committee added this clause to this section can not be known and must be left to conjecture; for it does not improve the style and must remain a dead letter, or must destroy the right of the people of the respective states, to manage their domestic affairs.

Section 2.

Par. 1. "The citizens of each state shall be entitled to all the privileges and immunities of citizens in the several states."

Par. 2. "A person charged in any state with treason, felony or other crime, who shall flee from justice and be found in another state, shall, on demand of the executive authority of the state from which he fled, be delivered up, to be removed to the state having jurisdiction of the crime.

Par. 3. "No person held to service or labor in one state under the laws thereof escaping into another, shall in consequence of any law or regulation therein be discharged from such service or labor; but shall be delivered up on claim of the party to whom such service or labor may be due."

As said in discussing the power to regulate commerce, the first paragraph of this section contains an important provision of the compact of the union between the states. For unless the citizens of each state could go into other states to trade, and be civilly treated while there, and be authorized to buy and sell property of every description on equal terms with the citizens, and hold, own and transmit the title thereof on the same terms, there could be no union of the states.

It will be observed that this paragraph does not require the states to extend to the citizens of the other states equal *rights* with its own citizens, but only requires the states to extend to citizens of the other states the same *privileges* and *immunities* extended to its own citizens; consequently, the citizens of sister states may do all things in any state that the citizens may do, except to vote and hold offices therein.

The second paragraph, providing for the capture and return of those who are charged with treason, felony, or other crime, is a part of the first, and necessary to the maintenance of the union, and to enable each state not only to protect its own citizens against lawlessness, but to protect the citizens of sister states.

Section 3.

Par. 1. "New states may be admitted by the congress into this union; but no new state shall be formed or erected within the jurisdiction of any other state; nor any state be formed by the junction of two or more states, or parts of states, without the consent of the legislature of the states concerned, as well as of the congress.''

Par. 2. ''The congress shall have power to dispose of and make all needful rules and regulations respecting the territory or other property belonging to the United States ; and nothing in this constitution shall be so construed as to prejudice any claims of the United States, or of any particular state.''

To give to this section the broad meaning the language indicates, makes it conflict with other provisions of the constitution, and imbues it with a latent ambiguity, to be explained by other provisions of the constitution and the proceedings in the convention relating thereto and the history of the settlement of the colonies and their charters.

The preamble to the constitution shows that this union is to consist of American states, or, as expressed therein, '' United States of America.''

Section four of article four requires the United States to guarantee to each state a republican form of government, and no new state can be admitted on any other terms than on full and complete equality ; therefore no new state can be admitted unless it has a republican form of government. These two conditions are so plainly expressed that they can not be disputed.

But the third condition has been made somewhat obscure by the decision of the supreme court in the Dred Scott case (in which that court in the course of its argument intimated that the congress probably had authority to naturalize Indians of the various tribes or nations) ; this third qualification, therefore, may be said to be ambiguous ; and its ambiguity may be explained by the proceeding of the convention and the relation of the citi-

zens and inhabitants of the several states to their respective states under state laws.   However, the purpose
of the supreme court in that case was to show that the
African negroes were incapable of being admitted into
the family of sovereign people on equal terms, jurisdiction and powers with the white people, and it did not
take into full consideration the status of the Indian
nations and inhabitants thereof to the states and the
union.

But the court did say in that case that :

"The words 'people of the United States' and 'citizens' are synonymous terms.   They both describe the
political body who, according to our republican institutions, form the sovereignty, and who hold the power
and conduct the government through their representatives.
They are what we familiarly call the 'sovereign people,'
and every citizen is one of this people, and a constituent
member of this sovereignty." *

"Every person and every class and description of persons, who were at the time of the adoption of the constitution recognized as citizens in the several states,
became also citizens of this new political body ; but none
other ; it was formed by them and for them and their
posterity, but for no one else.†

By the fifth section of the ninth article of the confederation each state was required to furnish its quota of
militia in proportion to the white inhabitants thereof
only.

The naturalization act passed by the congress in 1790
authorized the naturalization of aliens being free white
persons only.   And many of the members of the congress that passed that naturalization act had been mem-

---

* 19th Howard, p. 404.   † 19th Howard, p. 406.

bers of the convention that framed the constitution, and were among our ablest statesmen and lawyers. *

Therefore that naturalization act is entitled to great respect, as a contemporaneous interpretation of the constitution as to what class of people were entitled to be taken into the family of sovereign rulers of the United States. But as strong as this evidence is, we need not stop with it alone.

Before the formation of the more perfect union by which the people of the states were taken into it, as well as the political organization of the states, most of the states had laws prohibiting white people from marrying negroes, Indians or mulattoes ; though a few of the states had omitted to include *Indians* in their laws relating to marriage.

Indians, negroes and mulattoes, whether slave or free, being excluded from the militia force of the states, and being prohibited from intermarrying with the white people, they could not have constituted any part of the sovereign people, who ordained and established the constitution, or nation, of the United States of America ; but it has been suggested that the negroes are now citizens of the United States, and of the state wherein they reside. These suggestions come from those who have not closely examined into the intent and meaning of the fourteenth and fifteenth amendments to the constitution.

The first section of the fourteenth amendment simply declares that, ''all persons born or naturalized in the United States and subject to the jurisdiction thereof are citizens of the United States, and of the state wherein they reside.''

But the second section thereof concedes that declara-

---

* 19th Howard, p. 406.

tion to be untrue by offering a reward to the states to permit the persons indicated the right to vote in certain elections, among which the right to vote for delegates to conventions was not named.

If the negroes had been made equal sovereign citizens, by that amendment, with the white people, they would have a legal right to aspire to the hand in marriage of the highest lady in the land, and no law could be passed by any state to deny them that right; no amendment to the constitution, that would open the parlors of the white people to the equal approach and entrance of the negro race, would have been ratified by the states; it may, therefore, be assumed that the draftsmen of that amendment intentionally avoided making the negroes sovereign citizens. No one can be a citizen of the United States unless he is a citizen of one of the states, for that would destroy the fitness of the United States to execute its trusts in protecting the citizens of all the states alike. If the United States could have citizens independently of those of the states, it would not be competent to represent the states, for to the extent of the interest of the citizens of the United States, its interest would be hostile to that of the state; but as this question will be fully discussed in reviewing the fourteenth and fifteenth amendments to the constitution, further notice of it is deferred until then.

The fourth condition or limitation on the power of congress to admit new states, viz., that they must be contiguous to the body of American states, requires a more minute and extensive examination into the action of the convention, and of the states, and of circumstances relating to the granting of that authority to the congress.

As has been said heretofore in this review, every nation must have a people associated together as one peo-

ple, or body politic, or national family (as they are sometimes called), and that body politic, or national family,
must own and hold exclusive possession of a certain and
known part of the globe, and have a political policy or
government of some sort.

Hence, every nation consists of a certain people associated as one people, owning a certain part of the globe.
The territory they have appropriated to their exclusive
use is a necessary part of the nation, and it is utterly impossible to pass the sovereign title to the territory, without also passing sovereign control over the inhabitants
thereof in the same deed or act of cession, unless the sovereign control over the inhabitants should be reserved by
the deed of cession ; and no nation would be willing to
buy the territory on such terms.   In the treaties ceding
the Floridas and Louisiana province to the United States,
it was agreed in each treaty that the inhabitants should
be taken into the national family of the United States,
but the sovereign control over the inhabitants passed by
the treaty in each case to the United States ; in one case
the sovereignty over them was ceded by the kingdom of
Spain, and in the other by the republic of France, without
consulting the wishes of the inhabitants conveyed.

No people who authorize their government to trade
them off, by the sale or transfer of the territory they inhabit, can possibly be free, nor can any people who authorize their government to change the race or character of the people who constitute the body politic of the
nation, either by allowing a lower grade or race of
people to take part in managing the affairs, or by purchasing them as a part of a territory, particularly if this
lower grade or race so purchased are to be permitted to
take part in the management of the nation, as equals with
the former national family or body politic thereof.

While many nations authorize the purchase and ownership of provinces, with the right of sovereignty over the
inhabitants thereof, I do not know of a single nation
whose government has authority to dispose of any part
of the territory that constitutes the nation proper, or any
part of the class of people who constitute the body politic of the nation ; or that has any authority to change
the character of the people composing the body politic,
either by extending the rights and privileges of the national family to a lower grade of people, or by taking a
lower grade of people into the national family by purchasing the territory they inhabit.   However, the right
of franchise has often been extended to the same race of
people, and the right of citizenship was extended in
Rome, but to the same race of people. The only attempt
to degrade the national family that I know of is chargeable
to the United States, in its attempting to elevate the native-born of African descent—which proved a failure—
and the more recent attempt to raise the low grade or
race of people inhabiting the Philippine and other
islands—which is as likely to prove a failure. Whether
the United States has a sovereign government or not is
of little consequence, so far as this question extends.

Since the explosion of the doctrine of the divine right
of kings, we are forced to look to the people as the
original source of power, and since man is recognized,
by the whole of Christendom, to have been endowed by
the great Ruler of the Universe with free agency, and as
free agency and sovereignty are equivalent to each other,
man must be recognized as a sovereign by gift of nature ;
so that whenever sovereignty is lodged in a government,
it must be so lodged by authority of the people. And
as no government can exist without an association of
people into one body or national family, the body politic

of the nation, or national family, must continuously succor and feed the sovereignty as lodged in the government; for they can no more part with their sovereignty
than they can with their free agency, though they may,
by voluntary engagement, oblige themselves by compact
to maintain sovereignty in their government by a con-
tinual flow of their respective sovereignty to the government. Hence every government that is vested with sovereignty derives it by compact between the members of
the body politic, consisting of the people who constitute
the nation, whether the government thereof was formed
by compact or the result of growth. Authority in the
government to destroy or to change the body politic
from which it must continue to draw its sovereign authority, involves authority to destroy itself, or to change
its own character without consulting the people engaged
in feeding and keeping it alive; for when the body politic that gives it succor and life is changed or destroyed, the
government must cease to exist, unless it be built anew.
The sovereign authority of England is lodged with the
parliament and king of that realm; but they would not
dare to interfere with the body politic of that kingdom.
Should the parliament and king of that nation undertake
to extend to Canada, or any other province of that nation, equal representation in the British parliament, with
the right to vote on questions involving the policy of
that kingdom, it would be denounced as revolutionary and
void, and the king forced to prorogue that parliament and
call another. Inasmuch as such an undertaking would
be the exercise of rights inalienable from the people, they
could not have been granted, and should be held by the
people of the kingdom as unconstitutional.

When they take into consideration the principles announced by the great Declaration of Independence, the

fact that no government for the United States was ordained by the constitution, but in lieu thereof, three separate agents, to-wit, the legislative, executive and judiciary departments, that the legislatures of two-thirds of the states may demand a federal convention to propose amendments to the constitution, and when any amendments proposed by that convention shall be ratified by conventions in three-fourths of the states, they are to become the constitution on that subject, all logical reasoners will be forced to the conclusion that the sovereignty of the United States resides in the people of the states. If it is in the people of the states, they alone have the right to determine who shall be taken into the body politic and become members of the national family.

There is no authority in the letter of the constitution that allows the congress or the president to buy territory, or to sell territory, except to emigrants and settlers, and in sales to emigrants and settlers the sovereign title is never passed; not only is the eminent domain retained, but the purchaser becomes subject to the sovereignty of the nation. While as has been shown, every sale of territory by which the sovereign title passes, sovereign control over the inhabitants thereof also passes. Power to buy territory in the United States, if it exist, must, therefore, be drawn alone from implication.

Is it not strange that any citizen of the United States would be willing to draw a power by implication, that at once makes him a slave to his government, that not only denies him the right to choose his own associates, to constitute the body politic or national family, but lays him liable to be sold as a part of the territory he may inhabit; for the right to buy necessarily includes the right to sell?

But it is claimed by some, that the United States

did buy the province of Louisiana. The facts are, the United States held the superior title, *in trust*, to that province, and it was cheaper to buy out France's possession of it, than to go to war at that time for the possession thereof.

The status of that province, together with the history of the title of the United States to it, and the claim of France to it will incontrovertibly sustain my contention that nothing passed to the United States by what is known as the Louisiana purchase, except the actual possession of it.

As the evident object of England in planting her colonies in this country, was to appropriate the vacant and unclaimed part of the continent, the boundary given to the three colonies, viz., Virginia, New England and the grant to the Earl of Clarendon and others, included the whole of North America between Canada and the Floridas, being thought to extend from 31° to 48° north latitude. The charter to Virginia was amended in 1606, and made to extend two hundred miles north of, and two hundred miles south of Point Comfort in Virginia, and to extend across the continent the same width.

The second company, by amended charter of 1620, was made to extend from 40° to 48° north latitude, and to extend across the continent—in the language of said amendment, " to extend from sea to sea."

The charter to the Earl of Clarendon and others, in 1663, was the grant under which the Carolinas were settled. The boundary thereof was, " beginning at Lucke island in the southern waters of Virginia, thence west to the Southern seas, and south to the river Mathias, which bordereth on the coast of Florida," etc.

These amended charters were granted by James, styling himself King of England, Scotland, France and Ireland.

The charter to the Earl of Clarendon and others was granted by Charles II., styling himself King of England, Scotland, France and Ireland.

These three grants included all of North America between 31° and 48° north latitude, extending across the continent from sea to sea.*

In 1673, being sixty years after England had taken possession of the greater part of it, and ten years after she had taken possession of the whole of it, France claimed to have discovered the province of Louisiana, and governed the same by officers sent out from Paris, making New Orleans the capital of the province.

On November 3, 1762, some ninety years after claiming to have discovered it, France ceded that part of it that lay on the east of the Mississippi river, including New Orleans, to Spain ; but Spain retroceded it to France by treaty of Ildefonso, October 1, 1800.†

This treaty was laid before a called session of congress by President Jefferson, that met the 17th of October, 1803, which resulted in what is called the Louisiana purchase.

The fact that England had possession of said province at the time France claimed to have discovered it, and claimed it prior to the treaty of Paris of 1763, why was it not included in the treaty of alliance between France and the United States of 1778? The sixth section of that treaty reads as follows :

"Art. 6. The most Christian King renounces forever the possession of the islands of Bermuda, as well as of any part of the continent of North America which before the treaty of Paris, in 1763, or in virtue of that treaty, were acknowledged to belong to the crown of

---

* Poore's Charters.   † Id.

Great Britain, or to the United States, heretofore called British colonies, or which are at this time, or lately have been, under the power of the king and crown of Great Britain."*

But in addition to this claim, the charter to the Georgia Company, granted in 1732 by King George II., paid no attention to the claim of France to the province of Louisiana, for the grant to Georgia stretches entirely across said province to the full width of the grant to that colony by the express language of the charter, showing that England—at least at that time—claimed all that she had appropriated by planting her colonies in this country, and doubtless continued to claim the whole of it, which we have seen included all that part of the continent of North America between 31° and 48° north latitude, extending from the Atlantic to the Pacific oceans.

Having shown what England claimed, I will now show what the colonies claimed while the Revolutionary War was going on.

On the 15th of December, 1778, the legislature of Maryland adopted a declaration setting out that many of the states claimed large surplus and unsettled territory, that some of them claimed to extend to the Mississippi river or to the Pacific Ocean, and on the same day drew up instructions to the members of congress from that state, directing them to insist on so amending the articles of confederation as to authorize congress to fix the boundary of the states and to set apart said surplus territory as a fund to pay the war debts.†

* Statutes at Large, U. S., vol. 8.
† Henning's Stat. of Va., vol. 10, pp. 549–556.

The state of Virginia, on the 14th of December, 1779 (being about a year afterward), prepared and adopted a remonstrance to the Maryland resolutions and instructions, from which I make the following quotation :

. . "Congress have lately described and ascertained the boundaries of these United States as an ultimatum in their terms of peace. The United States hold no territory but in right of some one individual state in the union ; the territory of each state, from time immemorial, hath been fixed and determined by their respective charters, there being no other rule or criterion to judge by ; should these in any instance (when there is no disputed territory between particular states) be abridged without the consent of the states affected by it, general confusion must ensue ; each state would be subjected in its turn to the encroachments of the others, and a field opened for future wars and bloodshed ; nor can any agreements be fairly urged to prove that any particular tract of country, within the limits claimed by congress on behalf of the United States, is not part of the chartered territory of some one of them, but must militate with equal force against the right of the United States in general ; and tend to prove such tract of country (if north-west of the Ohio river) part of the British province of Canada. . .

"When Virginia acceded to the Articles of Confederation, her rights of sovereignty and jurisdiction within her own territory were reserved and secured to her, and can not now be infringed or altered without her consent. . . ." *

The action of the legislatures of these two states show that, in the midst of the war, the states claimed all of the territory within the boundary of their respective charters,

* Henning's Stat. of Va., vol. 10, p. 558.

and that the whole of said territory was claimed by England; therefore, it was claimed by both parties to the revolutionary war, and of course the whole of it was involved in that war, and passed to the several states according to the boundary of their respective British charters upon the acknowledgment of their independence.

As said by the supreme court, whatever England claimed, or was entitled to when war was declared, was involved in the war and passed to the colonies by the acknowledgment of their independence; and the treaty with England attempting to define the boundary of the United States did not affect the boundary thereof, for no territory was granted by that treaty. *

As long as the colonies remained mere municipal agents of Great Britain, the disparity in the size of them, as colonies, was a matter of no consequence, but when they were about to become sovereign states, that disparity excited jealousies among them, and three of the states delayed ratifying the Articles of Confederation on account of it, and insisted on the surrender of their surplus territory by the large states to aid in paying the expenses of the war. And the congress made repeated appeals to the large states to do so, but none were heeded until the congress pledged itself to hold the surplus territory so ceded by the states, for the benefit of all of the states, and to divide it up into convenient sizes and shapes to be formed into states, and as fast as either of said divisions should contain a sufficient population to constitute a state, to admit the same as a new state with equal sovereignty and freedom with the existing states,

* 12 Wheaton, 523 (U. S.), Harcourt, etc., v. Guillard, etc.; 12 Wheaton, 530 (U. S.), Henderson v. Poindexter.

which pledge was made with the resolution adopted on the — day of September 1780.

In consideration of this pledge the state of Virginia, on the 2d of January, 1781, authorized the cession of its surplus territory north-west of the Ohio river with certain reservations to soldiers, settlers, etc.

Although Virginia offered to cede its territory northwest of the Ohio river in 1781, the deed for it was not made until 1783, and was not delivered until the 1st of March, 1784. This deed, after reciting the act of the Virginia legislature and the reservation of certain parts for soldiers and settlers, proceeded as follows: "Now, therefore, know ye, that we, the said Thomas Jefferson, Samuel Hardy, Arthur Lee, and James Monroe, by virtue of the power and authority committed to us by the act of said general assembly of Virginia, before recited, and in the name, and for and on behalf of said commonwealth, do, by these presents convey, transfer, assign, and make over, unto the United States in congress assembled, for the benefit of the said states, Virginia inclusive, all right, title and claim, as well of soil as of jurisdiction, which the said commonwealth hath to the territory or tract of country within the limits of the Virginia charter, situate, lying, and being, to the northwest of the river Ohio, to and for the uses and purposes, and on the conditions of the said recited act." . . .*

All of the states, except North Carolina and Georgia, had followed Virginia's example and ceded their surplus territory to the United States, before the convention that made the constitution met; and it was believed that those two states would also cede their surplus territory to the United States.

---

* These proceedings may be found in volumes 10 and 11, Henning's Statutes at Large of Virginia.

I have not examined the deeds from each of the states to the United States, but there was no convenient or reasonable way for them to convey their surplus territory respectively, except to convey from a given boundary line to the extent of the boundary of their respective British charters, which vested the United States with the true and paramount title to what was known as the Louisiana province.

England's claim to the whole of that part of the continent of North America included between Canada and the Floridas from the Atlantic to the Pacific Oceans having been entered by actual settlement on each of said colonial grants for the purpose of taking possession of the whole grant in each case, while no part thereof was claimed or occupied adversely, by a well-settled rule of law each settlement spread over the whole grant to the extent of the boundary thereof ; and as but one constructive possession can exist at the same time, the settlement of France at New Orleans could not be made to extend further than the actual settlement and inclosures, if an adverse possession can be made available between nations, which is at least doubtful.

But as England continued to claim it, which is shown in various ways, notably by the grant to the Georgia Company in 1732, the adverse possession at New Orleans could not prejudice England's title to what is called the Louisiana province.

The whole of that part of the continent of North America between Canada and the Floridas, stretching across the continent from the Atlantic to the Pacific Oceans (which included the province of Louisiana), being claimed and occupied by England through her colonies at the beginning of the war of the revolution, the whole of it was involved in that war, and the title thereof passed from England to the states by the acknowledgment of their independence.

Consequently the United States, under the articles of confederation, covered and included the whole of said part of the continent of North America; and the United States, under the constitution of 1787, necessarily included the same country or territory; and that was the country or territory that was contemplated by the convention in authorizing new states to be admitted, by the use of the following language in the draft of the constitution by the committee on detail: "New states, lawfully constituted or established within the limits of the United States, may be admitted," etc. And doubtless the same country was recognized as being within the United States by the committee on style; but that committee, knowing that there was no authority granted by the constitution to congress or the United States to buy any additional territory, regarded the words "lawfully constituted or established *within the limits* of the United States" as surplusage, as no new states could be admitted unless they were lawfully constituted or established, and as no authority to buy territory was granted, no new states could be admitted unless they were within the limits of the United States; therefore said committee changed it to "New states may be admitted by the congress into this Union," etc.

There being no authority in the congress to naturalize any but white persons being free, or to admit any except free white people into the family of the nation, and there being no authority in the United States to acquire territory, the whole of the surplus territory ceded to the United States in trust by the respective states is obliged to be held for the exclusive use of the citizens of the United States and such free white people as congress may naturalize; and as no territory can be bought, no people can be purchased as part of any territory by the United States government or any of its departments.

These provisions wisely secure the purity of the body politic or national family of the United States, and firmly reserve to the white people alone the sovereign authority of the nation.

Should the people of the states (in whom the entire sovereign authority of the nation is lodged) desire to add territory to the United States, or to take a different race or grade of people into the national family or body politic of the nation, they may do so, provided they speak through a federal convention and ratify the same by conventions in three-fourths of the states ; those conventions being the only organ provided by the constitution through which the people can express their sovereign will on any subject.*

Many of the anti-slavery people of the free states were opposed to the United States getting possession of the Louisiana province, because it would evidently increase the slave territory and add other slave states to the union ; and some of them, conceding that said province was involved in the war, and although England's claim may have been better than that of France, still the United States was estopped from claiming it by reason of the treaty with Spain of 1795, fixing the western boundary in the middle of the Mississippi river. But that treaty, as well as the one with England, was passed on by the supreme court in the cases reported in 12 Wheaton, heretofore cited, did not profess to pass title to, or convey any territory by either party ; there were no words of purchase, conveyance, or grant of any territory in said treaty. But if there had been, the whole of the surplus territory of the several states had been ceded to the United States in congress assembled, in trust for a specific purpose (to wit), to be held for the

* See chaps. 1 and 2.

equal benefit of all of the states, and to be sold only to settlers and emigrants who would occupy it, and as fast as any particular division of it should acquire a sufficient population to entitle it to a representative in congress, to admit such division into the union as an equal state. Therefore, any agreement the United States may have made with Spain not to claim the territory west of the Mississippi could not have any binding force on the several states of the United States, because it would have been in violation of the trust by which the United States held that territory.

Second, Spain had no interest in the territory west of the Mississippi river, for the whole of the territory ceded by France to Spain laid on the east side of that river.

Third, there was no bargain or sale of any territory on the west side of the Mississippi river by the United States to Spain in that treaty, nor was any consideration offered or paid for any territory west of that river; consequently no estoppel can operate against the claim by the states of the territory west of the Mississippi river and none can possibly arise out of that treaty with Spain.

It is, however, claimed that Mr. Jefferson doubted the the existence of authority under the constitution to purchase the province of Louisiana, and urged an amendment to the constitution to authorize its purchase.

If Mr. Jefferson was guilty of knowingly and willfully violating his oath to support the constitution, instead of being revered as the great apostle of the liberty of the people, he should have been impeached and condemned as an arch enemy of constitutional government and human freedom. But there was never any foundation for that charge, and it must have been started and kept alive by his enemies, for it is a vile aspersion of his character.

Mr. Jefferson was an active participant in all of the proceedings of his state—Virginia—relating to the claim of that state to the territory within the boundary of its British charter; and was one of the members of congress from that state at the time they were constituted commissioners to convey the surplus territory of that state to the United States, and probably drafted the deed in person, part of which is hereinbefore quoted. As shown by that deed the whole of the territory of that state northwest of the Ohio river, to the full extent of the boundary as given by its British charter, was conveyed to the United States in congress assembled, in trust for the benefit of all of the states; and he knew it to be the duty of the United States to acquire possession of every foot of the territory so conveyed as fast as it should be needed to make states of, and there is nothing in any part of the proceedings relating to the acquisition of the possession of the province of Louisiana from France that shows the slightest doubt of, not only the authority, but the imperative duty to remove the obstruction to the possession of that province on the mind of Mr. Jefferson.

It is however true, that Mr. Jefferson entered into convention with the first consul of France relating to the acquisition of the province of Louisiana some six months before communicating with the senate or congress.

As the congress alone is authorized to contract debt, or put the United States under obligation to pay money, and by his convention said province was to cost the United States thirteen millions of dollars, Mr. Jefferson laid himself liable to impeachment for assuming legislative powers, however he felt justified by declarations and acts of congress; but whatever the congress may have declared on the subject, could be repudiated by the same congress or its successor, and if the congress had concluded that the previous resolutions, declarations and acts were insufficient to authorize so bold a step to be taken by the executive, that conclusion would amount to a decision that it was their duty to impeach the president.

Mr. Jefferson, however, thought the previous acts and declarations authorized him to act without waiting to confer with the senate or the congress, and in a message to congress on the 17th of October, 1803, explains to congress his reasons for so doing, which are as follows :

. . . "Previous, however, to this period we had not been unaware of the danger to which our peace would be perpetually exposed whilst so important a key to the commerce of the western country remained under foreign power. Difficulties, too, were presenting themselves as to the navigation of other streams which, arising within our territories, pass through those adjacent. Propositions had therefore been authorized for obtaining on fair conditions the sovereignty of New Orleans, and of other possessions in that quarter interesting to our quiet to such extent as was deemed practicable, and the provisional appropriation of $2,000,000 to be applied and accounted for by the president of the United States, intended as part of the price, was considered as conveying the sanction of congress to the acquisition proposed. The enlightened government of France saw with just descernment the importance to both nations of such liberal arrangements as might best and permanently promote the peace, friendship and interest of both, and the property and sovereignty of all Louisiana which had been restored to them have on certain conditions been transferred to the United States by instruments bearing date the 30th of April last. When these shall have received the constitutional sanction of the senate, they will without delay be communicated to the representatives also for the exercise of their functions as to those conditions which are within the powers vested by the constitution in congress.

"Whilst the property and sovereignty of the Mississippi and its waters secure an independent outlet for the produce of the western states, and an uncontrolled navigation through their whole course, free from collision with other powers and the dangers to our peace from that source, the fertility of the country, its climate and extent, promise in due season important aids to our treasury, an ample provision for our posterity, and a wide spread for the blessings of freedom and equal laws." . . . *

Said convention with France was laid before the senate on the same day this message was sent to the congress (being the 17th of October, 1803). The senate approved it, and on the 21st of October, 1803, by special message, the treaty as consented to by the senate, and ratified and exchanged between the nations, was laid before the congress. †

Said treaty was afterward sanctioned and carried into effect by the congress.

Mr. Jefferson realizing the danger he was in, if the congress should fail to adhere to its former declarations, doubtless felt some uneasiness about exercising legislative powers, and may have given expression to the same. But he never had any doubt of the right to quiet the possession of the province of Louisiana.

One of the objects named in the preamble to the constitution, is "to provide for the common defense," and the ownership of the Floridas being necessary to the public defense, their purchase was made under that authority, and the purchase thereof in discharge of the duty to provide for the public defense was entirely justified by the constitution.

---

* See Messages of Presidents, vol. 1, p. 358.

† Messages, etc., vol. 1, p. 362.

The treaty by which the two Floridas were acquired was entered into the 22d day of February, 1819, but was not ratified until the 19th of February, 1821 ; and by it Spain ceded to the United States the two Floridas, together with the island and city of New Orleans ; and the United States ceded to Spain the greater part of what now constitutes Texas. As the United States held this territory of Texas under the cession of the states in trust, there was no authority in the United States to cede it to Spain ; nor had the United States any authority to cede it under the decision of the supreme court in the Dred Scott case, for even if the original title thereto emanated from the Louisiana purchase, still it would be held in trust to make states of, and could not be sold ; but that territory has been re-acquired by the United States, therefore that sale need not be considered any further.

As all of the territory between Canada and the Floridas, stretching entirely across the continent, from the Atlantic to the Pacific oceans, was involved in the war, it passed to the states by the acknowledgment of their independence, therefore the whole within that boundary must be construed to be within the United States. In addition hereto, as the United States is required to provide for the public defense, they may buy territory contiguous to the United States where it may be necessary to provide for the public defense, and may admit new states formed of the territory so purchased. The new states authorized to be admitted into the union must, therefore, be within or contiguous to the existing states of America.

But if the constitution and the declaration of independence be considered as obsolete, and this question one of policy and economics, the objections to the acquisition of

such islands or remote territory, except as stations for
naval and commercial uses, is most dangerous, for such
islands or remote territory, as states, will require a separate
army and navy to maintain them, or each of them, which
can never be used to aid in maintaining the contiguous
American states ; while it is impossible to construct a fort,
port, or arsenal, or to use ships of war for the protection of
the coast and ports of any of the contiguous states of
America, without their contributing to the security of
each of the states of America. The bulk of the cost of
maintaining such isolated states would fall on the American states as tribute, or an additional expense. What
could the American states expect in return for this tribute?

The population of the Philippines is sufficient to furnish some part of the army to defend those islands, but
soldiers drawn from that mongrel population can not be
relied on to maintain the reputation the American citizens have won as soldiers ; nor can we expect from
them great scientists, inventors, or statesmen to add
glory to the citizenship of the United States. Then
what can we expect in return for the extra expense
to the American states? The taxation, under the constitution, is required to be equal, and the expenditures for each ought at least to approximate equality,
for unless they do approximate equality, some of the
states will be forced to pay tribute to other states. It
is true some of the American states pay more taxes
than other states, but the states that pay small amounts
of taxes have but little expended on them ; and isolated
states separated from the American states by the high
seas or foreign nations, can not be made to pay a tithe
of what they will cost the American states to maintain
them.

Furthermore, the people of the American states would expect to furnish the officers and other employes, to get some of their tribute money back, and that partiality to citizens of the American states would engender a spirit of resentment on the part of the citizens of such isolated states, which would likely result in manifestations of rebellious feelings on the part of the natives, strong enough to call for interference on the part of the military authorities.

In this way, whatever civil government may be established therein must gradually fall under the military authorities; and thus, although formed into states, they would soon become mere provinces of the United States. And the military feeling engendered by the glittering display a well-equipped army and navy would show, coupled with the impression that would necessarily take hold of the soldiery, that the army and navy alone represented the glory of this nation—particularly as the military would have at least partial control of the civil authorities in such isolated states—they would become so impressed with their importance as to make their authority felt in the *contiguous American* states, and speedily convert the Republic of the United States into an imperial nation with unlimited powers, or such as the empire would assume control of; for as no powers were granted to the United States, no limitations were imposed on the United States by the constitution.

Therefore, a new government would have to be established for the new empire.

This new government being without limitations, with a formidable army and navy at its disposal, would not be likely to surrender powers of much value to the people.

However, if we could secure mild-tempered and honest emperors for a long while, the powers of the empire might be limited by interpretation until an unwritten constitution, similar to that of the kingdom of Great Britain, would be established ; but if the emperors are to be chosen through bribery and fraud, no one can possibly tell how far the people will be enslaved or what tyranny may be imposed on them.

It is claimed that we now own the Philippine group of islands, the Hawaiian islands, and some of the West India islands, and the Territory of Alaska. The natural inquiry therefore, is, what shall we do with them ?

Since the theory upon which this nation is founded is that the sovereignty resides in the people only, and is inalienable from them ; according to the declaration of independence, the sovereignty must be equally vested in the people ; for if some of them can be subject to the will of others, those subject to others can not be sovereign. And by the thirteenth amendment to the constitution it is provided that "neither slavery nor involuntary servitude, except for crime, shall exist within the United States, or any place subject to their jurisdiction." Our new possessions can not, therefore, be held as provinces or as permanent territories.

No appropriation that may be made for the maintenance of the army and navy, necessary to protect states formed of any of said islands or territory, can in any possible way redound to the protection of the contiguous states of America, and, as under the limitations on the taxing powers, neither of said groups of islands as states can be made to pay a tithe of the cost of maintaining them, it will be impossible to equalize the burdens and emoluments between the American states and states formed of said isolated territory or islands. They therefore can not be admitted as equal states ; consequently the best that we can do is to get rid of them on the best terms consistent with the free institutions of the United States and the rules of humanity.

International law requires us to hold them until we can turn them over to a humane government. The constitution of the United States prevents us from selling said islands and territory to any buyer except the inhabitants themselves, for the reason that a sale of the islands and territory includes a sale of the inhabitants as a part of the land as hereinbefore explained. Therefore we are compelled to give them a chance of organizing a humane government for themselves, and to aid them in maintaining their government until the people thereof become strong enough to maintain it for themselves.

We having aided in a friendly way the establishing of free governments organized by the inhabitants thereof for themselves, they in grateful recognition of that service would prefer to give their trade to the United States. Whatever government may be established should be required to pay the expense the United States is put to in giving such aid, and in case of the Philippine group of islands, they ought to be required to pay the twenty millions of dollars the United States paid Spain for them, as well as the cost of aiding in establishing the government conforming to the will of the inhabitants thereof.

It is the duty of every government to carefully guard what is called the glory of the nation it represents. What is meant by the *glory* of a nation is its power to protect its institutions and the rights of its citizens, and to maintain its dignity and standing among nations, and to maintain its honor and adherence to its pledges and policy as a nation.

The United States of America, without said islands or isolated territory, with a merchant marine to carry its own commerce, and a navy to protect that marine, and conveniences to transport its soldiers from one point to another of the United States within the boundary thereof, will be able to successfully defend herself and compel other nations to respect the rights of her citizens ; but with said islands to be defended, whether as states or as provinces, the military power of this nation will be so weakened as not only to impair the glory of the United States, but may cause her to submit to insults to her flag that would not be tolerated as long as the nation remains compact and independent of the combined powers of the world.

ARTICLE V.

"The congress, whenever two-thirds of both houses shall deem it necessary, shall propose amendments to this constitution ; or, on the application of the legislatures of two-thirds of the several states, shall call a convention for proposing amendments, which in either case shall be valid, to all intents and purposes, as part of this constitution, when ratified by the legislatures of three-fourths of the several states, or by conventions in three-fourths thereof, as the one or the other mode of ratification may be proposed by the congress ; provided, that no amendment which may be made prior to the year one thousand eight hundred and eight, shall in any manner affect the first and fourth clauses in the ninth section of the first article, and that no state, without its consent, shall be deprived of its equal suffrage in the senate."

The language of this article is by no means clear as to the precise meaning the draftsmen intended to be given it; but an examination of the proceedings of the convention will show the manner in which it found its way into the constitution in that form, and will shed some light on the interpretation that should be given to it.   In con-

struing the constitution, every part should be made to harmonize with every other part if possible, and all should
yield to the great American principles upon which the
system of government is based.

As pointed out in the first, second, and third chapters
of this review, the whole sovereign authority was reserved to the people, and the government of the federal
union was to be but a corporate agent of the people of
the several states; and the people of the several states
were made directly subjects of the federal union under the
constitution of which this is a part, thereby making themselves bear the same relation to the more perfect union
that they bear to their respective states, viz., of being both
sovereign and subject; and having adopted sovereign
conventions as the only organ through which to express
their sovereign will, this article must be construed as
providing two modes of amending the constitution.

One mode of amending that instrument is by two-
thirds of each house of congress agreeing to and proposing amendments, which, when ratified by the legislatures of three-fourths of the states, shall be valid to all
intents and purposes as parts of the constitution, but this
mode of amending the constitution applies alone to
changing the manner of executing the powers theretofore
granted; for each house of congress, as well as the legislatures of the states, are but agents of the people, and
they can neither enlarge their letters of authority nor
reduce the duties imposed on them by the sovereign
people while acting through the regular organ for expressing their sovereign will. Besides, no power can be
added to any of the departments of either the federal
governmental agent or to the governmental agents of the
states, except by the sovereign authority; nor can any
of said departments be relieved of any duty theretofore

imposed on them by the sovereign authority except by that authority itself, and that authority speaks *only* through sovereign conventions.

Consequently the congress and the legislatures of the states have no authority to change the plan or system of the government, but may change the mode of executing the powers expressly granted to the congress or to any department of the United States, but can go no further.

The legislatures of the states are incompetent to grant such extensive powers; it was the ratification by the people in their respective states alone that gave validity to the constitution.*

This is as far as even Mr. Hamilton thought the congress and the legislatures of the states could go in amending the constitution.†

The other mode of amending the constitution is, by the call of the legislatures of two-thirds of the states for a convention, which the congress has no authority to refuse, but must act ministerially and make the call.‡

When this convention is called, the states must appoint the delegates to it ; and whatever amendment they may recommend, relating to any changes in the powers of the United States, must be submitted to conventions chosen by the legal voters of the states respectively, and when such amendments shall be ratified by such conventions in three-fourths of the states, they shall become part of the constitution to all intents and purposes.‖

That convention, like the one of 1787, may propose any amendment it chooses, even to the abolishment of the departments of the governmental agents : it can pro-

---

* McCulloch v. Maryland, 4 Wheaton, 116.
† See Letter 85, Federalist.
‡ See Letter 85, Federalist ; see Story's Com. on Con., sec. 1832.
‖ See letter of the convention to congress.

pose to do away with the judiciary department, or a re-modeling of it only, or a remodeling of the executive or the congress, and when ratified by conventions in three-fourths of the states these propositions will become part of the constitution to all intents and purposes. As the present constitution was a mere proposal until ratified by the people in their state conventions, it will require a ratification by the people in state conventions to make any change in the form or powers of the government valid.*

This was evidently the purpose of the convention when this article of the constitution was agreed to. For, the constitution was constructed on a series of resolutions offered by Hon. Edmund Randolph; among those resolutions was the following:

13. "*Resolved*, That provisions ought to be made for the amendment of the articles of union, whensoever it shall seem necessary, and that the assent of the national legislature ought not to be required thereto."†

This resolution was agreed to by the committee of the whole, just as it was when offered, but it was altered by the committee of detail in drafting it into the form of a constitutional provision, by leaving out the latter clause, to-wit, "*and that the assent of the national legislature ought not to be required thereto*," so that it was made to read as follows:

Art. 19. "On application of the legislatures of two-thirds of the states in the union for the amendment of this constitution, the legislature of the United States shall call a convention for that purpose." ‡

This draft of the constitution, after some changes as to other parts of it, was referred to a committee of re-

---

* McCulloch v. Maryland, 4 Wheat, 416.
† Elliott's Debates, vol. I, p. 145.   ‡ Ibid., p. 230.

vision, known as the committee on style, and that committee changed this article by attempting to insert in it a power not agreed to by the convention, and which it was doubtful that the convention would agree to.

As Hon. Gouverneur Morris of that committee claimed to have rewritten the whole of the constitution, and to have made some changes in it, to him personally may be ascribed the entire credit of the apparent confusion in this article. As he was so zealous an advocate of establishing a sovereign government, which could not possibly be done, as long as the states had authority to alter, amend or change the whole plan of its powers and duties, it may be that the confused form the authority to amend the constitution appears in, was intentional on his part. But by so covering that addition to the article he left uncovered the provision agreed to by the committee of the whole, of the convention, to-wit, that the states, or the people thereof, should have the right to amend the articles of the federal union without the assent of the congress, or of any other department or officer of the federal union thereto.

To have given to the congress and the state legislatures authority to enlarge the powers of the congress, or to reduce the powers of the congress, would have transferred the sovereign authority from the people to them, and would have established all that is claimed by the nationalist; for that would have vested the United States congress with sovereign authority, and consequently have divested the people of it.

Conventions being the only organs through which the sovereign people express their sovereign will, whatever amendments to the constitution may be proposed by a federal convention; changing the form of the government, or its powers; or the race of people to constitute the national family, must be acted on by conventions of the states, and not by the legislatures of the states, as claimed by the late Justice Story, in his Commentaries on the Federal Constitution.*

Suppose, after the legislatures of two-thirds of the states had called for a federal convention, the congress should neglect to call it. That duty being a mere ministerial one, could the states go on and hold the convention without its being called by the congress? I think they could ; at all events, should the states hold the convention and propose amendments, which would afterward be ratified by conventions in three-fourths of the states, there is no authority in the union that could nullify the amendments so made to the constitution.

The representatives in the congress being elected every two years, there is no probability that the members thereof would either fail or refuse to perform a plainly-declared duty under the constitution, especially if there was a reasonable hope of the amendments desired to be proposed by the federal convention being ratified by conventions in three-fourths of the states.

On the other hand, suppose the congress should desire to enlarge its own powers by amendments to be proposed by two-thirds of each house thereof, with a hope of having them ratified by the legislatures of three-fourths of the states, the legislatures of the states would not be likely to ratify them unless extraordinary influence could be brought to bear on them. This was done in reconstructing the states on the southern side of the late civil war, and it must be admitted that such amendments were accomplished by coercive means ; that an entire revolution of the American system of government would

---

* Story's Com. on Con., Sec. 1832.

have resulted but for a conservative judiciary, who prevented it by interpretation.

Or suppose the wealthy citizens of the country should desire to change the federal republic into an aristocracy of wealth, and provide for perpetuating their wealth in their own families. After influencing the congress to propose such amendments as they wanted, they might seek to control the election of the legislatures in enough states to ratify their amendments, by the skillful use of money in buying up the public newspapers, and engaging the services of able speakers to stump the states to be carried against the will of the people ; or they might induce the congress to take control of elections in the several states under pretense of regulating the election of representatives to the congress, and presidential electors, and deprive those citizens who were opposed to the revolution from voting, and in that way carry the election of representatives to the legislature, and by either mode secure enough of the states to ratify the amendments to the constitution.

If the congress and the legislatures of the states are authorized to so amend the constitution as to change the form of the government, the action of the congress and the legislatures of the states would be political in character, and therefore beyond the reach of the judiciary department, and there would be no remedy except in resorting to the great principle set forth in the Declaration of Independence, of exercising the right of the people to change their government at will.

The proviso that no amendments, prior to the year 1808, affecting the first and fourth clauses of the ninth section of the first article relates to the importation of African slaves, and has become obsolete by the thirteenth, fourteenth and fifteenth amendments to the constitution, as well as by the lapse of time.

304 CONSTITUTION OF THE UNITED STATES.

The second proviso, to-wit: "No state without its consent shall be deprived of its equal suffrage in the senate," still stands in full force and effect, and the constitution can not be so amended as to deprive any state of its equal suffrage in the senate, even by the sovereign people themselves without the consent of the state to be deprived thereof.

This provision is not as clear as it might have been made, it was never contemplated that any state could remain in the union without equal suffrage in the senate, either with or without its consent; but it was thought that some of the small states might prefer to consolidate themselves into one larger state, as provided in section three of article four, providing that "no new state shall be formed by the junction of two or more states without the consent of the legislatures of the states concerned, as well as of the congress."

Two states may consent to be merged into each other, and thereby be formed into a new state, which would necessarily cause one or the other to lose its equal representation in the senate; but as long as each remains a separate state, they must each be represented equally in the senate, as provided in section three of article one; and no state can change that provision by consent or otherwise.

Nor can all of the other states combine and deprive any one of the states of that equal suffrage in the senate as long as the constitution is adhered to.

"State," as used in this connection, means the political organization of the states.

ARTICLE VI.

Par. 1. "All debts contracted and engagements entered into, before the adoption of this constitution, shall be as valid against the United States under this constitution as under the confederation."

Par. 2. "This constitution and the laws of the United States, which shall be made in pursuance thereof, and all treaties made, or which shall be made, under authority of the United States, shall be the supreme law of the land; and the judges in every state shall be bound thereby, any thing in the constitution or laws of any state to the contrary notwithstanding."

Par. 3. "The senators and representatives, before mentioned, and the members of the several state legislatures, and all executive and judicial officers, both of the United States and of the several states, shall be bound by oath or affirmation to support this constitution, but no religious test shall ever be required as a qualification to any office or public trust under the United States."

The second and third paragraphs of this article so forcibly bear on the judicial powers that they were considered somewhat at length in the comments on the judiciary department; they however perform so important a part in construing the constitution that they should be considered more minutely, although it may cause a repetition of some of the thoughts heretofore expressed.

The first paragraph of this article assumes all of the debts or engagements of the confederation, and makes them debts and engagements of the more perfect union.

It is however true, the jurisdiction of the United States was extended by the constitution to other subjects of government and their taxing powers greatly increased, to enable them the better to provide for maintaining the governmental agency of the union and its general welfare, and to enable the officials to discharge their duties and trusts as public agents.

306 CONSTITUTION OF THE UNITED STATES.

By a well-established rule of international law a change in the form of government does not relieve the nation of its debts and engagements ; hence the debts and obligation of the confederation were in law obligations of the more perfect union. The government is not the nation, but simply the organ through which the nation expresses its will ; therefore every debt or engagement of the United States under their government as a confederation would remain debts and engagements of whatever government might have been formed ; hence the assuming of the debts and engagements of the confederation was no more than the United States were compelled to do. Furthermore, in the change from the confederation to the more perfect union each state that had constituted a part of the confederation became a member of the more perfect union without changing the character of the government from a federal republic, and without changing the name from that of "The United States of America," and without changing the people who composed the states of the union ; hence the United States under the new organization were bound to assume the debts and engagements of the confederation.

The second paragraph of this article makes the constitution, laws made in pursuance thereof, and all treaties made and to be made, the supreme law of the land. Laws made in pursuance of the constitution necessarily consist of laws that aid in putting it into practical operation, and differ widely from laws made under authority thereof ; the latter being laws that are authorized by the constitution, though not required to give that instrument force and effect. In one case the congress is in duty bound to pass the law to aid in the execution of the constitution, while in the other case the congress exercises its discretion. The laws made in pursuance of the constitution, treaties made or that may be made under authority of the United States, and the constitution itself, are declared to constitute the supreme law of the land ; and "the judges in every state shall be bound thereby, any thing in the constitution or laws of any state to the contrary notwithstanding."

This has been construed by the Supreme Court of the United States to include all laws enacted by the congress under or in conformity with the constitution, whether made in pursuance of that instrument, or made by authority thereof. The supreme court having appellate jurisdiction of all cases arising under any law enacted by the congress, that interpretation must stand until it shall be overruled by that court.

To more clearly bring the distinction between laws passed in pursuance of the constitution, and such as are enacted under or by permission thereof, it should be borne in mind that there are powers that are exclusively within the jurisdiction of the states, and there are powers of which the states and the United States are vested with concurrent jurisdiction. Among this character of powers there appears in the fourth article the following :

"Full faith and credit shall be given in each state to the public acts, records, and judicial proceedings of every other state. *And the congress may by general laws prescribe the manner in which such acts, records and proceedings shall be proved, and the effect thereof.*"

The several states being vested with eminent domain over the lands within their respective boundaries, and each state being authorized to construct its own government, and organize its own judiciary, and make its own local laws, each state must have authority to prescribe the evidences of title to the lands therein, the evidence of the public acts and how they shall pass and be proven, and determine which of the courts thereof shall constitute courts of record, and how the official acts of each shall be shown.

In each of these particulars, the courts of the respective states, as well as the supreme court of the United States, recognizes the laws of the respective states as the paramount law on these subjects, notwithstanding the act of congress may, and in many instances does, conflict with the state law relating thereto.

There are other instances wherein the jurisdiction of the states and of the federal union are concurrent, where the state law is permitted to prevail over the federal law, which might be shown.

But this is regarded as sufficient to prove that there is a broad distinction between laws passed in pursuance to the constitution and the laws passed under that instrument.

All treaties made or to be made under authority of the United States are declared to be the supreme law of the land; but treaties are the only character of laws made under authority of the United States that are declared to be the supreme law, and no other laws made under or by the permission of the constitution are to be regarded as any part of the supreme law.

As shown in considering the judiciary, this paragraph also expressly requires the judges of the state courts to be bound by the constitution and laws of the United States made in pursuance thereof, and by all treaties made and to be made under authority of the United States, as the supreme law of the land, etc.

This provision refers to the judges of the state courts in their official capacity, and was intended to bind them as judicial officers in the discharge of their judicial duties; for a subsequent paragraph of this article requires the judges of the state courts, in conjunction with all state and federal officers, to take an oath to support the constitution. This paragraph, therefore, can only apply to the office of the judges of the state courts, and requires them *as judges* to be bound. They must, therefore, exercise a judicial discretion in ascertaining the meaning of the different provisions of the constitution, also a judicial discretion in ascertaining whether the law they may be called on to obey was made in pursuance of the constitution, and also a judicial discretion in ascertaining whether the treaties they may be called on to obey were made under authority of the United States; and should the judges of the state courts find that the treaties were not made under authority of the United States, or that the laws involved were not made in pursuance of the constitution, they could not treat them as any part of the supreme law of the land without disregarding their oaths of office; and they must interpret the constitution for themselves, and can not rely on the supreme court of the United States to interpret that instrument for them.

It is claimed by the nationalist that the last clause of this second paragraph was intended to put at rest all possible danger of any conflict between the judiciary of the states and that of the United States. But the first clause of this paragraph declares what shall be the supreme law of the land, and the third paragraph requires the judges of the state courts, and all other officers of the states, and of the United States, to be bound by oath or affirmation to support the constitution, which necessarily includes all laws made in pursuance of the constitution; and all treaties made, or to be made, especially as the organization of the judiciary of the United States gives to the supreme court appellate jurisdiction of all

cases arising under the constitution ; laws made by the
congress ; treaties made by authority of the United
States ; controversies between citizens of different states,
etc., render it impossible for any conflict between the
jurisdiction of the state and federal courts, without said
provision.   So that it was a senseless and idle provision,
unless it was intended to perform some other function,
and it must therefore be construed to have vested the
state courts with judicial discretion, *not* to prevent possible conflicts between the state and federal courts.

Some light may be drawn from the proceedings of the
convention on this subject.

This provision, as adopted by the committee of the
whole, and as prepared by the committee on detail, in
transforming it from a resolution to a provision of the
constitution, differed from the wording of it by the committee on style.   The resolution was :

7. " *Resolved*, That the legislative acts of the United
States, made by virtue and in pursuance of the articles
of union, and all treaties made and ratified under the
authority of the United States, shall be the supreme
law of the respective states, as far as those acts or
treaties shall relate to the said states or their citizens and
inhabitants ; and that the judiciaries of the several
states shall be bound thereby in their decisions any thing
in the respective laws of the individual states to the contrary notwithstanding."*

This resolution, in conjunction with the other resolutions to go into the constitution, were put into the hands
of a committee to reduce them to proper forms as constitutional provisions, known as the committee of detail.

That committee made no change in the substance,

* Elliott's Debates. vol. I, p. 221.

though it changed the language somewhat so as to read as follows :

Art. 8. "The acts of the legislature of the United States made in pursuance of this constitution, and all treaties made under the authority of the United States, shall be the supreme law of the several states, and of their citizens and inhabitants ; and the judges in the several states shall be bound thereby in their decisions, any thing in the constitutions or laws of the several states to the contrary notwithstanding."*

It is clear from the foregoing quotation that the judges of the states were expected to interpret the constitution and ascertain whether a law was made in pursuance of the constitution, and also to ascertain if a treaty was made under authority of the United States.

It will be remembered, however, that at the time that provision was agreed to by the convention, the organization of the judiciary department did not vest jurisdiction in the federal court of actions arising under the constitution ; it was changed by the committee on style, or rather by the Hon. Gouverneur Morris, and as that change was made, it was necessary to change this paragraph also, but failing to change the paragraph under consideration, it stands in flagrant conflict with the organization of the judiciary department, and sustains Messrs. Jefferson, Jackson and Lincoln in denying that the supreme court was vested with exclusive authority to finally interpret the constitution.

Doubtless the Hon. Gouverneur Morris overlooked the conflict he was leaving against his hope of giving the supreme court such autocratic powers, as exclusive authority to finally interpret the federal constitution must

---

* Elliott's Debates, vol. 1, p. 227.

have vested it with. Or he feared that so radical a change "would alarm others or shock their self-love."

If the organization of the judiciary of the United States had remained as it was agreed to by the convention, and as expressed by the committee on detail, the constitution would have been above the Supreme Court of the United States, as well as above every other department of the United States, and of the states; and not subject to be changed or modified by interpretation by the supreme court.

As originally drafted the constitution could not be changed by interpretation by any of the departments, or any tribunal, except the sovereign people in sovereign conventions; therefore, all courts were compelled to give to that instrument their own construction, and it was highly important to designate what should constitute the supreme law, and to require the judges of the state courts to be bound thereby.

The language of this paragraph, as well as that used in the various provisions of the constitution bearing on the subject, shows that it vests the judiciary of the several states with authority to construe the constitution and determine for themselves whether any act of the congress be in pursuance of the constitution or simply authorized by it; and to determine whether any treaty was made under authority of the United States. However, since the change put into the constitution, giving to the Supreme Court of the United States "jurisdiction of all cases arising under the constitution or laws of congress," and since the supreme court so interprets the constitution as to authorize it to finally interpret that instrument and holds that every law passed by the congress shall constitute parts of the supreme law, the distinction between laws passed in pursuance of the constitution and those passed by authority thereof is made wholly unavailing.

As the United States constitutes a part of the governmental machinery of the states, they constitute a part of the governmental machinery of the United States ; every officer of each of the states, as well as those of the United States, ought to be required to take an oath to support the constitution of the United States.

ARTICLE VII.

"The ratification of the conventions of nine states shall be sufficient for the establishment of this constitution between the states so ratifying the same."

It should be remembered that this constitution was formed under authority of the confederation. An attempt was made to call or convene a confederate convention of delegates from the states, but that effort fell through. Afterward the congress of the confederation called a convention according to authority contained in the articles thereof to meet in Philadelphia, and it was in that convention and under that authority the states sent delegates to amend the articles thereof, to make them adequate to the exigencies of government and the better to preserve the union.

The Articles of Confederation, or the Constitution of 1777, as it was frequently called, expressly declared that the states should retain all of their sovereignty and jurisdiction as free and independent states.*

As sovereign states, each had a right to speak and act for itself in all matters relating to any changes in its form of government or its relations to other sovereignties; for, being sovereign, its will was supreme, and

---

* Articles 2 and 3, Confederation.

could not be limited. However, sovereign nations or states may bind themselves by voluntary engagements, by treaties, or compacts of union, without parting with their respective sovereignty.*

The states, in forming the compact of union under the Articles of Confederation, obligated themselves to abide by acts of the United States in the congress assembled, on all questions committed to the congress by the articles thereof ; and, as provided in said articles, agreed that the union should be perpetual unless changed by the congress and afterward confirmed by the legislature of every state.†

It will also be observed that at the time the constitution was constructed the states were sovereign, and must have continued so until altered by the adoption of the new constitution, if in fact the new constitution had the effect of changing the relation of the states to the union.

The congress, instead of proposing specific amendments to the articles of confederation, called a convention to propose them ; that convention was approved of by the legislatures of the states, as manifested in the appointment of delegates thereto. That convention changed the character of the confederation, not only by enlarging the powers thereof, but changed it from a confederation of the political corporation of the several states only, to a confederation including the sovereign people of the several states, so that (as shown in second chapter), under the Constitution of 1787, the union consists of a confederation of both the political corporations of the states and of the sovereign people of the several states. When the new constitution was completed by the convention, it

---

* Vattell's Law of Nations, Book I, Chap. 1, Sec. 10.
† Article 8, Confederation.

was reported to the congress, which approved it and referred it to the legislatures of the several states, with the recommendation that they call conventions respectively to ratify the same, as had been advised by the convention. The legislatures manifested their approval of it by calling conventions in their respective states to ratify the same ; and the states, in conventions consisting of delegates chosen by the people thereof for the express purpose of considering the provisions of the new constitution, with authority from the people themselves to ratify the same if approved by the said delegates. The delegates in said conventions in each of said states ratified the new constitution in the order of time, and with recommendation of the amendments thereto as shown in the second chapter of this review.

CHAPTER X.

RELATES TO THE AMENDMENTS TO THE CONSTITUTION.

ARTICLE I.

"Congress shall make no law respecting an establishment of religion, or prohibiting the free exercise thereof; or abridging the freedom of speech, or of the press; or the right of the people peaceably to assemble, and to petition the government for redress of grievances."

The provisions of the whole of this article are included within the spirit of the constitution, and if the United States government be considered as a mere agent of the states and people thereof, and a part of the government of each of the states, the congress can exercise no powers except those that are granted to it by the constitution, and neither of the powers expressly prohibited to the congress by this article is included in any grant of power to the congress by the constitution. Without the prohibitions contained in this article, the congress could not exercise either of the powers named without violating the constitution. However, the rights sought to be protected by the provisions of this article were held so dear to the people of the respective states, that the congress was expressly prohibited from interfering with them. In each of the states these powers were reserved to the people, and withheld from the grant of powers to their respective states in a bill of rights. There being no bill of rights connected with the constitution of the United States, this article and the other nine articles, ratified at the same time, it was hoped, in a measure, would supply its place.

That the congress should have authority to establish a national religion is so repugnant to free government and religious liberty, that it needs no argument to show the importance of expressly prohibiting the exercise of that power.   And authority in congress to abridge the freedom of speech or of the press, would arm the congress with power to distroy the freedom of the people, and enable it to mount over other barriers or checks placed upon it by the other provisions of the constitution : hence the prohibitions contained in this article can not be too highly esteemed.

However, notwithstanding this provision of the constitution, the congress in 1798 passed what was familiarly known as the alien and sedition acts.   Which declared it to be unlawful for any individual, or publisher of a newspaper, to speak or publish offensive language of or concerning the president or any of his cabinet, or any public officer, and prescribed a punishment, by fine and imprisonment.

That act soon passed out of favor, and was so heartily condemned by the American people as to become a dead letter before it expired by limitation.   Justice Chase, of the supreme court, who more harshly than either of the other justices executed said law, was arraigned for impeachment, not so much for executing that act as for his coarseness in executing it, and indulging in political bias while on the bench, particularly in his charges to the juries.   The impeachment failed on account of his services in the Revolutionary War and in the organization of the government.   The alien and sedition act is now held to be repugnant to the constitution by the American people generally, though during the late civil war the papers that published news favorable to the rebellion were suppressed, in flagrant violation of this article of amendment to the constitution.

ARTICLE II.

"A well-regulated militia being necessary to the security of a free state, the right of the people to keep and bear arms shall not be infringed."

The third paragraph of section 10, article I, of the constitution, prohibiting the states from keeping troops, or ships of war, in time of peace, and the provisions of paragraphs 13, 14 and 15, of section 8, of article I, giving to the United States authority to regulate the land and naval forces, and to provide for calling out the militia, and of organizing, arming, and disciplining the same, made it necessary to qualify those provisions, by this article of amendment to the constitution, to enable the states to maintain a militia.

ARTICLE III.

"No soldier shall, in time of peace, be quartered in any house without the consent of the owner, nor in time of war but in a manner to be prescribed by law."

The quartering of the soldiers in the houses of the citizens has been resorted to by tyrants to discover the patriots who love their country more than their ruler, to vent his spleen on, and to show his power to the people, by punishing those patriots, to hold others in such awe as to prevent them from rebelling against his usurped powers.

But, furthermore, power to quarter troops in the houses of the citizens, is utterly inconsistent with the sacredness with which the home government and the security of the home castle are held under the laws of all English speaking people. And power to quarter troops in one's house at a time he does not want them there, not only curtails his liberties, but infringes on his right to use his own property as he pleases, in a lawful way.

This article, therefore, was necessary, not only to quiet the fears of the people, but as a limitation on the power of the public officials, and as security against changing the character of the government by gradual usurpations.

ARTICLE IV.

"The right of the people to be secure in their persons, houses, papers and effects, against unreasonable searches and seizures, shall not be violated ; and no warrants shall issue but upon probable cause, supported by oath or affirmation, and particularly describing the place to be searched and the persons or things to be seized."

This article, like the third, guards the people against the use of probable forces to aid the officials in enforcing usurped powers, should they become corrupt enough to desire a change in the government, by searching for evidences of what they might term treason on the part of patriotic citizens to deter others from asserting their rights and liberties as secured by the constitution. But, to be subject to be searched by arrogant officials, clothed with small official powers, would be extremely annoying and insulting to one's family as well as to himself ; still, where one is suspected of concealing persons or things unlawfully, and there are reasonable grounds for that suspicion, backed by oath or affirmation of the guilt of the accused, the authority to search is granted in this article by a negative pregnant ; for the provision against unreasonable searches grants the right to make reasonable searches, when applied for under oath or affirmation of the guilt of the accused.

This article is also valuable to allay apprehensions of unreasonable searches, and to protect the people against their use to aid in changing the form of government, and to prevent the people from being oppressed by corrupt officials.

ARTICLE V.

"No person shall be held to answer for a capital or otherwise infamous crime, unless on a presentment or indictment of a grand jury, except in cases arising in the land or naval forces, or in the militia when in actual service, in time of war or public danger; nor shall any person be subject, for the same offense, to be twice put in jeopardy of life or limb; nor shall be compelled in any criminal case to be a witness against himself, nor be deprived of life, liberty, or property without due process of law; nor shall private property be taken for public use without just compensation."

This article contains as important guards to the liberties of the people as any provision in the constitution.

As no one can be punished for a capital or otherwise infamous crime, unless on a presentment or indictment by a grand jury, and in addition to the presentment or indictment of a grand jury there must be a verdict of a trial or petit jury, and conviction of the guilt of those accused of capital or otherwise infamous crime, as shown by the sixth article of amendment, which is as follows:

ARTICLE VI.

"In all criminal prosecutions the accused shall enjoy the right to a speedy and public trial, by an impartial jury of the state and district wherein the crime shall have been committed, which district shall have been previously ascertained by law; and to be informed of the nature and cause of the accusation; to be confronted with the witnesses against him; to have compulsory process for obtaining witnesses in his favor, and to have the assistance of counsel for his defense."

Therefore, an accused not only is entitled to the indictment or presentment of a grand jury, and a verdict of a petit jury, but he is entitled to a speedy and public trial; and can not be tried in a prison or bastile which has been a cradle or nursery for so much tyranny and mischief in the world. In our mother country persons had been put in prisons on spurious charges for political purposes, and held there without a trial, or when granted a trial it was conducted in the prison in the presence only of the minions of the tyrant, often private enemies of the prisoner.

These two articles supported by the second paragraph of section nine of article one of the constitution, providing for the writ of *habeas corpus* renders it utterly impossible to deny to any one a speedy and fair trial before a jury of his own state and district.

These rights are again strengthened by the eighth article of amendment, which provides that excessive bail shall not be required. This, of course, applies only to bailable cases. These articles of amendment, to wit, the fourth, fifth, sixth, and eighth, include the necessary provisions for the protection of the personal liberties of the citizens not contained in the constitution, as it was when originally adopted by the states, and as long as they are respected and observed, it will be impossible for the public officials to rise above the people; for no one can be either denied or shielded from a speedy public trial, before an impartial jury of the state and district in which the crime shall have been committed. As said in discussing the judiciary, the shielding of any one from such a trial, without extending that protection to all, is a denial of equal protection to those not so shielded, and society has as much right to enforce justice as the accused has to demand it. Indeed, there is more danger to the liberties of the people in shielding a class of offenders from a speedy public trial by a jury of their state and district, than can arise out of a denial of such a trial to any one; because, the

precedent of shielding from justice lays the foundation for
the establishment of privileged classes, in repugnance to
civil liberty; for civil liberty can not exist on any other
foundation than equality of rights and immunities between
all citizens.   That the congress has violated these fundamental principles in divers ways we are constrained to
admit, notably, among the instances in which they were
ignored, are : first, the passage of the alien and sedition
acts ; second, the passage of what is known as the fugitive slave acts, protecting civil officers against trial and
punishment for violating state laws, although they could
not be tried for capital or otherwise infamous crimes
committed in any state, by the federal judiciary or any
tribunal of the United States.   If the congress had authorized the fugitive slave law to be executed by the
military arm of the United States, the soldiers could have
been tried and punished for any offense committed under
orders of superior officers, by court martial of the United
States, although the crime may have been committed entirely in any one of the states, and by the United States
authority, it would have been excusable in shielding them
from punishment under state laws, enacted by the states
while in rebellion against the United States.   For every
federal law, whether it be a provision of the constitution
or an act of congress passed in pursuance thereof, constitutes a part of the supreme law of the land, and the state
judges are bound by it, and whenever a state passes a law
in conflict therewith for the purpose of preventing the
federal laws being executed, such state would be in rebellion against the United States, to that extent at least.

The Supreme Court of the United States not only sustains the validity of that act of congress, but carries it
far enough to cover cases of those who, while acting
under orders of the president, wantonly take human life,
and as shown in a former chapter of this review, actually

shielded one Mr. Neagle, who shot and killed Ex-Chief Justice Terry of the State of California, from a trial before the courts of that state, although said Naegle could not be tried in any court or before any tribunal of the United States, because the crime had been committed entirely within that state.

These cases are sufficient to show a gradual taking away of the most valuable limitations in the constitution by the public officials.

ARTICLE VII.

"In suits at common law, where the value in controversy shall exceed twenty dollars, the right of trial by jury shall be preserved ; and no fact tried by a jury shall be otherwise re-examined in any court of the United States, than according to the rules of the common law."

This article has been made use of to indicate an intention on the part of the makers of the constitution, to vest the federal courts with a common law jurisdiction ; but the only function that this article can reasonably be made to perform on that subject, is to prescribe the mode of re-examining cases in the federal courts ; and the federal court should look alone to the organization of the judiciary to ascertain the jurisdiction thereof. Suppose this article could be twisted into vesting the federal courts with a common law jurisdiction ; it may well be inquired what common law they would have jurisdiction of ; and if it is claimed that they were thereby vested with the jurisdiction of the common law of England, a pertinent inquiry arises as to what part of the common law of England, for much of the common law of England relates to the king and royal family, and to a distinction between what is known in that country as the nobility and the common people ; and, surely, it will not be contended that this article inaugurates the English distinctions in society, or that it establishes a royal family, or a king.* But if this article be interpreted so as to make it refer to the common law of the respective states, as modified by the statute of each individual state in which a suit may arise, and to be enforced in the state adopting the same, there is no conflict between its provisions and the other part of the federal constitution. The common law of the states in which any suit may arise and be prosecuted, should alone be enforced therein by the federal courts. For, by the rules of the common law, as modified by the statutes of the state in which a contract may be made, always constitutes a part of the contract itself, and without considering the laws existing at the time to interpret, it would be utterly impossible to correctly decide on the right of the parties to any contract.

Adopting this interpretation of this article, it provides valuable protection to each citizen who may sue or be sued in a federal court against the arbitrary rulings of an autocractic judge, by securing to them a jury to try their controversies according to the rules of law in the state where the contract was made, in all cases where the amount in controversy shall be twenty dollars, or upwards.

ARTICLE VIII.

"Excessive bail shall not be required, nor shall excessive fines be imposed, nor cruel and unusual punishment inflicted."

These eight articles of amendment to the constitution contain limitations on the United States, and its departments, of a highly valuable character, though they are not the only limitations thereon ; for that instrument constitutes limitations on all powers granted, and excludes all powers not granted from the jurisdiction of the United

---

* Par. 8, Sec. 9, Art. 1, Con.

States. So that the greatest limitations on the United States consist in the failure to grant powers to them.

The government is like attorneys, in fact, who have no powers unless they be embraced within their letters of attorneys ; the United States, or the departments thereof, have no powers unless the grant can be found in the federal constitution, which is the letter of attorney given by the people to them.

Because of a rule of interpretation to the effect that the enumeration of specified rights reserved to the people might be held in particular cases to exclude other rights not expressed, the ninth article was adopted, as follows :

ARTICLE IX.

" The enumeration in the constitution of certain rights shall not be construed to deny or disparage others retained by the people."

This article entirely does away with that rule of interpretation. Therefore the naming of limitations on certain powers has the effect of emphasizing and strengthening the prohibition against the exercise of the named powers, without affecting the reserved powers.

But the amendments to the constitution do not stop at the ninth article of amendment, but go further, and by the tenth article of amendment settle all doubts about the reserved powers, which is in the following language :

ARTICLE X.

" The powers not delegated to the United States by the constitution, nor prohibited by it to the states, are reserved to the states respectively, or to the people."

I have referred to this article frequently in this review, and deem it useless to say more about it in this connection, than that it is utterly impossible to give to it any force at all, unless it serves to require a strict construction of the constitution; for as heretofore contended, the constitution speaks only by the language thereof; therefore it is impossible to delegate powers by it to the United States otherwise than by express language, particularly as all powers not delegated to the United States by the constitution, nor prohibited by it to the states, are expressly reserved to the states respectively, or to the people.

How can the powers delegated to the United States by the constitution be distinguished from those that are expressly reserved to the states respectively, or to the people, except by the letter of the constitution?

The supreme court, in the case of McCulloch v. State of Maryland, and in the case of Gibbons v. Ogden, heretofore quoted and referred to, in the consideration of the organization of the judiciary department, admitted that if there was any thing in the constitution of 1787 like the provision in the constitution of 1777, requiring the constitution of 1787 to be strictly construed, the interpretation given to that instrument in those two cases would not have been authorized by the constitution; hence that court could not have noticed this article of the constitution.

ARTICLE XI.

"The judicial power of the United States shall not be construed to extend to any suit in law or equity commenced or prosecuted against one of the United States by citizens of another state, or by citizens or subjects of any foreign state."

At a very early period in the history of the United States, the supreme court, by a divided court, held the United States to be a sovereign nation, and on that theory took jurisdiction of suits brought against several of the states by individual citizens of other states, or by subjects or citizens of foreign states. The argument of some of the judges composing the majority of that court, in the case of Chisholm v. The State of Georgia, would lead to depriving the states and the people of all sovereign authority, and ultimately vesting the whole of that authority in the United States. To avoid that tendency, and to avoid the annoyance to the states, said eleventh article of amendment to the constitution was proposed by the third congress, on the 5th of September, 1794, and was declared by a message from the president to the congress, dated 8th of January, 1798, to have been ratified by the legislatures of three-fourths of the states.

This article of amendment takes away from the federal courts jurisdiction of all cases wherein any individual may be the plaintiff against the state. The jurisdiction of the federal courts never extended to controversies between citizens of the same state, or the citizens thereof and their own state, so that should the supreme court, by its interpretation of the constitution, reduce the states to artificial persons, as other corporations are held, still the federal courts could not take jurisdiction of controversies to which a state may be a party, unless the controversy shall be between two or more states; because this eleventh article of amendment expressly takes away from the federal court jurisdiction of suits against the states by citizens of another state, or citizens or subjects of any foreign state; and the constitutional provision, in constituting the judiciary department, *does not vest* the federal judiciary with jurisdiction of controversies between citizens of the same state, nor between any state and its own citizens.

To have vested the federal judiciary with jurisdiction of controversies between any state and its own citizens would have completely destroyed the federal principle

and the power of the states to maintain their home
government.

In the formation of the constitution, no new powers
were delegated to the states, though the states were, by
that instrument, limited in the exercise of powers that
they were vested with under the articles of confederation,
which was necessary, in order to enlarge the powers of
the United States sufficiently to make them adequate to
the exigencies of government.

It was not only necessary to take certain powers from
the states to be given to the federal union, but certain
other powers were necessarily taken from the states which
were not given to the union but reserved to the people.
Section ten of article I was thought sufficient to define
all of this class of powers; but by a refinement of legal
reasoning, it was feared that the enumeration of certain
rights, whether granted to the United States, or those that
were prohibited to the states, or those reserved to the
states or to the people, might be interpreted to grant
greater powers to the union than was intended. To
settle that danger the ninth article of amendment provides that the enumeration of certain rights shall not be
construed to disparage other rights reserved to the people; and the tenth article of amendment provides that all
powers not delegated to the United States nor prohibited
to the states by the constitution, are reserved to the
states respectively or to the people, which ought to allay
every doubt on the subject, and require every grant of
power to the United States to be strictly construed, as
hereinbefore contended.

The state governments had absolute control over their
own citizens while they were acting as subjects thereof,
though, while acting as sovereigns, they had absolute
control over the governments or corporations thereof;
and neither of these rights was granted by the constitu-

tion of the United States, nor prohibited by that instrument to the states; consequently, they were expressly reserved to the states respectively or to the people.

The governments of the states are but corporations of limited powers defined by the constitution thereof, and the Supreme Court of the United States in the case of McCulloch v. The State of Maryland, before quoted, held the United States are sovereign in respect to the powers granted to them, and that the state governments are sovereign in respect to the powers reserved to them; yet that would not authorize the United States to take jurisdiction of engagements entered into by the states in the exercise of their sovereign authority under their constitution; unless it was possible for one sovereign to be under the control of another sovereign, which is utterly impossible. For if sovereignty is supreme and beyond control, except to the extent it may voluntarily obligate itself, no sovereign authority can be made subject to the control of another sovereignty, without destroying its sovereignty. This ought to have guided the supreme court, without the eleventh article of amendment to the constitution, but that court seems not even to have submitted to the limitations imposed on it by this eleventh article of amendment, for, beginning with the Dartmouth College case, it has invariably adhered to the theory that private corporations granted by a state constitutes contracts, and that the states can not impair the obligation of those contracts.

It must be conceded that no state can impair the obligations of contracts made under any law of such state, between citizens of any state of the union, or between citizens of this country and citizens or subjects of foreign nations. But any state may not only impair the obligation of its own contracts, but it may repudiate any contract it may make, and there is no power in the United States to pre-

vent it, but, as before shown, the states have gotten rid
of a large part of the evil effects of that ruling of the
supreme court, by reserving the right by a general statute,
or a provision of the constitution thereof, requiring all
charters to private corporations to be subject to alteration,
amendment or repeal, at the option of the state.   So that
the purposes of this eleventh article of amendment to the
constitution is now practically executed, though not recognized to its full extent as a part of the constitution.

The first ten articles of amendment to the constitution
were required by the states, and would have been attached to the several ordinances adopting the constitution as conditions precedent, but for the fact that such
conditions would have been worded in different language
by each state, and would have been an impediment to putting the constitution into operation ; therefore, the friends
of the constitution assured those who opposed the adoption of it as it was, that the required changes by the states
should be proposed by the first congress, and submitted
to the state legislatures for ratification.   The congress in
good faith proposed twelve amendments, but the state
legislatures failing to ratify the first two, the last ten only
became part of the constitution.

As before stated, the eleventh amendment was prompted
by suits against the states by citizens of other states, and
aliens.

ARTICLE XII.

The twelfth article of amendment, relating to the election of president and vice-president, has been given and
fully discussed in the chapter on the executive department.

ARTICLE XIII.

Sec. 1. "Neither slavery nor involuntary servitude,
except as a punishment for crime whereof the party shall

have been duly convicted, shall exist within the United States, or any place subject to their jurisdiction."

Sec. 2. "Congress shall have power to enforce this article by appropriate legislation."

This article was proposed by the thirty-eighth congress on the 1st of February, 1865, and was declared, in a proclamation of the secretary of state, dated the 18th of December, 1865, to have been ratified by the legislatures of twenty-seven of the thirty-six states, viz.: Illinois, Rhode Island, Michigan, Maryland, New York, West Virginia, Maine, Kansas, Massachusetts, Pennsylvania, Virginia, Ohio, Missouri, Nevada, Indiana, Louisiana, Minnesota, Wisconsin, Vermont, Tennessee, Arkansas, Connecticut, New Hampshire, South Carolina, Alabama, North Carolina and Georgia.

The evident object of this article of amendment to the constitution was to abolish the institution of slavery throughout the United States. As all of the states were responsible for that institution, each state being bound to deliver up fugitive slaves, on claim, to their owners as shown in the third paragraph of section two of article four of the constitution ; and as property in slaves was an artificial right, *not* a natural right, there ought to be some way for the states to withdraw their support from that institution.   But there was no way for them to do so provided in the constitution, consequently it could not be done except by the exercise of the sovereign authority of the people of the several states, and the only organ through which the people can express their sovereign will is a sovereign convention. The federal convention alone could propose such a radical change in the government, and the state conventions are the only organs through which the sovereign will of the people can be expressed in ratification of such a change. It is, however, true that the congress may propose amendments which, when ratified by the legislatures of three-fourths of the states, shall become parts of the constitution. But when we reflect that the United States consists of a union of the sovereign people of the several states, and also of a union of the political organizations of the several states, and that both the United States, and the several states, are but agents of the people of the several states, and neither of said agents has any powers except those that were delegated to them respectively by the people, their powers to amend the constitution must necessarily be limited to changes within the scope of the powers granted to them ; therefore, they can not change the character of the government, nor enlarge its powers, nor relieve it of any of the duties imposed on it by the sovereign authority. However, as all of the former slave states have changed their respective constitutions, and abolished the institution of slavery no difficulty can ever arise on this point ; still it is necessary to know how far the congress and the state legislatures can go in amending the constitution ; whether they can abolish any species of property in a state desiring to maintain it ; and if they can abolish property in birds or dogs, or in animals *feræ naturæ* that have been made property of by the state ; and whether, if they can abolish the rights of property in such animals, can it be done without compensation being paid to the owners for them, as was done in the abolition of slavery?

The right of property in slaves was by the constitution required to be recognized by every state in the union, and it is provided that private property shall not be taken for public use without just compensation in the fifth article of amendments ; but this thirteenth article of amendment was proposed and ratified at a time when the people adhering to the union were excited and desired to punish those who had taken part in the rebellion, and but little attention was paid to the constitution, or the rights of the states or the people thereof, and no provision was made to compensate the owners of the slave property. This breach of the constitution has also been adjusted by the states, in amendments to their respective constitutions abolishing slavery therein.

ARTICLE XIV.

Sec. 1. "All persons born or naturalized in the United States, and subject to the jurisdiction thereof, are citizens of the United States and of the state wherein they reside. No state shall make or enforce any law which shall abridge the privileges or immunities of citizens of the United States ; nor shall any state deprive any person of life, liberty, or property, without due process of law ; nor deny to any person within its jurisdiction the equal protection of the laws."

Sec. 2. " Representatives shall be apportioned among the several states according to their respective numbers, counting the whole number of persons in each state, excluding Indians not taxed. But when the right to vote at any election for the choice of electors for president and vice-president of the United States, representatives in congress, the executive and judicial officers of a state, or the members of the legislature thereof, is denied to any of the male inhabitants of such state, being twenty-one years of age, and citizens of the United States, or in any way abridge, except for participation in rebellion, or other crime, the basis of representation therein shall be reduced in the proportion which the number of such male citizens shall bear to the whole number of male citizens twenty-one years of age in such state."

Sec. 3. " No person shall be a senator or representative in congress, or elector of president and vice-president, or hold any office, civil or military, under the

United States, or under any state, who, having previously
taken an oath, as a member of congress, or as an officer
of the United States, or as a member of any state legislature, or as an executive or judicial officer of any state,
to support the constitution of the United States, shall
have engaged in insurrection or rebellion against the
same, or given aid or comfort to the enemies thereof.
But congress may by a vote of two-thirds of each house
remove such disability."

Sec. 4. "The validity of the public debt of the United
States, authorized by law, including debts incurred for
payment of pensions and bounties for services in suppressing insurrection or rebellion, shall not be questioned.
But neither the United States nor any state shall assume
or pay any debt or obligation in aid of insurrection or rebellion against the United States, or any claim for the
loss or emancipation of any slave ; but all such debts,
obligations and claims shall be held illegal and void."

Sec. 5. "The congress shall have power to enforce,
by appropriate legislation, the provisions of this article."

This amendment was proposed to the legislatures of
the several states by the thirty-ninth congress on the 16th
of June, 1866. On the 21st of July, 1868, congress
adopted and transmitted to the department of state a
concurrent resolution, declaring that "the legislatures of
the states of Connecticut, Tennessee, New Jersey, Oregon,
Vermont, New York, Ohio, Illinois, West Virginia, Kansas, Maine, Nevada, Missouri, Indiana, Minnesota, New
Hampshire, Massachusetts, Nebraska, Iowa, Arkansas,
Florida, North Carolina, Alabama, South Carolina, and
Louisiana, being three-fourths and more of the several
states of the union, have ratified the fourteenth article of
amendment to the constitution of the United States,
duly proposed by two-thirds of each house of the thirty-
ninth congress ; therefore,

"*Resolved*, That said fourteenth article is hereby declared to be a part of the constitution of the United States, and it shall be duly promulgated as such by the secretary of state."

The secretary of state accordingly issued a proclamation, dated the 28th day of July, 1868, declaring that the proposed fourteenth amendment had been ratified, in manner hereafter mentioned, by the legislatures of thirty of the thirty-six states, viz.: Connecticut, June 30th, 1866; New Hampshire, July 7th, 1866; Tennessee, July 19th, 1866; New Jersey, September 11th, 1866 (and the legislature of the same state passed a resolution in April, 1868, to withdraw its consent to it); Oregon ratified it September 19th, 1866; Vermont, November 9th, 1866; Georgia rejected it November 13th, 1866, but ratified it July 21st, 1868; South Carolina rejected it December 20th, 1866, but ratified it July 9th, 1868; North Carolina rejected it December 4th, 1866, but ratified it July 4th, 1868; New York ratified it January 10th, 1867; Ohio ratified it January 11th, 1867 (but the legislature thereof passed a resolution in January, 1868, to withdraw its consent to it); Illinois ratified it January 15th, 1867; West Virginia ratified it January 16th, 1867; Kansas, January 18th, 1867; Maine, January 19th, 1867; Nevada, January 22d, 1867, Missouri, January 26th, 1867; Indiana, January 29th, 1867; Minnesota, February 1st, 1867; Rhode Island, February 7th, 1867; Wisconsin, February 13th, 1867; Pennsylvania, February 13th, 1867; Michigan, February 15th, 1867; Massachusetts, March 20th, 1867; Nebraska, June 15th, 1867; Iowa, April 3d, 1868; Arkansas, April 6th, 1868; Florida, June 9th, 1868; Louisiana, July 9th, 1868; Alabama, July 13th, 1868; Georgia again ratified the amendment February 2d, 1870; Texas rejected it November 1st, 1866, but ratified it February 18th, 1870; Virginia rejected it February 19th,

1867, but ratified it October 8th, 1869. It was rejected by Kentucky, January 10th, 1867; by Delaware, February 8th, 1867, and by Maryland, March 23d, 1867.

This amendment requires the fifteenth amendment to complete it, which more definitely points out the class of persons the fourteenth amendment was intended to affect, which is as follows:

ARTICLE XV.

Sec. 1. "The right of citizens of the United States to vote shall not be denied or abridged by the United States or by any state on account of race, color, or previous condition of servitude."

See. 2. "The congress shall have power to enforce this article by appropriate legislation."

The fourteenth amendment was not only voted for by the native born of African descent before its adoption, and before they were made capable of being voters, but at a time a large portion of the valid white citizens of the seceding states were denied citizenship, and their right to vote by an act of congress; and even by that arbitrary method of reconstructing the seceding states, it is at least doubtful whether a sufficient number of the states ratified it to make it a part of the constitution, for it required a resolution of the congress, declaring it had been ratified by three-fourths of the states, and an order by that department, to induce the secretary of state to promulgate it as a part of the constitution.*

The fifteenth amendment, however, was promulgated by the secretary of state without any command from the congress.

As shown in discussing the authority to admit new states, *every* nation must have a people associated to-

---

* Revised Statutes of United States.

gether as one people, who may be known and recognized as but one political body or people, capable of appropriating a designated part of the globe to their exclusive use; for if there is any doubt about the character or the identity of the people who lay claim to that designated part of the globe, their claim will not be regarded by other nations, races, or tribes of people.

The dual system of governments for the United States was ordained and established by white people for themselves alone, and negroes, mulattoes and Indians were excluded from the body politic or national family of people, who ordained and established the nation of the United States.

A national family being the foundation upon which every nation must rest, for whenever the political association of the people of a nation—or, as it is expressed by the supreme court in the Dred Scott case, *national family*—shall be destroyed, their country, territory, or other possessions will necessarily revert to the God of nature, and again become free to the occupancy of any other tribe, race, or nation of people.

As shown in discussing authority to admit new states, no people can be free who commit to their government authority to change the character of people who may have been ordained to constitute this political association or national family, either by extending to inferior tribes within the country authority to participate in the management of the national affairs, or by expanding the boundary thereof so as to take in an inferior tribe or race of people to participate therein.

And, as shown in the first chapter of this review, the only organ for giving expression to the sovereign will of the people is through sovereign conventions.

Therefore, any change in the character of the people who compose the political association of this nation, or the national family, requires the assent of the sovereign will ; and, as shown in discussing the fifth article of the constitution, such changes must be made by a federal convention and ratified by conventions in three-fourths of the states.   Hence the native-born of African descent could not have been added to the family of sovereign citizens of the United States by any amendment proposed by the congress and ratified by the legislature of any number of the states, even if ratified by the legislatures of all of the states ; but, for the purpose of ascertaining the intent and effect of the fourteenth and fifteenth amendments to the constitution, the manner of proposing them, and the way it is claimed they were ratified is waived without conceding authority in the congress and state legislatures to make such amendments.

The first clause of the first section of the fourteenth article of amendment simply declares as a fact, that "All persons born or naturalized in the United States and subject to the jurisdiction thereof are citizens of the United States and of the state wherein they reside."

As shown by the fifteenth amendment, this was intended to make the native born of African descent believe they were to become citizens thenceforth.   But the second section of this fourteenth amendment concedes to the several states the right not only to deny the truth of the declaration in the first clause of the first section, but concedes to the states authority and power to disregard it, for the second section offers the states an inducement to acknowledge so much to be true as will permit the native born of African descent to vote in elections for the *choice of electors for president, representatives in congress; the executive and judicial officers of the state and members of the legislature thereof,* and that their right to vote in either of said elections shall not be abridged except for participation in rebellion or other crime. It is a settled rule of interpretation that the naming of particular rights excludes all others from the grant.

Remembering that sovereign conventions were ordained as the only organs through which the people can express their sovereign will, and that the states were not required by the proposition in this second section to extend the sovereign right to native born of African descent to vote for delegates to sovereign or constitutional conventions, or to hold office in the state, shows that the draftsman of this fourteenth amendment did not intend to make the African inhabitants sovereign citizens, for, as sovereign citizens, no laws could be made prohibiting them from intermarrying with the white people, or from attending the same public schools. And the danger of daughters of the white people being entrapped into marriage with the black bucks, while attending school together, would have defeated its ratification by the states ; which probably presented itself to the draftsman of the amendment.

But, whatever may have influenced the draftsman, or the congress that proposed it, or the states that were counted as ratifying it, this amendment, by itself, and with the aid of the fifteenth, fails to make the native born of African descent sovereign citizens of the states or of the United States ; and the congress itself recognizes this fact.

For, being authorized to enforce said amendments by legislation, the congress, in what was known as the civil rights bill, authorized colored inhabitants to carry their suits to the United States courts, whether they were plaintiffs or defendants, on a plea that they were denied justice in the state courts on account of race, color, etc.

This act of congress appears to be based on the idea that native born of African descent became citizens of the United States by said amendment, and by virtue of being citizens of the United States they become citi-

zens of the state wherein they inhabit ; there is nothing
in this act requiring equal protection under the laws of
the state wherein they reside, but the states are required
to extend to that class of persons equal protection under
the laws, and, as they are authorized to take their cases
into federal courts, the laws referred to can not apply to
state laws, of which the courts of the United States have
no jurisdiction.   Therefore that act attempts to vest a
class of persons with privileges that may not be enjoyed
by full citizens of some of the states wherein they reside ;
and in many other ways the congress treated them as
being peculiarly under the protection of the United States,
and characterized them as citizens of the United States
and, therefore, citizens of the state wherein they reside,
though the United States being merely a name to designate
the states united, and without power to protect or govern
any people except as the agent or trustee of the states,
there can not be any citizens thereof, except the citizens
of the several states in the union.

   If the United States could have citizens independent
of those of the several states, the United States could
not in good faith represent the states united ; but to the
extent of its own citizens it must have an existence independent of the states, and to that extent its interest
would conflict with that of the states ; and to that extent
the United States would become a rival of the states.

   The first section provides that, "no state shall make
or enforce any law which shall abridge the privileges or
immunities of citizens of the United States ; nor shall
any state deprive any person of life, liberty or property,
without due process of law ; nor deny to any person
within its jurisdiction the equal protection of the laws ;"
which applies only to citizens of the United States while
under the jurisdiction of the state.   Furthermore, the

first section attempts to transfer all citizenship from the states to the United States.

The fifth section provides that, "the congress shall have power to enforce, by appropriate legislation, the provisions of this article."

If these provisions had been upheld by the judiciary, they would effectually have transferred the whole police jurisdiction of the states to the congress of the United States, and have converted the states into mere provinces, and the United States into an unlimited empire, but, fortunately for the people of the United States, at the time these amendments first came before the supreme court for interpretation, there were able and patriotic judges on the supreme court bench who eliminated the revolutionary features by interpretation.*

The justice who wrote the opinion of the court, in the course of his argument, intimated that the object of these amendments might have been to get rid of the effects of the decision of the supreme court in the Dred Scott case, but that question was not involved in those cases, and it was not duly considered by the court, and should be deemed *obiter dictum*, and no authority ; and no regard has been shown it by the judiciary or any department of the United States.

Free societies of people may unite themselves together by voluntary engagement or compact, and each society retain its freedom and sovereignty as a perfect state, provided they enter into that union on perfectly equal terms.

And they may institute a common agent to represent the union without impairing the freedom or sovereignty of these societies within the union, provided equality be preserved in the compact of the union, and provided fur-

---

* Slaughter's House Cases, 16 Wall. 36.

ther, the respective societies consist of one race of people, or at least of kindred races of people. For, if some of the members or societies of such a union reject any race or tribe of people from their societies or political organizations, and other members permit those races or tribes into their society or political organizations, the several members of such a union could not retain equal freedom and sovereignty therein.

If the native born of African descent were made sovereign citizens by these amendments to the constitution, they must have been made citizens of the states wherein they reside, and therefore citizens of the United States, and they not only have the right to travel in the same railroad coaches, but to send their children to the same public schools the children of white people attend, for the black children may learn much from associating with the white children ; and they have the right to patronize the same hotels, churches, theaters and to intermarry with the whites, and they can not be denied either of these, or any other equal right, by either state or federal laws. If they are sovereign citizens, it needs neither argument nor the citation of authorities to show that they can not be discriminated against in any way whatever, for sovereignty is supreme and can not be limited otherwise than by voluntary agreement, which may be broken at will by the sovereign, and no act of the law-making power can become a law that allows greater privileges to one sovereign than to another.

That the children of that race of people are excluded from the schools provided by the public for white children, and are prohibited from intermarrying with the whites, or occupying the same seats in theaters, or riding in the same railroad coaches with the white people, and in many other ways discriminated against by the laws of the states, which are recognized as valid by every

department of the United States, shows that the African
inhabitants are not sovereign citizens of the states or of
the United States; for, if they were sovereign citizens,
every discriminating act of the legislature of any state
would be unconstitutional and void.

But they are inhabitants of the United States and
of the state wherein they reside, and as mere inhabitants they are entitled to protection under the laws
of the United States and of the state wherein they
reside. As the native born of African descent owe no
allegiance to any other nation, prince or potentate,
and have always resided in the United States, it is
difficult to define the exact relation they bear to the
United States and the state wherein they reside. They
are surely entitled to the protection of both, and may be
said to be wards of both. However, they may be wards
of the United States without being wards of any state,
as in case of their going to a territory of the United
States, they not being full citizens of the state they leave
to go to such territory, by leaving, all obligations between them and the state they migrate from would be
severed; in that case, the African inhabitants of the territory would still remain wards of the United States.
Citizens of the states who migrate to the territories of
the United States remain citizens of the states they migrate from until the territory shall be formed into a
state; for the territories belonging to all of the states as
equal owners, though held in trust in the name of the
United States. No one can become a citizen of any of the
territories of the United States, however long they may
reside therein, as citizenship must always be on land and
can not float in the air or be held in abeyance; hence,
it remains where it last took root.

However, persons leaving a foreign nation to settle in
a territory, who are entitled to be naturalized, must ac-

quire some right under the laws of the United States, and must be entitled to protection of the authority having control of the territories while residing therein, which makes them a species of wards to the congress.

The second clause of the first section having been eliminated by decision of the supreme court in the Slaughter-House cases, *supra*, and the declaration in the first clause of the constitution being unenforcible, there is but little remaining of this amendment.

The second section requires the negroes to be enumerated in the same way the whites are counted for representation of the states in the congress and for the selection of presidential electors, if the states will allow them to vote in certain specified elections.

The third section disfranchises those who had taken an oath to support the constitution of the United States and afterward engaged in the rebellion, but the congress was authorized to relieve them of that disability by special act or acts, and all who were engaged in the rebellion have either died or had their disabilities removed by special acts of congress, so that this section is now obsolete.

The fourth section thereof gives the war debt a constitutional sanction, and provides that neither the United States nor any state shall pay for any slave that had been freed by the thirteenth amendment to the constitution.

As the states have manumitted the slaves by state laws and no one is claiming pay for them, and there being no disposition to repudiate the war debt, this section ceases to perform any functions. However, these two sections present curious features of the human mind, which may prove a valuable lesson to students of statesmanship.

The members of congress who proposed this amendment, while preparing and proposing it, were under oath

4

to support the constitution, and as such officers they were bound to protect all citizens alike in the enjoyment of their private property. Property in slaves was guaranteed by the constitution, so that in preparing and proposing this amendment they were engaged in open rebellion to that instrument while under oath to support it. Therefore it is curious that they could have been impressed with the seriousness of the crime of those who had taken an oath to support the constitution, after being absolved from it, by going out of office before engaging in rebellion against that instrument, remain so blind to their own rebellion against the plain letter thereof.

But the states having abolished slavery in their respective borders, and extended to their former slaves the right to vote, and to acquire, own and dispose of property in the same way the sovereign white citizens do, these two amendments no longer perform any functions except to threaten the tranquillity of society, by leading the blacks to believe they have greater rights than they really have, which emboldens them to attempt to grasp other privileges not due them.

The right to vote may be made of great value to the manumitted slaves. If they vote as their individual opinions lead them to believe to be their best interest, each exercising his own personal judgment, and if they demean themselves decently and respectfully toward the white as well as toward each other, they will have the respect and sympathy of all good citizens to aid them in the strife of life, and their votes will be solicited in the same way the votes of the whites are sought by candidates and parties.

But while they continue to vote at the dictation of any one party, like a herd of alarmed buffaloes "running all together," without exercising their own personal reason or friendships, how can any individual or party respect them? In so doing, but for the indulgent sympathy of the whites, they might be harshly treated, and more strictly bound and limited in the enjoyment of privileges under the state laws.

Furthermore, the states united, must have a common agent or representative, else they can not be united. To destroy that common agent would disintegrate the union of the states. That common agent must be common to all of the states as equals, and can not have any interest independent of the union of states, without coming in conflict with the union ; and whenever it undertakes to represent any people, except the people of the several states, it is bound to place itself in opposition to the interest of the states of the union, and to that extent its ability to serve the several states, as fully as its duty requires, must necessarily be destroyed, and the purposes of the union must be thwarted, unless a new common agent could be procured.

The supreme court, however, has decided in more than one case, that there may be citizens of the United States and citizens of the states, consisting of different persons, and that a person may be a citizen of one without being a citizen of the other, but how can that be as long as the United States is simply the common agent of the states united? It is true the territories are under the exclusive control of the congress, therefore they can not be controlled by any one of the states, and persons who migrate to a territory from a foreign nation, as soon as they take out their naturalization papers, will become wards of the United States, as they can not become citizens of a territory held in trust by the congress for the use of all of the states alike, as equal owners of the beneficial interest thereof ; but the congress in acting as the guardian of that class of wards to the nation, will be acting as the agent of all of the states, and in harmony with all of the states, and simply carrying into effect the obligation of the states united as to that class of persons, or inhabitants of the territories.

The Indians occupying territory within the United States, subject to the jurisdiction thereof, are in like manner wards of the United States.

A state may authorize emigrants from foreign nations to vote therein before they have been in this country long enough to be naturalized according to the naturalization acts of congress; but the right to vote does not make them citizens, and they would not be entitled to the privileges and immunities of citizens thereof in any other state.

There has been no case, that I know of, before the supreme court, involving this question.

However, it was incidentally referred to in the Dred Scott case, hereinbefore cited, and the court held that the right to vote might be extended to persons who were not citizens, and that the mere right did not make them citizens, which expression of the court is fully sustained by text-writers on the subject.

Therefore, by extending to the colored male inhabitants the right to vote, a state does not make them citizens, particularly as the states extending that right to the colored race prescribed limitations and restrictions on them. And the states may take away from the native born African inhabitants the right to vote at any time, though that is not likely to be done as long as they behave themselves with only tolerable decency and patriotism.

Therefore, the colored race of people, although born in the United States, can not constitute any part of the national family of sovereign citizens.

INDEX.

www.ingramcontent.com/pod-product-compliance
Lightning Source LLC
Chambersburg PA
CBHW020240290326
41929CB00045B/628